FIVE MINUTES WITH GOD

FIVE MINUTES WITH GOD
Rusty Hills

ISBN-10: 1941972454
ISBN-13: 978-1941972458

Library of Congress Control Number: 2014950104

Published by Start2Finish
Fort Worth, Texas 76244
www.start2finish.org

Printed in the United States of America

Cover Design: Josh Feit, Evangela.com

DEDICATION

To the Elders of the Chase Park Church of Christ—Thank you for your vision in implementing this program and for the confidence that you showed in me in allowing me to carry it out.

and

To the Chase Park family—Thank you for your unwavering support and encouragement of this program and of me. It has meant more than you will ever know. I love you all.

INTRODUCTION

How many of us have made the commitment to begin a daily Bible reading program with the goal of reading through the Bible in a year, only to forget, fall behind, get discouraged and give up? Sound familiar? We all want to study the Bible more, but our busy lives and hectic schedules make devoting time to personal Bible study difficult. Likewise, every church understands the importance of Bible study and prayer in the lives of her members, and most have, at some point, attempted to implement some kind of daily Bible reading program, probably with disappointing results. It was out of this dilemma that *Five Minutes with God* was born.

Five Minutes with God is a different concept in daily Bible reading. It doesn't challenge the reader to complete the entire Bible or even one of the testaments in a year's time. Instead, it encourages the reader to focus on shorter passages of Scripture and to read them intentionally and with greater understanding. It, in essence, narrows the field of vision to one particular idea or thought and helps the reader to see that portion of God's Word more clearly. By focusing, in this year, on a survey of the Old Testament books, readers are able to journey through history from the very beginning of time to the days just before the birth of Christ in order to become acquainted with God and his relationship with humanity. The accompanying devotional thoughts are designed to help further clarify the reading and encourage deeper thought into the meaning of each passage. Some of the thoughts are intended to instruct while others have the purpose of motivating, but all of the readings and thoughts will hopefully inspire in the reader a greater appreciation of God and the many wonderful aspects of his character along with a better understanding of our struggle against sin and the great desire and plan of God to provide a way back to him.

THE OLD TESTAMENT

Except for the few exciting stories that we learn as children and maybe the occasional psalm, we tend to largely neglect the Old Testament when it comes to our daily Bible study. The language is sometimes difficult and the subject matter is often boring or seems very disconnected from our own life and times. Yet, on closer examination, we find that this estimation, at least the latter part of it, is altogether false. Though we do not live under the old covenant today and therefore are not answerable to the laws of the Old Testament, there is a vast wealth of knowledge and understanding that can be gained from the inspired words of this ancient collection of books. In fact, the apostle Paul would later write, by inspiration, "For whatever was written in former days was written for our instruction, that through endurance and through the encouragement of the Scriptures we might have hope" (Romans 15:4). Though we are separated from the people and places of the Old Testament by thousands of years and thousands of miles, we have much in common with them. We all live in the same world, we all have the same God, and we are all part of the same story—the story of a loving God who desperately desires a relationship with his greatest creation and his unrelenting effort to redeem them and to prepare them for an eternal abode with him. The Old Testament provides much of the background in helping us to understand our place and role in that wonderful story.

The Old Testament teaches us about God. From the very first sentence of Genesis, the unlimited power and wisdom of God is on full display. As he moves and works among the nations of the world, his transcendence and sovereignty are clearly evident. But beyond his immutable power and unapproachable glory, we learn of the character of God through the pages of the Old Testament. We see his perfect righteousness and his disdain for evil. We are witness to his unwavering faithfulness. We also learn that God, in all of his power and glory, is also a God of unconditional love and unending mercy. He loves mankind with an everlasting love and pursues a relationship with him passionately and unrelentingly. The picture of God that is painted in the pages of the Old Testament gives us every reason to stand in awe and wonder of him and to fall before him in praise and worship.

The Old Testament teaches us about sin. In its pages, we learn of its entrance into this world and of the destructive work of Satan in his efforts to draw us away from God. We learn of the power of sin to separate us from God and of its devastating consequences to both our physical and spiritual lives. The Old Testament also warns us time and again in unmistakable terms of the weakness of human flesh and the propensity for sin that we all struggle with. Finally, we learn of the aversion to sin that characterizes God and of the great price that he was willing to pay through his Son to defeat sin and to redeem mankind to himself. By the instructive examples of the Old Testament, we are taught to hate sin as God does, to avoid it when we can, and to repent of it when it finds its way into our lives.

The Old Testament teaches us about us. We learn of our beginning and of the amazing fact that we were caringly created in the form and image of our Creator. We see powerful examples of both the incredible faith and faithfulness of which we are capable and the depths of depravity to which we can fall. Most of all, we learn of our desperate need for the love, mercy, and grace of God. We witness, through the lives of others, the drastic highs and lows of life, and the wonderful blessings of strength and help that are available from God on any of life's paths. We see the helplessness and hopelessness of a life without God and the blessed hope of a life that is sheltered under his mighty wings.

The Old Testament teaches us about salvation. Though the atoning sacrifice of Christ would not come until later, there is much that the Old Testament helps us to understand about the salvation that God would offer through his Son. First of all, we see the need for salvation. As we witness the devastating consequences of sin, we come to understand our need to be saved from its curse. In the Old Testament, we also find the constant willingness and desire of God to save his people. Without that desire and his extraordinary efforts, we would have no hope of being saved. Finally, we learn that, even before the foundation of the world, God had a plan for salvation. Through the story of the Old Testament, we see the unfolding of that plan to prepare the world for the coming of his Son so that sin and death could be forever defeated and mankind could have the salvation that they so desperately needed.

The story of the Old Testament is our story, told through the eyes and experiences of those who have gone before us. Their victories, failures, struggles, and successes are recorded as a shadow of our own journey through this world toward eternity. So, as you read their stories, do not think that your life is so far removed from theirs that there is no benefit to be found in them.

HOW TO USE THIS BOOK

This book is different from other daily devotional books that you may be familiar with. In most of those books, there is a reading from the Bible that is suggested for each day, but that text is not crucial to understanding or benefitting from the day's devotional thought which typically stands alone as an independent reading to give inspiration or motivation for the day. Not so, with *Five Minutes with God*. In reality, this book is part devotional book, part Bible study. This daily reading program was designed in such a way that the Word of God is at the core of it and that the reading of that word is crucial to it. The writings contained in this book were never intended to overshadow or replace the reading of God's word but rather to illuminate and point the reader to it. As you spend time with these devotionals each day, understand that the reading of the Biblical text is essential to the understanding of the thought because it is directly related and connected to it. The assigned reading for the day will be relatively short (usually one chapter or less) and is prominently displayed at the top of each page. Please take the time to read that passage before reading the accompanying thought. Because the thought is often designed to shed light on the meaning of some portion of the Biblical reading, you might find it helpful to re-read the passage after considering the day's thought.

Finally, it is my desire and prayer that these daily devotionals serve as a springboard, launching you into more and deeper Bible study. While some might view the brevity of these readings as a shortcoming of this system, I am of the belief that the short passages allow the reader to explore the text in more detail and to glean nuggets of truth and understanding that might otherwise be overlooked. Likewise, the thoughts that are given in this book are just that—thoughts—and they are wholly mine. Read them, consider them, and then meditate on the passage with the intent of increasing your own understanding of its purpose and teaching. Most of all, remember that this daily devotion is about God, his word, and the relationship that you have with him because of Christ. My prayer is that, through this study, you will grow in your knowledge and in your love and devotion for God, his Son, and his body, the church.

To God be the glory!

Day 1

Today's Reading:
Genesis 1:1-31

The Bible's story—the story of God, time, the world, mankind, sin, and salvation—begins "in the beginning." In the beginning, there was nothing. Nothing that is, except for God, who has always been. Our first encounter with God is one that should leave us in absolute awe of his all-encompassing power and wisdom. At his command, the physical universe appears, coming into existence out of nothingness. Over the course of six days, he speaks the world into being with flawless design and in meticulous detail. As our ability to explore and our capacity for understanding our world and universe has grown and expanded over the centuries, we are constantly amazed at the intricacies of its inner-workings and boggled by the understandings that continue to elude us. Yet, those things that will always remain mysteries to us were perfectly understood, planned, and designed in the mind of God. The apostle Paul would later write, "For his invisible attributes, namely, his eternal power and divine nature, have been clearly perceived, ever since the creation of the world, in the things that have been made" (Romans 1:20). These first words of the Bible give us an explanation of the amazing origin of our world, but even more importantly, they introduce us in a powerful way to the omnipotent, omniscient God of the universe. What a marvelous beginning to a marvelous book!

What are some things that we learn about
God from this first chapter of the Bible?

DON'T FORGET TO PRAY AND HAVE A GREAT DAY!

Day 2

 Today's Reading:
Genesis 2:1-25

While Genesis 1 tells us about the beginning of the world, chapter two reveals the beginning of God's relationship with his greatest creation, mankind. From the very beginning, there was a special place in the heart of God for humankind. He was the centerpiece and masterpiece of God's creative work, as well as the purpose of all creation. While God merely spoke the world into creation, his work of creating man was much more personal and hands-on. Rather than simply commanding man into being, God skillfully and lovingly formed him from the dust of the earth. Like a potter with his clay, God carefully shaped this special creation into his own image and then, with his very breath, he breathed into man the breath of life. While there is wonder and beauty in all of God's creation, nothing compares to man, for while the rest of creation was entirely the work of God's mind and hands, mankind was more the work of his heart. But God did not stop there. He also wanted man to be happy and fulfilled, so God provided for him. He created a perfect utopia of an environment for man to live in; one that would meet every need and be free from struggle and hardship. God also knew that man needed companionship, someone to share life with and to be a helper for him, and so, he created woman to fill that all-important role. Thus, God's creative work was done and the world and life that God intended for man was complete and perfect… at least for a little while.

In what ways is man created in the image of God?

DON'T FORGET TO PRAY AND HAVE A GREAT DAY!

Day 3

Today's Reading:
Genesis 3:1-24

God desired (and still desires) a close relationship with his special creation. He wanted to be a Father to them—to provide for them, care for them, protect them, and love them. He wanted to walk and talk with them in close communion. But he wanted that relationship to be one of mutual desire and choosing; one that was genuine and voluntary. After all, a relationship that is forced is, in reality, no relationship at all. And so, God gave man the freedom of choice. This masterpiece of creation that God had so lovingly shaped and formed with his own hands into his very image, this being that he had breathed life into with his own breath, this life that he had so carefully and attentively provided for, would now have the opportunity to choose whether or not to return the love that had been shown to him. The choice was his—to walk with God or to go his own way, to heed God's loving guidance or to listen to the other voices, including his own, that would lead him away from God. It was a choice that would shape not only the lives of Adam and Eve but also of every person who would ever live. By their choice, sin entered the world, and the earth and all her inhabitants have suffered sin's consequences ever since. Though much has changed since Adam and Eve made the choice to eat of the forbidden fruit, every human being is still faced with the same life-shaping choice—to accept God's love and enter into a faithful relationship with him or to reject God and go his own way. What will your choice be?

Why was it so important for God to give mankind freedom of choice?

DON'T FORGET TO PRAY AND HAVE A GREAT DAY!

DAY 4

Today's Reading:
Genesis 6:1-22

Much has changed since that fateful day in the Garden of Eden when Adam and Eve were deceived by Satan and disobeyed God's one prohibitive command. In the many years that have passed since the first man and woman were evicted from the paradise of Eden, not only has the earth been populated, but it has also been filled with sin. So wicked had mankind become, in fact, that God was filled with grief and regret as he looked down upon the sad state of his creation. Yet, even in his anger, God's love and grace remained intact as he considered the one life that stood out above all the others—Noah. The story of Noah is an amazing story of faith and obedience. Given the monumental task of constructing an ark to be used for the saving of his family, and given very specific instructions for its construction, Noah was meticulous in his following of God's commands. For years he worked to complete the ark, all the while warning those around him of the coming destruction and preaching a message of repentance. His faithful obedience not only saved his family from the flood but provided a wonderful example for every generation that would come after him. Peter would later compare the building of the ark to the obedience of baptism (see 1 Peter 3:20-21). What a blessing the Old Testament is, so full of wonderful examples that teach us so much about God and our relationship with him.

What do you think would have happened if Noah had followed his own ideas instead of God's instructions for the ark? What can we learn from that scenario?

DON'T FORGET TO PRAY AND HAVE A GREAT DAY!

DAY 5

Today's Reading:
Genesis 7:1-24

This reading reveals one of the very dark days in the earth's history—the day that God brought his vengeance upon a world overcome with sin and destroyed mankind with a flood. Perhaps, more than anything else, this drastic action by God is a testament to the destructiveness of sin, both physically and spiritually. So unbearable is sin in the eyes of God that he found no acceptable alternative to a purging deluge of water to deal with it. Sin—the transgression of God's law—is often viewed by our world as being harmless, inconsequential, and even, in the minds of some, nothing more than a hyper-moralistic myth. Yet, one of the vital messages of the Old Testament, seen so very clearly in this text, is that sin is not only real but has a truly devastating effect on the world and is disastrous when it comes to our relationship with God. If we are to have any hope for a faithful relationship with God, we must take sin seriously and be diligent in our efforts to avoid and defeat it. But surprisingly, the story of the flood is also as much about God's grace and mercy as it is about his aversion to sin. As committed as he was to "blotting out" every living thing from the earth through the flood, he did not act without providing a means of hope for humanity through the salvation of Noah and his family. Even in His anger, God remains faithful and offers hope to sinners.

In what ways is sin a destructive force in our lives today?

DON'T FORGET TO PRAY AND HAVE A GREAT DAY!

DAY 6

 Today's Reading:
Genesis 8:1-22

B ut God remembered Noah…" The ark that had served as a safe haven for all those on board during the dismal days of the flood had literally been a Godsend, but it could not sustain them forever. Therefore, God, in his remembrance of Noah, caused the waters to recede and, just over one year after entering the ark, Noah and the rest of its inhabitants walked out onto dry ground. They had been spared by the grace of God. He had provided for them, watched over them, and preserved them. He had, in fact, remembered them, and in response Noah remembered God. In his first recorded act after exiting the ark, Noah built an altar and offered sacrifices to God. As this man of faith looked around at a world laid bare by flood waters, he was surely aware of the fate that humankind had met and of the undeniable grace that had been shown to him by God. There was seemingly no thought of self-preservation, no hint of arrogance, no show of self-reliance; Noah knew, without a doubt, Who it was that had saved him. With a heart full of gratitude and humility, he sought to give thanks and praise to the God of his salvation through the offering of sacrifices. Again, we are reminded through this great example of a vital characteristic of a faithful relationship with God—a humble and grateful recognition of God's grace and mercy.

In what ways can we show our gratitude
for God's grace and mercy upon us?

DON'T FORGET TO PRAY AND HAVE A GREAT DAY!

Day 7

Today's Reading:
Genesis 9:1-17

The rainbow—it is still a sight that thrills us every time that we are blessed to see one in the sky. While many in the world may see the rainbow as nothing more than a physical phenomenon resulting from the passing of light rays through water droplets; to the Christian, it represents so much more. Understanding its origin and meaning from this text, the rainbow becomes an inspiring reminder of God's love and faithful promises. After essentially pressing the reset button on humanity, God made a commitment to Noah and to all of his descendants that he would never destroy the earth in such a manner again. To seal his promise and as a sign of his covenant with mankind, God placed a rainbow in the sky to be a reminder of this great promise to every generation. But a closer examination of this text reveals that the rainbow also served to remind God of his promise and covenant with mankind. Sin would always be a problem with humanity, and no doubt, there would be times when God would look down upon the wickedness of the earth and be tempted to take a similar action to what he did in the days of the flood. Yet, his promises are true and faithful, and with each rainbow that appears in the sky, God is reminded of his everlasting covenant with mankind. Certainly, a day of final fiery destruction will come when the Lord returns, but until then, God, who promised, is faithful and therefore will never again bring a global flood upon the earth.

What does it mean to you to know
that God is faithful in keeping his promises?

DON'T FORGET TO PRAY AND HAVE A GREAT DAY!

DAY 8

 Today's Reading: Genesis 11:1-9

The tower of Babel represents another important turning point in the development of mankind and civilization. Imagine a world with only one language. At first blush, it might seem like a positive and helpful situation, but this text shows what is possibly the inevitable conclusion of such circumstances—a humanity that feels no sense of limitation and no respect for their proper place with regard to God. This infamous tower is representative of mankind's constant attempts to assume the place of God for himself and to ascend the spire of prideful notoriety and authority. There is no humility or submission in that mentality; no recognition of the transcendence of God or of our answerability to him. One of the great and important messages of the Old Testament is that only God is God and no man can assume his place. God will not be mocked, and he cannot be replaced. He is a benevolent, loving, and merciful God but make no mistake: He is God! This text might answer some fundamental questions about the plurality of languages and civilizations in our world, but the more important lesson from this event is the stern warning given to mankind against the prideful attempt to put themselves in the place of God.

Why do you think that mankind so often tries to take the place of God?

DON'T FORGET TO PRAY AND HAVE A GREAT DAY!

Day 9

Today's Reading:
Genesis 12:1-9

From our very first introduction to the great life of Abraham, his faith in God is being tested in ways that most people would not be able to imagine. To leave your home and extended family for an unknown location and future would certainly be a great test. But with this and every command that God issued to Abraham, there were always the abiding promises of God. He was not asking Abraham to make sacrifices and obey difficult commands for nothing. There were always the assurances of greatness, land, offspring, care, and protection. God required a great deal with regard to Abraham's faith and obedience, but he promised even more in return. It occurs to me that the same thing is true for us. Though our tests may not be as obvious or challenging as those of Abraham, we certainly face times and circumstances that require our faith, devotion, obedience, and sacrifice. We will struggle, question, and be challenged at times in our spiritual lives, but we must never forget that the promises of God are faithful, and they are far greater than what God asks us to give up for him. Like Abraham, we have been promised a home in a land flowing with milk and honey and blessing upon blessing. If we will learn from the example of Abraham and faithfully obey the call and commands of God, we will be partakers of the great and eternal promises of God.

What sacrifices have you made for God and what
promises of his correspond to those sacrifices?

DON'T FORGET TO PRAY AND HAVE A GREAT DAY!

Day 10

 Today's Reading:
Genesis 17:1-27

Sometimes our challenge is not so much to deal with the difficult situations of life or choices that our faith demands as it is to deal with the unknowns of how God will work out our circumstances for good. In our limited ability to understand our own lives and our complete inability to know our physical future, we often struggle to see how God can possibly use the challenges that we face to bring about those things that he has promised. Our faith is tested, and we often try to work out our own solutions, essentially giving up on God. This is exactly the situation that Abraham finds himself in. God had promised to make Abraham a great nation with countless generations, but without an heir, Abraham finds himself struggling to trust God to keep those promises. After two attempts to solve this dilemma on his own, Abraham seems somewhat frustrated when God insists that the heir will be one from Sarah's own womb, despite her old age. But God delivered on his word, proving that nothing is impossible with God. Paul would later write that "for those who love God all things work together for good..." (Romans 8:28). What a comfort it is to know that we serve a God who is not only faithful in keeping his promises but who is able to work any circumstance out for good to the accomplishing of his perfect will!

Think about a challenging or trying time in your life.
How did God use those circumstances to bring about good?

DON'T FORGET TO PRAY AND HAVE A GREAT DAY!

Day 11

 Today's Reading:
Genesis 18:1-15

Have you ever laughed at God—looked at your own circumstances and compared them to the things that God has asked of you or promised you and reacted with doubt or unbelief? How can he possibly cause anything good to come out of this? How can this possibly accomplish his will? Though we may not actually laugh as Sarah did, to question or doubt the ability or promises of God may not be that uncommon for us. Our nature is often to be skeptical and pessimistic concerning our own difficulties. But faith—real, true, living faith—demands that we fight against our own doubts and fears and trust in the wisdom and power of God. We may not always be able to see the path of resolution and blessing that God has placed before us and to trust in the unknown may not always seem like the logical thing to do, but God's ways are higher than our ways and often far beyond our ability to see or understand. Sarah laughed at the prospect of bearing a son, but God again demonstrated his ability to perform his will and keep his promises. Over and over again, God reminds us through his word that nothing is beyond his ability and that he is well capable of blessing us in whatever way we most need. He is a faithful God! The question is: are we willing to accept the challenge of faithfully trusting him?

Why is it often hard for us to trust in God's care and promises?

DON'T FORGET TO PRAY AND HAVE A GREAT DAY!

Day 12

 Today's Reading:
Genesis 22:1-19

Can you imagine the challenge to Abraham's faith that this command of God must have posed? Any of us who are parents certainly understand the protective and nurturing instinct that we have toward our children. To consider voluntarily taking their lives is unthinkable. Yet, for Abraham, there was even more at stake. All of the great promises that God had made to him were reliant upon an heir. If Isaac was killed, then all of the promises of God would die with him. But it is this very point that made the willingness of Abraham to sacrifice his son so important and such a great lesson for us. You see, this test was not just about a father's love for his child; it was about his love for Jehovah and about whether that love was one that surpassed every other love and desire of his heart. It was also about his faith and trust in God—a faith that was so complete that he trusted God to do the impossible and to fix the unfixable. In human terms, to kill someone is permanent, but Abraham was to go even further. After killing Isaac, he was to offer him as a burnt offering to God. Not only would his life be taken but his body would be destroyed. Yet, the Hebrew writer gives us the insight that Abraham believed that the same God who had given him Isaac through the aged and barren womb of Sarah could also bring that dead and destroyed body back to life (Hebrews 11:17-19). Through this text, we are reminded in a vivid way of the kind of all-surpassing love and absolute trusting faith that we are to strive for in our own relationship with God. May God help us to continually grow in these areas!

What is the greatest test of faith that you have ever experienced?
What helped you to pass that test?

DON'T FORGET TO PRAY AND HAVE A GREAT DAY!

Day 13

Today's Reading:
Genesis 27:1-29

This scene from the life of Jacob is troubling to us. We expect these men who made up the line of patriarchs leading to the nation of Israel to be morally and ethically upright in every way. It is distressing to see Jacob involved in this underhanded plot to deceive Isaac and steal Esau's blessing. We are left in somewhat of a quandary to understand why God would allow this travesty to happen and how he could continue to bless Jacob despite this obvious wrongdoing. Remember, first of all, that the Lord had foretold these things while Esau and Isaac were still in the womb (Genesis 25:22-23). Later, in selling his birthright to Jacob, Esau would demonstrate a weakness of character that would prove him to be unqualified for spiritual leadership. By the way, the selling of his birthright to Jacob created an agreement between the brothers wherein Esau essentially forfeited his firstborn status and gave to Jacob all of the privileges of the firstborn, including the blessing of the father. It seems that there was plenty of blame to go around in this situation and everyone involved bore some of the fault. The bottom line seems to be that all of the players in this scene were human. They were all imperfect and subject to bad judgment and improper behavior. But God used these imperfect people and their imperfect ways to bring about his perfect will, and therein lies comfort and hope. As humans, we are all imperfect and have lives that are full of mistakes, shortcomings, and failures. But God is a perfect God who can use even our imperfections to bring about his perfect will. To God be the glory!

What are some imperfections that you have?
How has God used those imperfections to his glory?

DON'T FORGET TO PRAY AND HAVE A GREAT DAY!

DAY 14

 Today's Reading:
Genesis 29:1-30

Have you ever felt like you were deceived, mistreated, or cheated? Most of us have felt that way at one time or another. Can you imagine how Jacob must have felt when he learned that he had been tricked into marrying the wrong woman? Now, after yesterday's reading and considering what Jacob did to his brother, you might be thinking that he got what he deserved, but be that as it may, the fact remains that Laban acted deceptively in giving Leah to Jacob instead of Rachel. Think about the reaction of Jacob: first, he treated Leah properly. He had made a commitment to her, and though he had done so unknowingly, he remained faithful to that commitment. Second, he remained true to his love for Rachel. Despite Laban's underhanded actions, Jacob loved Rachel deeply and wanted to have her as his wife, so he worked to achieve that goal. Third, he acted with integrity toward Laban. Jacob did not return dishonesty for dishonesty. Instead, he held true to the arrangement that he made with Laban even though it required an additional seven years of service. Here is the point: in the world, some people are going to be dishonest at times. They are going to show a lack of integrity and fairness in their dealings with us. They are going to lie, cheat, and steal with no regard for our well-being. However, their attitudes and actions do not have to dictate ours. We do not have to treat others disrespectfully just because they treated us that way. We can choose to turn the other cheek and do the right thing regardless of how we are treated. We can choose to walk with God instead of walking in the way of sinners. Let's choose the better path!

Why is it often so hard to maintain our integrity when we are treated unfairly? What can we do to help us in those situations?

DON'T FORGET TO PRAY AND HAVE A GREAT DAY!

Day 15

 Today's Reading:
Genesis 37:1-36

What do you do when your dreams fall apart? How do you cope when the plans that you have for your life just don't work out the way you had envisioned? In the case of Joseph, this scenario became all too real when, as a seventeen year old young man, he literally dreamed of greatness in the form of a position of prominence and authority over his brothers and even his father. He would rule over them. But even while these dreams were still fresh in his mind, he was taken by his envious brothers, thrown into a pit and eventually sold into slavery. He was being taken to Egypt never to see his family again, at least as far as he knew at the time. This was not the life that he had imagined. His visions of grandeur had been crushed; his dreams shattered. But God had a plan that was much bigger and grander than Joseph had ever imagined! He knew perfectly well where Joseph needed to be and how to get him there, and although Joseph had to endure hardship for a time, God was always in control. And thus it is with us. There is no doubt that we all experience those times when our lives take an unexpected and undesirable turn, and we feel like our dreams have fallen apart and all hope for a meaningful future is over. We fret and worry and mourn our circumstances and maybe even wonder why God has deserted us. But, like Joseph, God has a plan for us—one that is bigger and grander than we can even imagine. We must simply, as the old song says, "trust and obey." If we will remain faithful to him and trust him with our lives, he will lead us to exactly where we need to be.

Why do you think that Joseph had to endure
such hardship in order to fulfill God's plan?

DON'T FORGET TO PRAY AND HAVE A GREAT DAY!

Day 16

 Today's Reading:
Genesis 39:1-23

F our times in this chapter, either by direct statement or observation, it is stated that the Lord was with Joseph. Whether Joseph was a slave, the overseer of Potiphar's house, or a falsely accused prisoner, the Lord was with him to bless him and cause him to flourish. It occurs to me that we are often very cognizant of God's presence and blessings when good things happen in our lives, but we are not as quick to acknowledge his abiding presence when our circumstances are difficult. Our reaction to trials is, more often, to petition him for help when we are struggling, almost as if he is not presently with us, but in answer to our prayers, he might come to our aid. However, this chapter seems to purposefully make the point that at the low points in Joseph's life, God was there. Though Joseph found himself in difficult situations and under unfair circumstances, God was there to turn his negatives into positives. Of course, though Joseph had no way of seeing this at the time, all of these episodes in his life were part of God's bigger plan to preserve his people. I am reminded of the words of Paul in Romans 8:28: "And we know that for those who love God all things work together for good, for those who are called according to his purpose." While it may be an unsettling reality of life that difficulties and trials will come, we can take courage in knowing that God is always there to provide the strength and help that we need. And who knows—maybe that hardship that we are struggling with is a negative that God will turn into a positive as he works to bring about his greater plan in our lives.

How has God turned negatives into positives in your life?

DON'T FORGET TO PRAY AND HAVE A GREAT DAY!

Day 17

 Today's Reading:
Genesis 41:1-36

It is very interesting to consider the ways that God worked throughout the Old Testament. He often used godless nations and people to accomplish his will. In this case, God worked in the lives of both Joseph and Pharaoh to reach his desired outcome. Through the dreams that were given to the Egyptian king and the wisdom granted to Joseph to interpret those dreams, a plan was set in motion to save the Egyptian nation from a devastating famine and, in the process, to save Joseph's family and God's people. What is the lesson to be learned from this series of events? That God is firmly in control of all things! God can use any nation, any person, or any situation to bring about his will. It does not have to be someone who is willing to acknowledge and submit to him. He can use unbelievers or even enemies to accomplish his will, not by an involuntary manipulation of their free will, but simply through his perfect knowledge and understanding of the world and its happenings and through his perfect providence. If all of this seems difficult to grasp, it is surely because of the transcendent greatness and glory of God that is far beyond our ability to comprehend. We truly serve a great God who continues to be active in our lives and world to providentially bring about his will and purpose. To him be all the glory and the praise!

Why do you think that Joseph had to endure
such hardship in order to fulfill God's plan?

DON'T FORGET TO PRAY AND HAVE A GREAT DAY!

DAY 18

Today's Reading:
Genesis 41:37-57

As we have considered the story of Joseph over the last few days, we have concentrated much of our attention on God, and rightly so, for his hand of blessing and care was certainly at the center of Joseph's success. However, we must not overlook the important role that Joseph's faithfulness played in these events. Throughout all of the trials that Joseph endured, his confidence in God and his determination to be faithful to God never wavered. When he met with success, he never became boastful or self-reliant in his attitude. Through his faithfulness to God's plan, even Pharaoh acknowledged God and gave him the glory. As Joseph carried out his given task of preparing Egypt for the coming famine, he never doubted the word of God or wavered in his duty to carry out the task that God had instructed. Remember that, though all of this was the plan of God, never was the free will of Joseph or any other person overruled. Joseph's actions were by his own volition and due to his trust in God and commitment to his faithfulness to him. While Joseph's life might teach us much about the power, wisdom, and purposes of God, it also teaches us a great lesson about the importance of our own faithfulness. Whether our circumstances are good or bad, easy or difficult, there is no greater or wiser course that we can take than the one that leads us to trust God and to commit ourselves to be faithfully obedient to him.

In what ways can our trust in and
commitment to God be demonstrated?

DON'T FORGET TO PRAY AND HAVE A GREAT DAY!

Day 19

Today's Reading:
Genesis 42:1-24

It doesn't make sense. Why would a man who is a foreigner, one who came to Egypt as a purchased slave, one who had spent years in an Egyptian prison, be placed in such a position of authority? Why would he be put in charge of Egypt's storehouses of grain, arguably their most valuable commodity during this time of severe famine? From a purely physical and historical point of view, it simply does not make sense. It shouldn't have happened... and yet it did! In these unlikely events from the life of Joseph, we see the marvelous providential care and working of God in all of its glory. Through the inspired pages of God's word, we are allowed to see behind the veil, as it were, to understand the purposes of God and to see his providence in action in extraordinary ways. Not even the malicious acts of jealous brothers, the slanderous lies of an immoral woman, or the unbelief of a godless nation could prevent God's will from being accomplished. Aren't you glad that we do not serve an uncaring and inactive God, but rather One who is constantly watching over us and working toward our good and ultimate salvation? Though we cannot always see his purposes as clearly as we can in the life of Joseph, we can be sure that, as long as we are walking with him, he is leading us in the direction of that will and purpose. It is in this "encouragement of the Scriptures" that we find the hope that Paul refers to in Romans 15:4. Thank God for the treasure of the Old Testament!

How would you explain the concept of
providence to someone who didn't understand it?

DON'T FORGET TO PRAY AND HAVE A GREAT DAY!

Day 20

 Today's Reading:
Genesis 45:1-28

Not only do we learn much about God and his working through the life of Joseph, but we also learn a great deal about ourselves and our dealings with life. Joseph experienced an immense amount of adversity in his life, much of it at the hands of his brothers, and while he had no control over those events in his life, Joseph was responsible for how he would respond to them. Would he be filled with bitterness, resentment, and hatred toward his brothers who had acted so treacherously toward him? Would he be angry with God and with life in general for all of the lost opportunities of his past? Certainly, if anyone has ever been justified in feeling those things, Joseph was. Yet, we find a remarkable peace with the past and recognition of God's work in the attitude and words of Joseph as he reveals himself to his brothers. With extraordinary faith and insight, Joseph is able to look beyond his own losses and hardships to see the bigger purposes of God at work. Instead of blaming his brothers for his circumstances, he credited God with providing a means of salvation for himself and many others. What a wonderful lesson for us! Adversity may be an unwelcome reality in all of our lives, but the way that we respond to that adversity can make all the difference. Often, all that is needed, in order to see God's hand of blessing in any circumstance of life, is faith—an obedient trusting of God to keep his promises and to work in our lives to bring about his will for our good. May God help us to have that kind of faith!

What are some things that we can do to find
strength to deal with adversity in a good way?

DON'T FORGET TO PRAY AND HAVE A GREAT DAY!

Day 21

**Today's Reading:
Genesis 46:28-47:12**

When we think of the Israelites in Egypt, we typically think of the bondage and hardship that they experienced in the days of Moses as recorded in the book of Exodus, but let us not forget that their dwelling in Egypt did not begin that way. When the family of Jacob came to Egypt to find relief from the famine and at the behest of Joseph, they were welcomed in by Pharaoh as guests, for the sake of Joseph. They were given a dwelling place in the best land that Egypt had to offer, and they were provided with all that they needed. Theirs was a happy and fruitful beginning in the land of Egypt. While it would not always be a good place for them, it was the perfect place at the time and for the purpose. It was the place that God had chosen for them and had led them to in order to preserve them. Some might would argue that God made a mistake in bringing them to Egypt, knowing the suffering that it would cause them in later generations. Surely he could have provided for them in another way. However, God's plans are always perfect for his purposes, both in the lives of the Israelites and in our lives today. Though his plans may lead us through dark and undesirable places at times, those places are a perfect part of God's bigger plan to teach us and mold us into what he would have us to be and to ultimately lead us to salvation.

*How do the struggles and difficulties of
our lives ultimately work for our good?*

DON'T FORGET TO PRAY AND HAVE A GREAT DAY!

DAY 22

**Today's Reading:
Genesis 50:1-26**

J acob, the grandson of Abraham and the man whose God-given name, Israel, would become the name of a nation, had died. Few deaths in the Old Testament receive the detailed attention that this one does. Joseph and his brothers mourn the loss of their patriarch, and for the sake of Joseph, the entire country of Egypt mourns with them. In a mixing of cultures and traditions, the body of Jacob is embalmed according to Egyptian standards and is then taken to the land of Canaan for burial with his fathers according to his request. Although death is a natural part of the cycle of life, it is anything but ordinary as an event in the life of a family. Regardless of the circumstances, death is traumatic and life-altering for those who are left behind. But while most of the recordings of this text have to do with the physical remains of Jacob and the dealings of those who survived him, we are also reminded that death represents a significant transition for the soul of man. In the final verse of chapter 49 which records the death of Jacob, we read this concluding statement: "and [he] was gathered to his people." While the body ceases to live upon death, the spirit, being separated from that body, goes to join the spirits of those who have gone before it in the unending halls of eternity. Jacob had not been a perfect man, but when all was said and done, he had trusted in God's faithfulness and committed his soul to the loving care of his Lord. As important as it was to Jacob that his body be laid to rest alongside those of his wives and ancestors, how much greater must it have been for his soul to be gathered into the presence of his faithful fathers and to rest in the comfort of his God.

How should the Christian view death?
Why is it often hard to see death in that way?

DON'T FORGET TO PRAY AND HAVE A GREAT DAY!

DAY 23

 Today's Reading:
Exodus 1:1-22

As the book of Exodus opens, we find that many years have passed and much has changed for the children of Israel and in Egypt. The number of Israelites, which began at 70 when they first came into Egypt, has multiplied greatly so that they have become a large and mighty population. Also, the reigning power in Egypt has changed so that the new ruler had no relationship with and felt no obligation to Joseph. He sees the Israelites, not as welcomed guests in his land, but as a threat to the security of Egypt. To deal with this threat, he seeks to control the Israelites by making them slaves. He also orders all male babies to be killed as a means of limiting their population and strength. Seemingly through no fault of their own, the children of Israel have fallen into very difficult circumstances and a time of much sorrow. Some might be tempted to ask, "Where is God, and why is he not doing something to help his people?" The only mention of God in this text is his blessing of the midwives who feared him and, therefore, refused to follow the Egyptian command to kill the male babies. But in that brief mention, a powerful truth is revealed in answer to the query: "Where is God?" Even in the midst of these dark days, God is working in unseen ways on behalf of his people. His plan to dis-play his mighty power and bring his people out of captivity is set and is already underway, though it will not become apparent to the Israelites for many years. Thus it is in our lives that even when our days are dark and we can't see God's hand at work, we can be assured that he is there, working in unseen ways for our good and salvation.

Why do you think that we often doubt
or question God during difficult times?

DON'T FORGET TO PRAY AND HAVE A GREAT DAY!

Day 24

 **Today's Reading:
Exodus 2:1-10**

While we are familiar with many of the more prominent heroes of the Bible, that holy book is also filled with a great many unsung heroes who, though not very well known or often acknowledged, are just as critical to the story of God's people and his plan for redeeming man. The book of Exodus might be dominated largely by the person of Moses as God's chosen leader to bring his people out of Egyptian bondage, but have you ever considered that if it were not for several individuals involved in saving him, he could not have lived to become what God had planned for him? There was Moses' mother who defied the orders of the Pharaoh in sparing his life and then, unbeknownst to Pharaoh's daughter, later became Moses' nurse. Then, there was Moses' sister who was watching as the baby was discovered by Pharaoh's daughter and "conveniently" volunteered to find a nurse, making it possible for Moses' own mother to care for him during his infancy. And of course, there was the daughter of Pharaoh who became an unwitting accomplice to God's plan by saving Moses' life and raising him in the very house of Pharaoh. Like the midwives of yesterday's readings, these women all played a role in bringing God's plan to pass whether they realized it or not. What about us? You see, God's plan to bring salvation to as many as possible is still underway (see 2 Peter 3:9), and you and I have a role to play in that plan. We may not be among the most well-known and prominent modern-day heroes of faith, but our contribution to the saving work of God is still crucial. May God help us to courageously do our part!

What can you do today to be a part of God's plan to save someone?

DON'T FORGET TO PRAY AND HAVE A GREAT DAY!

Day 25

Today's Reading:
Exodus 2:11-25

S ome of the greatest heroes of the Bible's story are also some of the most unlikely candidates for such prominent roles in God's work. Moses is certainly one of those. As we will see over the next couple of days, Moses was well aware of his shortcomings and very reluctant to accept God's calling. His attempts to decline God's assignment were possibly not so much a case of false humility or cowardly avoidance as they were an awareness of his difficult position and the obstacles that it would create for God's mission. In many ways, Moses was a man without a people. Born a Hebrew but raised as an Egyptian, he had sided with his people and killed an Egyptian in defense of a Hebrew. Wanted as a murderer by the Egyptians and labeled as a traitor by the Hebrews, he fled for his life away from everything and everyone that he knew. During the forty years that Moses spent shepherding his father-in-law's flocks in the land of Midian, one would have hardly guessed that he was bound for greatness. However, one of the wonderful lessons of God's word is that God is not bound by our thinking nor is he limited by our shortcomings. God is not nearly as interested in where we came from or what our limitations are as he is in what he can do through us. By his power, he can take the most unlikely candidate for greatness and do great things. The key, on our part, is simply to be willing to do his will and allow him to use us. If we are willing, then God can do great things, even with us!

What are some of the limitations of your life
that you feel hinder your usefulness to God?
Are any of those limitations things that God cannot overcome?

DON'T FORGET TO PRAY AND HAVE A GREAT DAY!

Day 26

 Today's Reading:
Exodus 3:1-22

We are often quick to criticize Moses for his lack of faith and his questioning of God's plan in this text. But honestly, when confronted with the consuming presence and transcendent glory of God as Moses was as he stood before the burning bush, who wouldn't see themselves as inadequate and unworthy. "Who am I..." would probably be the thought and question that any rational person would have in such a position. Moses' true shortcoming in this reaction to God's calling was not in his doubting of his own ability. In fact, from a purely physical standpoint, every one of his objections was legitimate. But, Moses fell woefully short by doubting God's perfect will and ability to overcome his human weaknesses. It is in this realization that we find one of the most important lessons that this episode from Moses' life has to teach us. As we consider our own calling from God to be an ambassador for Christ in the world and to strive to bring others to him, we are often painfully aware of our own shortcomings and weaknesses. We, like Moses, can often find ourselves making excuses and giving a wide array of reasons for why God should not depend on us. However, we must not underestimate God's ability to overcome our weaknesses and use us to accomplish his will. God never calls us to do anything alone; he always promises to be with us and to help us, even as he did with Moses. Therefore, our confidence is not in us but in him who works through us!

How can we learn to look past our weaknesses and see God's strength?

DON'T FORGET TO PRAY AND HAVE A GREAT DAY!

Day 27

 Today's Reading:
Exodus 4:1-17

A s we continue to examine this interaction between God and Moses, it occurs to me that for every excuse and obstacle that Moses offers, God has an answer and promises help. Beginning back in chapter 3, we notice: Moses says, "Who am I...?" God says, "I will be with you" (3:11-12). Moses says, "What shall I say to them about Your name?" God says, "I AM WHO I AM" (3:13-14). Moses says, "What if they don't believe me?" God says, "Show them My power" (4:1-9). Moses says, "I am not eloquent." God says, "I made your mouth. I will help you" (4:10-12). Moses says, "Please send someone else." God says, "I'll send Aaron with you but you are going!" (4:13-17). There was not a single question or objection that God was not prepared for and that he did not offer a solution for. He had thought of everything, and he provided Moses with every tool that he would need to accomplish the task that he was being charged with. What are some of our most common excuses? "I don't know enough." God's answer: 2 Timothy 3:16-17. "I'm not talented enough." God's answer: Romans 12:3-8; Ephesians 4:11-16. "I'm not good enough." God's answer: 1 John 1:7-2:2. "I just don't think I can do it." God's answer: Philippians 4:13; Hebrews 13:5-6. Yes, God has thought of everything and provided for every weakness that we have. So let us take courage and give ourselves to him, to fulfill his calling and do his will.

Take a few minutes to read God's answers to our
excuses that are referenced in this reading.
What do you learn from these verses?

DON'T FORGET TO PRAY AND HAVE A GREAT DAY!

DAY 28

 Today's Reading:
Exodus 5:1-23

Have you ever asked, "Why, God?" It is often a somewhat natural response to the difficult circumstances of life. Why has God allowed this suffering to take place in our lives? Why has he brought these hardships to us? Why hasn't he protected us from this adversity? Moses was sent to Egypt to deliver God's people from bondage, but his presence seems to have only aggravated the situation, making their lives and servitude even more difficult. The Israelites become angry with Moses, and Moses complains to God, not understanding how this turn of events fits within God's plan. Of course, as we read this passage within the overall scope of the story of God's deliverance of his people from Egyptian bondage, we understand that this, and every facet of this story works to bring about a demonstration of the glory and power of God Almighty. While that purpose and outcome might have been difficult for the Israelites to see in the midst of less-than-desirable circumstances, it is clearly seen in hindsight. Is not the same true for us? While in the midst of trials and tribulations, it is often impossible for us to see the hand of God at work or to understand his purposes. Like Moses, we might find ourselves asking, "Why?" But it is in those times that we must strive to be strengthened in our faith. Our paths may sometimes lead through dark and difficult places, but God is always there to see us through and to deliver us by his mighty hand.

Where can we find strength when we don't understand
or can't see God's purposes in the events of our lives?

DON'T FORGET TO PRAY AND HAVE A GREAT DAY!

DAY 29

Today's Reading:
Exodus 6:1-13

"I am the Lord." This phrase seems to be a sort of theme for this text. Its literal rendering is, "I am Yahweh." Yahweh, the Hebrew name for God, is more than just a name. It is a term that encapsulates every perfect and transcendent quality of God that makes him God and a name of which only he is worthy. When we read the story of the exodus, we might see only the mighty works of God done for the purpose of delivering his people from Egyptian bondage, but God had much more in mind. Through a powerful demonstration of both his vengeance and his care, Yahweh would reveal himself to his people in a way that would allow them to truly know and understand him and the meaning of his holy name. Never before had God revealed himself on such a large scale, but he wanted his people to know that he was a faithful God and one who would keep the covenant that he had made with their forefathers. He wanted them to know of his mercy, love, and care, but also of his righteousness and holiness. Above every so-called god that they had been exposed to in Egypt or that they would find in Canaan, he wanted them to know and revere him—Yahweh. One of the problems that we face today, even in the religious world, is that we have lost sight of who God is. We no longer know him as Yahweh or Jehovah. In our modern world, our understanding of God has been watered down so that we are no longer brought to our knees in his presence. In our arrogance, we presume to tell God what we will believe and how we will live with little regard for what he has commanded us. Certainly, one of the great purposes of the Old Testament is to help us to truly know and understand Yahweh. May God help us to listen to its instruction.

How can we develop the awe and
reverence that we need to have for God?

DON'T FORGET TO PRAY AND HAVE A GREAT DAY!

Day 30

Today's Reading:
Exodus 6:28-7:13

This scene reminds me of the commercials or television shows that give the viewers a warning that goes something like this: "These stunts are performed by highly-trained professionals using specialized equipment and in a controlled environment. Don't try this at home." You see, as God sends Moses and Aaron to go before Pharaoh, demanding the release of the children of Israel, he does not send them empty-handed. With the ability to perform miraculous signs, they are prepared to demonstrate the power of God to the king. But in an act of clear defiance, Pharaoh calls his own sorcerers to imitate the miraculous workings of Moses and Aaron by turning their own rods into serpents, just as Aaron had done. But in an unexpected twist, Aaron's serpent promptly swallows the serpents belonging to the sorcerers. What is the lesson for us? Beyond the obvious demonstration of the superiority of God's power over that of humans, the lesson may be that it is never a good idea to attempt to act like God. Only God is God! Only he can control nature and work in ways that are unbound by natural laws and limitations. When any human attempts to put himself in the place of God and to take on the authority or work that God has reserved for himself, he is not only doomed to failure but also places himself squarely in the path of God's judgment and wrath. Ours is not to replace God but rather to recognize him as God and to submit to his holy will.

What are some ways that we can be guilty of
attempting to take the place of God today?

DON'T FORGET TO PRAY AND HAVE A GREAT DAY!

Day 31

 Today's Reading:
Exodus 7:14-25

With this text, the well-known plagues of Egypt begin. Pharaoh's heart was hard and he had refused to obey God's command to let His people go. Therefore, to afflict Egypt with these bouts of severe suffering would be necessary in order to demonstrate God's power and authority and to convince Pharaoh to submit to his demand. For the Egyptians, the Nile River was, literally, their source of life. They depended on it to water the land during its flood stage, to provide drinking water, and to provide fish for food. So important was this body of water, in fact, that the Egyptians worshipped it as a representation of one of their most revered gods. The turning of this essential body of water to blood for seven days was, therefore, a devastating blow to the Egyptians. It is hard to image the suffering that this plague would have created—seven days without water to drink, to water livestock, or to use for other necessary activities; seven days of enduring the putrid stench of rotting blood and fish carcasses; seven days of being constantly reminded that this worshipped source of life and vitality had been turned into a source of death and decay. It is important to remember that this and all the plagues were about more than just punishing the Egyptians or forcing the release of God's people. They were about God demonstrating the power and authority over the world that only the true and living God can have. They were about proving that no false god and no earthly ruler could stand in the way of Yahweh and prevent his will from being done. That is a vital truth that we still need to be reminded of in today's world.

What false gods does our world tend to worship today?
How do those gods compare to the true and living God?

DON'T FORGET TO PRAY AND HAVE A GREAT DAY!

Day 32

Today's Reading:
Exodus 8:1-32

As we continue to see these loathsome plagues be brought down upon the land of Egypt by the mighty hand of God, there is a pattern of behavior that develops in Pharaoh that is not all that uncommon among men. When Pharaoh and his people were suffering under the weight of a plague, he was willing to heed the word of God and bow to his will, agreeing on several occasions to let the Israelites go. But as soon as the plague was removed, Pharaoh's heart was once again hardened, and he quickly withdrew his concession. Thus it so often is with men today. During very difficult and burdensome times in our lives, we may petition for the help of God, begging for his blessings and offering, in return, our repentance and faithfulness to his word. However, as soon as the trial has passed, we lose the willingness to submit to God's will and seemingly forget about our promise of repentance. Like Pharaoh, we, in essence, hold our obedience to God for ransom, only to double-cross him after receiving his help. But make no mistake—just as with Pharaoh, God is not fooled. He knows our hearts and motives perfectly. His patience and mercy is not a sign of his gullibility but rather a proof of his love. God gives us blessing after blessing and opportunity after opportunity, motivated by his desire to see us repent of our sins and come to him in faith and obedience. He is nothing if not longsuffering and merciful in his dealings with us, and yet, he is also ultimately just and righteous. May we learn from the mistakes of Pharaoh and truly submit our hearts and lives to the will of God.

How can we acknowledge and show appreciation
for the patience and mercy of God?

DON'T FORGET TO PRAY AND HAVE A GREAT DAY!

Day 33

 Today's Reading:
Exodus 9:1-35

One of the most fascinating elements of the Old Testament is to be able to see and understand the working of God in the world and in the lives of men to bring about his will and purposes. In this text, Pharaoh was far from being a godly man; he neither believed in God nor was he willing to meet God's demands, even amidst the relentless barrage of plagues that were coming upon his nation. Yet, God knew and was involved in Pharaoh's life for the working out of his own plan. In fact, this text tells us that God reveals to Pharaoh through Moses that "for this purpose I have raised you up, to show you my power, so that my name may be proclaimed in all the earth." Before Moses was ever called by God to go into Egypt and lead the Israelites out of captivity, God's plan was in place. He had chosen this man to be Pharaoh over Egypt, knowing that his arrogance, stubbornness, and hard-heartedness would allow for God's power and glory to be shown. God had allowed him to sit on Egypt's throne and given him this position of authority for the working of his greater purposes. It is this kind of "behind the scenes" view of God's involvement in the world, provided by the Old Testament, that gives us some insight into his involvement in our lives today. While we may not be able to see God's hand at work or know exactly how the circumstances of our lives will work to accomplish God's will, we can have great confidence that God is working and that his good purposes will be accomplished (see Romans 8:28).

Why do you think we often struggle to see
God's hand at work in our world today?

DON'T FORGET TO PRAY AND HAVE A GREAT DAY!

DAY 34

Today's Reading:
Exodus 10:1-29

What are we to make of the statement, "the Lord hardened Pharaoh's heart"? There is no doubt that Pharaoh was a stubborn and hard-hearted man who seemed determined to keep the children of Israel captive at all costs. However, in his moments of weakness due to the devastation of the plagues when Pharaoh seemed willing to acknowledge God and bow to his will, are we to understand that God interfered with his free will by hardening his heart, thus causing him to change his mind? Certainly not! The message of the Bible as a whole is that God's character and intent with regard to man is such that he cannot and will not manipulate man's free will for His own purposes. Therefore, we are left to wonder what this statement means. It is important to note that, in many instances in the Scriptures, there is little or no distinction made between God causing something to happen and allowing or permitting something to happen. In the cases of Pharaoh's heart being hardened, God caused the hardening of his heart only in the sense that he removed the plague, according to Pharaoh's request. The removal of the plague then allowed for a reversal of Pharaoh's attitude and decision regarding the Israelites. While that reversal of attitude was foreknown to God, it was never out of Pharaoh's hands to make his own decisions. In a similar way, God might allow events to take place in our lives and, at times, use those events to accomplish his purposes, but he will never overrule or otherwise manipulate our free will. He is truly a just and righteous God!

Why is our free will necessary to the
character and righteousness of God?

DON'T FORGET TO PRAY AND HAVE A GREAT DAY!

Day 35

 **Today's Reading:
Exodus 11:1-10**

The horrible plagues that God has brought upon Egypt have been devastating to the Egyptians' way of life. Their water has been tainted, their land defiled, their livestock killed, and their vegetation destroyed. Their bodies have been ravaged with boils and even their sky has been darkened. But with the promise of the tenth plague, there is no doubt that the worst is yet to come. This final plague, the death of the firstborn male of every household of Egypt and of their livestock, visited upon the nation by God himself, would finally break the will of Pharaoh and secure the freedom of the children of Israel. While it may seem to us that the severity of God's wrath was too much in this case, we must remember that God had given Pharaoh nine previous opportunities to comply—nine plagues that demonstrated God's power and that warned of his judgment, nine reasons to heed his word and obey his command, nine occasions to repent of his sins and submit to God's will. As much as the plagues are a testament to the severity of God's judgment, they are also a reminder of his longsuffering and forbearance. Whether in ancient Egypt or in today's world, God is a patient God who provides opportunity after opportunity for people to recognize their need for him and to come to him in faith and obedience. He is slow to anger and abundant in mercy because he is "not wishing that any should perish but that all should reach repentance" (2 Peter 3:9). May we heed God's warnings and submit to his will while we have the opportunity.

*What can we learn from the Pharaoh about
our own repentance and God's longsuffering?*

DON'T FORGET TO PRAY AND HAVE A GREAT DAY!

Day 36

Today's Reading:
Exodus 12:1-28

The Passover—it was Israel's greatest feast and their most treasured event. Before bringing the tenth plague upon Egypt, God gives his people instructions on, not only how to be protected from the plague, but also on how to commemorate this event throughout their generations. As we, through the blessing of God's inspired word, consider the cross of Christ, we cannot help but notice the obvious similarities between the Passover of Exodus and the atoning sacrifice of Jesus on the cross. We often attribute those similarities to God's intentional fashioning of the events of the cross after the time-honored emblems of the Passover so cherished by the Jews. However, it occurs to me that our ordering of the design of those two events is actually backwards. God did not fashion the crucifixion after the Passover; rather he fashioned the Passover after the crucifixion. While the events surrounding the tenth plague were certainly an important part of Israel's history, every element of the instructions that God gave to them in preparing for that night and for commemorating it was for the ultimate purpose of foreshadowing the crucifixion of Christ—the "passing over" of those who had been covered with the blood of the Lamb and thus protected from the penalty of sin—spiritual death. While the Passover of Exodus was certainly important, it did not compare to the efficacy or importance of the atoning death of Christ on the cross. The cross did not point backward; the Passover pointed forward.

What instructions has God given us for
commemorating Jesus' death on the cross?

DON'T FORGET TO PRAY AND HAVE A GREAT DAY!

Day 37

Today's Reading:
Exodus 12:29-51

As I think about the exodus of the children of Israel from Egypt, I am reminded of their coming into Egypt. The father and brothers of Joseph, along with other family members, had come to Egypt under difficult circumstances. God had sent Joseph ahead of them to prepare the way and to provide a means of salvation for them from the famine. They were treated with favor at first because of Joseph, but they eventually became slaves to the Egyptians. Throughout their 430 years of history in Egypt, this family had grown into a great nation of people. Despite Egypt's disdain of them and the hardships that were placed upon them, they had flourished by God's bountiful hand. Now, as they leave Egypt, they do so as a people who are clearly under the care and protection of the Almighty God. They have departed with their lives, their possessions, their livestock, and much of Egypt's wealth. As I envision the long procession of Israelites on their way out of Egyptian bondage, I am reminded of the constant love and care of a faithful God. Throughout their long tenure in a foreign land, he had never forgotten his covenant with Abraham, Isaac, and Jacob and was now, at long last, leading them toward their promised land. What a reminder that is of my own relationship with God. As I consider my life in this world, I am so very grateful for a faithful God who has not forgotten his covenant with us through Christ and who continues to care for and lead his children through this world and toward the promised land of heaven.

In what ways does God care for us as we journey through life?

DON'T FORGET TO PRAY AND HAVE A GREAT DAY!

DAY 38

Today's Reading:
Exodus 13:1-22

D on't forget! That seems to be the theme of this chapter as God gives some preliminary instructions and laws to his newly freed people. As humans, we tend to have very short memories at times. Lessons that we learn and commitments that we make, both in times of hardship and in times of rejoicing, often seem to be quickly forgotten as soon as our circumstances change. The Israelites witnessed, first-hand, the power and glory with which God had delivered them. They were, no doubt, awed by his might and grateful for his care during the weeks leading up to their exodus from Egypt. But that country and its struggles were quickly becoming part of their past and God knew how quickly they would forget all that he had done for them, how soon they would begin to murmur and complain, and how easily they would give themselves to idol worship. Even before the Israelites were beyond the reach of their previous captors, God begins to put memorials and laws into place to serve as a preventative measure against that forgetfulness. We may think it sad that God's people would be so quick to forget about him and all that he had done for them to bring them out of bondage and to give them a land, but, unfortunately, we are sometimes guilty of the same shortcomings. Yes, the propensity to forget is still alive and well in our world today. Though we were rescued from sin at the enormous cost of God's only Son, and though Christ willingly bore our sins on the cross and suffered immensely for our transgressions, we are, far too often, quick to forget about his great love and sacrifice as we rush head-long into sin. May we be constantly reminded of all that God has done for us through Christ.

What things and practices has God put into
place to constantly remind us of his goodness?

DON'T FORGET TO PRAY AND HAVE A GREAT DAY!

DAY 39

 Today's Reading:
Exodus 14:1-31

What stands out to me in this passage is the faith and confidence that Moses demonstrates in God on this occasion. The same Moses who did not want to take on the task of being the deliverer of the children of Israel and who questioned and doubted God even after returning to Egypt has grown mightily in his faith. As he stands with the Israelites, hemmed in by the Red Sea and watching the armies of Egypt bear down on them, Moses does not flinch. While others panic and cry out in hopelessness, Moses is still and calm, responding, "Fear not, stand firm, and see the salvation of the Lord, which he will work for you today." Notice that, when Moses says this to the people, he has not been given any instructions by the Lord yet. He does not know what God's plan is for dealing with the Egyptians. He simply knows that the God who delivered them out of Egypt by His mighty hand would also deliver them on this occasion. It occurs to me that this kind of faith does not come naturally or easily. For Moses, it developed as a result of the many times that he had followed the instructions of the Lord and witnessed God's faithfulness and power. For us, the discipline of unwavering faith is developed in much the same way. Life's circumstances will often lead us down dark and difficult paths. We might often wonder why and even question God's care, but it is in this crucible of trial that we are often able to see the faithfulness and power of God most clearly, and it is only through these trials that we learn to trust God most completely. May God help us to have a faith and confidence in him that will allow us to "Fear not, stand firm, and see the salvation of the Lord."

Is there a time when you witnessed the "salvation of the Lord" in your own life? If so, how did that event help to strengthen your faith?

DON'T FORGET TO PRAY AND HAVE A GREAT DAY!

DAY 40

 Today's Reading:
Exodus 16:1-36

The grumbling and complaining in this passage had become the common rhetoric of the Israelites whenever they became discontent with their circumstances. In this case, it was a lack of food that had prompted their complaints, and in response, God provided manna. This heavenly bread that would appear with the morning dew would sustain the nation until they came into the land of Canaan, but it came with some requirements and restrictions that were designed to teach the Israelites some important lessons about God and their relationship with him. First, God required the Israelites to gather the manna each day. In certain situations in times to come, God miraculously provides food stores that will not run out. But it was important for the Israelites to understand that effort was required of them in order to benefit from what God was providing. Secondly, they were only allowed to gather enough manna for one day's provisions (except for the day before the Sabbath). This restriction provided a daily reminder for the people that they were constantly reliant upon God for their survival. Each night's last thought and each morning's first thought was likely that they would have nothing to eat unless God provided it. These lessons of God's care and their own obedient effort were important to Israel and are still important to us, for our circumstances are not as different from theirs as they might initially appear. While God provides for us both physically and spiritually, those provisions come with requirements and restrictions.

What are some of the requirements and restrictions that
God has placed on his blessings toward us today?

DON'T FORGET TO PRAY AND HAVE A GREAT DAY!

Day 41

 Today's Reading:
Exodus 17:1-16

On this occasion, Israel faced the first adversary that they had encountered since leaving Egypt. In the battle against Amalek, we find an interesting and unusual attribute of this fight. The outcome of the battle was not to be determined by the strength or weakness of the armies on the battlefield, but rather by a simple gesture of Moses as he overlooked the battle. As long as Moses kept his hands raised, the army of Israel prevailed, but whenever he put his hands down, they began to be defeated. As the battle wore on, Moses grew weary in trying to maintain the difficult posture. Seeing the struggle of their leader to fulfill God's command, Aaron and Hur come to his aid by providing a rock for Moses to sit on and then by standing at Moses' side to hold his arms up. Through their combined efforts, the victory was won. God showed the Israelites that victory would not come by their power; victory would come by the mighty power of God. They would succeed or fail based upon their submission and obedience to him. Another important and practical lesson in this text is that we often need the help of others as we face the battles of life. This battle was not won based on the actions of any one person. Joshua was on the battlefield leading the troops, but he could not prevail without Moses fulfilling God's command. Likewise, Moses could not fulfill God's command without the help of Aaron and Hur. It took all of them, helping one another and fulfilling their given roles to complete the task. So it is with us. We each have a place and a role within the kingdom of God, and our victory will only be won as we work together to achieve success.

Can you think of others in your life who might need help in their spiritual struggle? What can you do to help them be victorious?

DON'T FORGET TO PRAY AND HAVE A GREAT DAY!

Day 42

 Today's Reading:
Exodus 18:1-27

M oses was the divinely chosen leader of the people of Israel. It was a position and responsibility that he took very seriously. The scene that is described in this text had, apparently, become a normal day-to-day routine for Moses as he sat from sunup to sundown answering questions, settling disputes, and judging in matters that were brought to him by a seemingly endless line of Israelites. It took a fresh set of eyes to see the fallacy in this system, and Jethro, Moses' father-in-law, provided that new perspective. You see, Moses was diligent in his service and determined to be the leader that God had called him to be, but in his efforts to fulfill that calling, however noble they may have been, he had created a system that was inefficient and unsustainable. Like many of us, Moses was trying to take care of everything himself and was unwilling to ask for help. In so doing, he was wearing himself out and creating discontentment among the people. Jethro's solution: delegate. Recruit some help. Find capable and trustworthy men and let them take some of the load. What's the lesson for us? Whether in our work in the kingdom or in our own personal lives, there are times when we will surely find ourselves unable to bear the load alone; times when we are overwhelmed by the scope or burden of the work before us. In those situations, Jethro's advice continues to ring true— find dependable and trusted people to help carry that load. Don't be too stubborn or proud to ask for help. The result of that concession will surely be greater success and more effective work for the Lord.

Why do you think we often try to do everything ourselves
instead of asking for help? How can we remedy this problem?

DON'T FORGET TO PRAY AND HAVE A GREAT DAY!

DAY 43

Today's Reading:
Exodus 19:1-25

In this chapter of Exodus, the children of Israel arrive at Sinai. This will be a very important place and time for this people as God delivers to them, through Moses, the law that will serve as their governing document in all matters, both civil and religious. But before giving them the law, God went about the task of showing them who he was. They had witnessed his power, but if they were going to be obedient and faithful to him, it was vital that Israel understand the nature and essence of God. They needed to see his transcendence and unapproachable glory. They needed to stand in awe of his holiness and bow before him in humility. And so, God showed himself to them, not in physical form but in thunder and lightning, smoke and fire—a demonstration of power and glory that left no doubt that God was one to be revered, obeyed, and feared. You know, it occurs to me that much of the reason that many are not willing to fully commit to God today is that we don't really know God. We have an image of God but do not understand the holiness and glory of Jehovah, the great I AM. We forget that we were created by him and for him and that we exist and are sustained by his will and merciful hand. We often do not feel the need to bow in his presence or to humble ourselves before him. We do not understand what a privilege it is to go before him in prayer or to lift our voices to him in worship. We have lost the sense of fear and awe with which we should approach him. Oh that we might learn to esteem God with the reverence and honor that is due him!

What are some of the ways that we can
show proper reverence and honor to God?

DON'T FORGET TO PRAY AND HAVE A GREAT DAY!

Day 44

**Today's Reading:
Exodus 20:1-21**

The Ten Commandments. Even in our modern world they stand, at least in the eyes of some, as a symbol of our responsibility to respect God and his commands. Though there was much more to the Law of Moses than these ten commands, these preliminary instructions provided a basic model for one's behavior and relationships in the world. The first four commands dealt with man's relationship with God and centered on the idea that God was the only true and living God and was to, alone, receive man's worship and obedience. He was to be respected, loved, and obeyed. The last six of the commands dealt with man's relationship with man and centered on the idea of treating others with love, fairness, and respect. In the New Testament, Jesus sums up the whole law in two commands: Love God with all of your heart, soul, mind, and strength, and love your neighbor as yourself (Matthew 22:37-39). It is easy to see the application of these two principles in the Ten Commandments. The Ten Commandments are no longer in force today since they are part of the old law and covenant; however, all but one of them ("Remember the Sabbath") have been reaffirmed in some way under the new covenant so that they still become binding principles for Christians today. In fact, Jesus teaches us that God expects an even greater level of faithfulness and obedience than the old law required, demanding not just the actions but also the hearts and minds of his people (see Matthew 5:21-48). May we learn from the Ten Commandments what God would have us to do concerning our relationship with him and with others, and may it motivate us to ever grow in our love and faithfulness towards him.

*Do loving God and loving man still sum up
the whole law of God? Why or why not?*

DON'T FORGET TO PRAY AND HAVE A GREAT DAY!

DAY 45

 Today's Reading:
Exodus 24:1-18

A couple of days ago, the thought focused on the glory, majesty, and holiness of God and the resulting humility and awe that should be produced in us as we come before him. With those thoughts in mind, can you imagine being in Moses' position and going into the presence of God as he did on Mount Sinai? Moses had directly interacted with God before, such as the occasion before the burning bush, but we get a sense from this passage that this was a completely different experience. This occasion was special and unique. As Moses disappeared into the cloud that consumed the mountain, he entered into the presence of God in a spectacular way. I see, in this scene, an important lesson to be learned about God. God did not want to be just a provider and protector for Israel. He did not want to be merely a giver and enforcer of laws. He wanted more than to be just an object of their worship like the multitude of false gods were to other nations. God wanted a relationship with Israel. He wanted to be their God and for them to be his people. He wanted their obedience and worship to be based in faith and love, not simply out of obligation or fear. So, even as he was delivering the law to Moses, he did so in a way that demonstrated his personal interest in and involvement with them. That desire of God is still present for us today. He does not just want to be feared or obeyed. He wants to have a relationship with us that is based on love, faith, and devotion. He wants to be a Father to us, caring for, providing for, protecting, and loving us. So great is that desire that he came to us, not in a cloud of smoke and fire, but in the person of his Son to dwell among us and to give himself for us in order to secure that relationship. What a wonderful God he is!

Why do you think that God desires a personal relationship with us today?

DON'T FORGET TO PRAY AND HAVE A GREAT DAY!

Day 46

Today's Reading:
Exodus 25:1-22

If God was going to have a covenant relationship with the Israelites, he would have to provide a means by which he could be made available to them—a meeting place of sorts where they could come to worship and petition him. This special place, the tabernacle, would be a constant reminder of the Israelites' relationship with God, serving as their place of worship and, literally, the center of their encampments and their lives. This portable structure would hold several items, each built according to God's explicit instructions and each serving a specific purpose, but none was more special or important than the Ark of the Covenant. This sacred item was a symbol of their covenant with God and would be filled with reminders of God's protection, his provision, and his law. Atop the ark sat the mercy seat of God. This ornate covering represented the very place where God would come down to meet with his people. It was the place where atonement of sins was sought and received. But, because of sin, the Ark of the Covenant and mercy seat of God had to be separated from the people. It could not be touched by man under penalty of death. A veil separated it from the rest of the tabernacle and only the High Priest could enter its presence on one specially appointed day of the year. It was as close as man could get to God because of the guilt of sin. We have no ark of the covenant today. No mercy seat. There is no need for one because sin no longer represents an insurmountable obstacle. Christ came to destroy sin's power and to deliver us from its chains. The veil has been torn away and we have un-fettered access to God. He lives within our hearts and we can enter into his very presence in prayer. Thanks be to God and to his marvelous Son who has freed us from sin and given us the blessing of reconciliation.

How did Christ destroy sin's power and how can we overcome it?

DON'T FORGET TO PRAY AND HAVE A GREAT DAY!

Day 47

 Today's Reading:
Exodus 32:1-35

The golden calf—in some ways, it represents all that is wrong with our religious world, even today, and reveals many of the inherent weaknesses of humanity. In Moses' prolonged absence, the children of Israel had become impatient and maybe somewhat bored. In their discontentment, their memories of God's mighty power and benevolent care had been dulled, and their recently vowed commitment to God had waned. Interestingly, it seems that the Israelites were not enticed by something that they were currently seeing or experiencing, and thus allowed their hearts to stray from God. Rather, it would appear that their hearts strayed first, and in that straying, they began to look for something to fulfill their wayward desires. That "something" came in the form of a golden calf—an idol made from their own gold jewelry and fashioned by the hand of Aaron at their request. They credited this god for bringing them out of the land of Egypt; they worshipped and sacrificed to it, and they even called the idol by the holy name of Yahweh, a name reserved only for God Almighty. In these acts, they violated the first three of the Ten Commandments given to them by God not long before this event took place. What does this have to do with our world today? Well, it seems that people are always looking for something new, different, or innovative to implement into religion—a new teaching, a new belief, a new way of worship, a new concept of "church," and the list goes on and on. In so doing, we, like the Israelites, often push God to the side and dismiss him in favor of our own type of golden calf. While there may sometimes be a need to evaluate and update our methods in doing the Lord's work, we must never choose to dishonor and replace God with something of our own creation.

What are some things that can and do become
"golden calves" in our religious world today?

DON'T FORGET TO PRAY AND HAVE A GREAT DAY!

DAY 48

 Today's Reading:
Exodus 33:1-23

This text provides a rich and beautiful glimpse into the relationship of Moses with the Lord. If the children of Israel were dismayed over the pronouncement that God would not go up among them as they went into the Promised Land, Moses was completely devastated. The thought of not being able to continue their ritual of speaking "face to face" in the tent of meeting was more than he could bear. Therefore, much of this chapter is devoted to the pleading of Moses for God to not take his presence away from them. Within Moses' words, there is a statement that I want to bring to your attention—one that should have a great deal of significance for us today as God's people. In verse 16, Moses says to the Lord: "For how shall it be known that I have found favor in your sight, I and your people? Is it not in your going with us, so that we are distinct, I and your people, from every other people on the face of the earth?" One of the reasons that Moses was so desperate for God to remain with them was so that they could be distinct from all the other nations because of his favor toward them. Though in the New Testament God similarly offers his favor to those who are in Christ today, it seems that the more common trend for us is to look for ways to be anything but distinct. We want to fit in, to be like the world. And so, to accomplish that goal, we often strive to look, sound, and act like those around us. Yet, how often does the Bible tell us to be different and distinct from the world? (See Romans 12:1; 2 Corinthians 6:17; Titus 2:14; Revelation 18:4) May God help us to ever desire to be closer to him and farther away from the world.

Why do you think that we so often try to be like everyone else?
How are we to be distinct as God's people?

DON'T FORGET TO PRAY AND HAVE A GREAT DAY!

Day 49

 Today's Reading:
Exodus 34:1-35

We have seen and will continue to see many fascinating attributes of God as we journey through the Old Testament. After all, that is a big part of its purpose for us today. But maybe none of those attributes of God are as awe-inspiring or praise-worthy as is his merciful love and longsuffering. As he describes himself in this very passage, he is "slow to anger, and abounding in steadfast love and faithfulness." It seems that no matter how far the Israelites wander away from him or how grievous their sins, he is always willing to forgive them and take them back. As he rewrites his commands on new stone tablets to replace the ones that Moses had broken in his anger over the sins of the people, God also re-establishes his covenant with Israel. He will continue to care for them, bless them, and give them victory over their enemies, not because of their worthiness but because of his own faithfulness. If God gave us the Old Testament to teach us these important lessons about himself, then surely we need to understand him in the same way today. He is still a merciful and patient God who is slow to anger and abounding in love and faithfulness. As humans, we constantly miss the mark and fall short of his glory and, yet, he saw fit to make a way for us through His Son. Though we might, at times, shun him and follow after other things, he continues to love us as his children. God's love and longsuffering are truly amazing, and as I look at the imperfections and failures of my own life, I am certainly thankful for a God such as him! Aren't you?

How has God shown His faithfulness to you?
How have you shown your love and thankfulness to him in return?

DON'T FORGET TO PRAY AND HAVE A GREAT DAY!

Day 50

 Today's Reading:
Exodus 40:1-38

What a glorious event this must have been for the Israelites. For some time, they had been building and preparing the different elements and furnishings for the tabernacle. Though it was to be temporary and portable in nature, it was, nonetheless, a magnificent structure that represented God's presence among them and acted as the holy place where their worship would be performed and where the Lord would meet with them. In our modern era, we might be tempted to quickly draw a parallel between the tabernacle of old and our church buildings of today. After all, at first glance, there seem to be some important similarities between them as they are both buildings dedicated largely to the worship of God. However, we must remember that the two are far from the same. While the tabernacle was truly a special and holy place, our church buildings today are only buildings—locations designed to provide comfortable and convenient places for our gatherings. If there is a modern-day parallel to the tabernacle, it is the body and life of the Christian and of the collective body of Christians, the church. God dwells, not within a physical structure, but within the hearts of his people. In that relationship with God, we are blessed far above the people of God under the old covenant. Christ has removed that veil that served to separate God from man and has allowed us to have access to him. So give thanks and live so that the tabernacle of your body and life brings honor and glory to God!

If our bodies are tabernacles, how should our
lives represent God's presence and holiness?

DON'T FORGET TO PRAY AND HAVE A GREAT DAY!

Day 51

 Today's Reading:
Leviticus 1:1-17

S acrifices were a very important part of the religious lives of the Israelites. While these sacrifices were offered at different times and for different purposes, there were some aspects of the process that were consistent and vital to the sacrifice being pleasing to God. Though the sacrificial system of the Old Testament is no longer in place, there is still much that it can teach us about God and his expectations of his people, both then and now. You see, while God's requirements and desires for his people with regard to their worship and obedience might have changed, his heart and character has not. So, what can we learn about God from sacrifices that can be helpful to us today? For one thing, when someone brought a gift to God to offer as a sacrifice, God required that it be "without blemish" (or in the case of a grain offering, the "firstfruits"). God did not want the unwanted and worthless animal—the sick, the lame, the injured, or the weak. He wanted the "unblemished" animal—the best that the worshipper had to offer, for it was that sacrifice that the worshipper offered with thought, purpose, and love. While God does not require animal sacrifices from his people anymore, he still wants and requires sacrifices "without blemish." He still wants the best that we have to offer. In our worship, our service, our giving, and our lives, God desires that we commit ourselves to him with the same thought, purpose, and love that he wanted from the Old Testament worshipper. The form of the sacrifice has changed, but the motivation and attitude behind it is still the same.

What are the sacrifices that we offer to God today?
How can those sacrifices be "without blemish"?

DON'T FORGET TO PRAY AND HAVE A GREAT DAY!

Day 52

Today's Reading:
Leviticus 10:1-20

Those who served as priests among the Israelites had a great responsibility to keep the law of God and to ensure that God's laws and requirements were followed with regard to the sacrifices that they made on behalf of the people. Nadab and Abihu serve as a classic example of the seriousness of that charge to keep God's commandments in the carrying out of their priestly duties. As part of those duties, the priests prepared an incense offering to God twice daily. Every detail of that incense offering was pre-determined by God, including the mixture of ingredients that made up the incense and the source of the fire used to offer the incense. A censer was to be used to retrieve hot coals from the altar that sat outside the holy place, the altar on which animal sacrifices were offered. The fire from that altar was the only source that God had authorized for the incense offering. Nadab and Abihu made the mistake of using unauthorized fire, that is, fire from a source other than the altar of burnt offerings, in the making of the incense offering. These priests probably thought, like many people would, that it really didn't matter where the fire came from. After all, fire is fire, right? What they failed to consider is that the source of fire mattered simply because God said it did when he dictated a specific source. In this example, we find another of those lessons learned about God from the Old Testament sacrificial system. That lesson is that when God gives a command, he means it and expects his people to follow it. Too often, we try, like Nadab and Abihu, to use our own logic and reasoning to figure out new or better ways to do things. In some cases, there is no problem with that, but when it comes to those things that God has directly and specifically commanded, we must not stray from his mandates. We must remember that if God has given a specific command, then only our obedience to that specific command will please him.

If our bodies are tabernacles, how should our
lives represent God's presence and holiness?

DON'T FORGET TO PRAY AND HAVE A GREAT DAY!

Day 53

 **Today's Reading:**
Leviticus 11:1-23

This chapter begins a series of commands concerning things that were clean and things that were unclean. Beginning with clean and unclean animals, God directs Israel to avoid those animals that he identifies as unclean. Possibly the most common question today concerning these commands is "Why?" What was the purpose for the many restrictions that God placed upon his people? While there may be several reasons for these restrictions, possibly the most important one, and the one from which we learn the most, is that God desired for his people to remain separate and apart from the nations that surrounded them. He did not want them to take part in the idolatrous ways of those around them or to be defiled by their unholy practices. God's greatest concern for Israel was always their spiritual well-being and faithfulness. While it was unavoidable that they be in contact with nations and people with other gods and other standards of living, God desired for his people to remain pure and holy, untouched by the sinful practices of those around them. While restrictions regarding clean and unclean animals might not be in place today, God still certainly wants the same spiritual faithfulness and purity for his people in Christ. He remains determined that those who come to him through Christ must leave the world behind, with all of its sin and uncleanness, and be wholly devoted to doing his will. Like the Israelites of old, we must make a choice about whom we will serve and how we will live. May we always choose God!

What are some ways in which we are called to be unlike the world today?

DON'T FORGET TO PRAY AND HAVE A GREAT DAY!

DAY 54

 Today's Reading:
Leviticus 16:1-34

It was, in many ways, the most important day of the year for the Israelites. On this day, and this day alone, the High Priest was allowed to go beyond the veil into the Holy of Holies for the purpose of sprinkling the blood of sacrifices on the mercy seat of God. On this day, through a series of ceremonies and sacrifices performed according to God's strict commands, the sins of the Israelites were confessed and atonement was provided. Yet, those sins could not be completely cleansed, for the blood of bulls and goats could never have sufficient power to remove the stain of sin. No matter how meticulously the High Priest and Israelites followed God's instructions for these sacrifices, they would never be enough. So, the Day of Atonement would be a day, not only to atone for their sins, but also to remind them of all of the accumulated sins of their lives. What a frustrating and hopeless feeling that must have been for the Israelites, but even in the inadequacy of the sacrifices offered on the Day of Atonement, God had provided hope through the promise of an eventual sacrifice whose blood would be powerful enough to cover every sin and to cleanse them completely. Through their own experiences, the Israelites learned, as we do through their story recorded in the Old Testament, that sin carries a curse that is not easily removed. One cannot simply obey a command or make a sacrifice and cleanse himself of the stain of sin. Rather, disobedience toward God carries a penalty that can only be removed by the power of God himself. But thanks be to God that he was willing to offer the greatest of all sacrifices, his own Son, to pay the price for sin and provide a means of cleansing for mankind.

Why do you think that God required these sacrifices
if they were unable to completely remove sins?

DON'T FORGET TO PRAY AND HAVE A GREAT DAY!

DAY 55

 Today's Reading:
Leviticus 17:1-16

Blood. In our modern medical understanding, we know well the vital importance of blood to the health and well-being of the body. We understand the purpose that blood serves and the role that it plays in maintaining good health. However, that medical knowledge is relatively new to humankind. For that reason, it is striking that this ancient writing reveals a truth about blood that would not be understood by humankind until thousands of years later. For the believer, this is one of many faith-building evidences of the divine source of the Bible. For the skeptic, it is another difficult dilemma that must be dealt with. For the people of God to whom these words were originally given, it was a reminder of the vast importance of blood in their relationship with God. By God's design, the blood of animal sacrifices was a necessary part of their worship, atonement, and everyday dealings with him. Without the shedding of blood, there could be no peace with God and no acceptance by him. You see, the statement that "life is in the blood" was true not only in physical terms, but also in spiritual terms. Even under the old covenant, spiritual life was not possible without blood. Still today, one cannot approach God and hope to find forgiveness or acceptance without the presence of blood. No, we do not make animal sacrifices today. There is no blood shed on a daily basis in order to demonstrate our devotion to God. The blood that we depend on is the blood of the Son of God that was shed for our sins. Without being washed in that blood, we cannot hope to have a relationship with God. Yes, there is life in the blood, and nowhere is that more true than in the eternal life to be found in the blood of Christ.

How do we go about being washed in the blood of Christ?

DON'T FORGET TO PRAY AND HAVE A GREAT DAY!

DAY 56

**Today's Reading:
Numbers 10:11-36**

After nearly a year of encampment at Sinai, the order is given for the Israelites to break camp and commence their journey toward Canaan. It has been an eventful period for the nation. They have received God's law, quickly violated that newly established covenant by fashioning and worshipping an idol, experienced God's wrath for their disobedience, witnessed his mercy and forbearance, constructed the tabernacle and all of its furnishings, and put many of their God-given procedures and practices into place as instructed. But now the time has come to begin to make their way to their final destination. While this text may seem to be nothing more than a somewhat tedious description of the procedure and ordering of the tribes of Israel as they packed up the tabernacle and prepared to leave, there is a lesson to be learned from it. Notice, in verse 13, that everything that was done was "according to the command of the Lord by the hand of Moses." Every detail of their activity, from the order of the tribes to the assignments with regard to the tabernacle, was by God's design and command. Every instruction had a purpose and nothing was left to chance. What does this tell us about God? It tells us that he is a God of details. God did not manage the Israelites as he did because he was an overbearing, power-hungry dictator; he did it because he knew what was best for them and was directing them in ways that they did not know how to go for themselves. The same is true for us. We have often painted God as One who does not care how we do things as long as we do them for him, but God is still a God of details. He knows what is best for us and his guidance is for our good. We must learn to listen to him, submit to his will, and pay attention to his details.

*Why do you think that we often want to do things our
own way instead of following God's instructions?*

DON'T FORGET TO PRAY AND HAVE A GREAT DAY!

Day 57

 **Today's Reading:
Numbers 12:1-16**

Maybe it is human nature to become envious of and bitter toward those who are in positions of authority over us. As I consider this scene of dissention against Moses, it occurs to me that Aaron and Miriam were probably both the least likely and most likely to fall victim to these feelings. As Moses' siblings, their love and respect for him should have been greater than most, but also as his siblings, their submission to his leadership might have been particularly challenging. Regardless of their feelings, God made his feelings on the matter and his relationship with Moses very well known. In his words, we find a unique relationship between the Lord and his chosen leader. While there may have been others that the Lord used as prophets to reveal his word, there was no one else to whom he revealed himself as he did to Moses, allowing Moses to see his form and speaking to him face to face. It is a beautiful picture of the relationship that God wants to have with mankind and that Christ would eventually make possible through his death. It is a relationship that is unhindered by the baggage of sin, one that allows for close communion and fellowship. It is the relationship of a God of love with the people who are the object of his love. Through Moses, we are given a glimpse of what God wants for us. What a wonderful blessing that is!

*In your view, what is the greatest blessing of the
opportunity to have a personal relationship with God?*

DON'T FORGET TO PRAY AND HAVE A GREAT DAY!

Day 58

 **Today's Reading:**
Numbers 13:1-33

From a strategic or military point of view it seemed like the right thing to do. What army preparing to go into battle doesn't want to know what they are up against? Under normal circumstances, to spy out the land would be the prudent step to take. But these were anything but normal circumstances. This land was the land that God had promised to Abraham and to Isaac and to Jacob. It was God's intention to fulfill that promise, and it made no difference what the land or the enemy looked like. Israel was not going to win that land by their own strength and skill. They were going to gain the land because God was going to fight for them and give them victory. There was no enemy, no matter how big or strong, that could stand against the strength of God. Under the circumstances, the decision to send spies into the land was not pragmatic, it was faithless. They trusted in their own strength instead of relying on the strength of God. They followed their own wisdom instead of heeding the word of the Lord. It would be a decision that would cost an entire generation of Israelites their lives and put off the inheritance of their promised land by forty years. It occurs to me that, though we are very critical of the Israelites' lack of faith, we are often guilty of the same mistake. How often do we apply our own judgment or trust in our own strength instead of trusting in God's wisdom and faithfully following his word? Like the Israelites, if we are to enter our promised land (Heaven), we must do so by faith.

In what ways can we be guilty of relying on our own wisdom and strength instead of trusting in God?

DON'T FORGET TO PRAY AND HAVE A GREAT DAY!

Day 59

 Today's Reading:
Numbers 14:1-25

Among the darkness of the Israelites' disbelief in this scene, there is the brightest of lights shone through the faith and conviction of two men: Joshua and Caleb. They had been among the twelve spies who went into the land of Canaan. They had seen the fortified cities, the strong armies, the fierce men who made them look like grasshoppers in comparison. They were under no delusion that Canaan was not the place that the others had described. Yet, when they looked at that land and its inhabitants, all they saw was the overwhelming goodness and strength of the Lord. They saw a blessed land that had been promised to them and their forefathers as an inheritance. They saw people and armies in that land who would be fighting, not against Israel alone but also against God Himself, and who would have no chance of being victorious. They were not driven by fear, but by faith. Though Joshua and Caleb would not prevail against the rest of Israel, they would eventually be the only two of their generation to enter that land and to inherit the promises of God. What enemies and battles do you face? What are the trials and temptations that stand between you and your promised land? We all have them—challenges, hardships, and struggles of one kind or another. The key to our success over those things is the same as that of Joshua and Caleb. We must allow the strength of God to overshadow the strength of our enemies. We must realize that God is bigger than the biggest problem that we might face. We must be driven by faith and not by fear.

What are your enemies? What can you do to
strengthen your faith in fighting those battles?

DON'T FORGET TO PRAY AND HAVE A GREAT DAY!

DAY 60

Today's Reading:
Numbers 14:26-45

Once again, God's anger had been aroused against this stiff-necked and rebellious people who seemed determined to follow their own way instead of his. Though Moses had seemingly talked God out of destroying them completely, the price that they would pay for their disobedience would truly be devastating. For every day that the spies had spent in the land, they would spend a year wandering in the wilderness. Forty years of being a people without a home. Instead of enjoying the blessings of a land flowing with milk and honey, they would know only the difficulties of a lifetime of wilderness wanderings. Their children would be born and grow up in the harshness of that environment and be forced to suffer the consequences of their sins. Ultimately, they would fall in that wilderness—each and every one of that rebellious generation (with the exception of Joshua and Caleb) would die before the nation would be allowed to cross the river and enter Canaan. As devastating as the physical consequences of the Israelites' disbelief and rebellion were, they fail to compare to the eternal spiritual consequences that our own disobedience can bring. You see, much like the children of Israel, we are journeying toward a great promised land that God has prepared for us. In order to reach that destination, we must separate ourselves from the world, live by God's word, and put our faith in him. Along the way, we will face enemies of different kinds—adversity, trials, and temptations that would turn us back and cause us to fail, but we must journey onward, knowing that not only is the prize that awaits us a truly glorious one, but also that the penalty for failing to enter the promised land is unthinkable.

What do you most look forward to about Heaven?

DON'T FORGET TO PRAY AND HAVE A GREAT DAY!

DAY 61

**Today's Reading:
Numbers 16:1-40**

In the course of the Biblical narrative, God often allows us to encounter questions and comments that transcend time and circumstance and that teach us vital lessons about ourselves and our relationship with God. In this telling of the rebellion of Korah, we find just such a question. "Is it a small thing...?" Korah had been greatly blessed by God and placed in a position of honor as a Levite and priest. He had been given the privilege of serving before the Lord in the tabernacle. Yet, for Korah, this honor was not enough. He was envious of Moses' authority. He desired to have the preeminence. He had taken the blessings of God for granted and had failed to appreciate all that he had been given. It occurs to me that even among Christians, many are often guilty of the same attitude as Korah. Regardless of all that God has given us, we want more. We often crave notoriety, desire worldly acceptance, or chase after physical accomplishment. When those aspirations take precedence over our devotion to God, we need the gentle reminder of the sort of question that was asked of Korah. Is it a small thing to you that God has made you his child? That he has given his Son for you and redeemed you to himself at such a great price? Is it a small thing to you that you have been allowed to wear the name of Christ and to be a part of his glorious body? Is it a small thing to you that you have been saved from your sins and given the blessed hope of an eternal home in Heaven? May we never take for granted the wonderful blessings of God.

What are some of the great things that God has blessed you with today?

DON'T FORGET TO PRAY AND HAVE A GREAT DAY!

Day 62

**Today's Reading:
Numbers 20:1-13**

During Moses' tenure as leader of the children of Israel, he had seen many amazing works of God and, in most cases, had been the hand through which those works had been accomplished. So, one might wonder what made such a difference on this occasion? Why did Moses not follow the command of God, and why was there such a severe penalty for his indiscretion? In searching for answers to those questions, we find an eternal principle that continues to demand our attention today. Notice the words of Moses as he speaks to the people about the water that will be brought forth from the rock: "Hear now, you rebels: shall we bring water for you out of this rock?" Moses' failure can be attributed to one simple word: WE. It seems that he had allowed some seed of self-importance and arrogance to find its way into his heart. In using the word "we," Moses accepted at least partial credit for the miraculous provision of water. He failed to exalt the Lord and give him all the glory, and it cost him the opportunity to lead the people into the Promised Land. How often, in our own lives, are we guilty of a similar attitude? While God may not work miracles through our hands today as he did through Moses, he is, nonetheless, active in blessing us with many talents and opportunities and in working to bring about his will for our good. But when good things come to us, when our work and efforts meet with success, when we are blessed beyond measure, to whom do we give the glory? Do we acknowledge God's gracious hand and give him thanks and praise for those things, or do we express a sense of selfish pride in our accomplishment? May we always be willing to give God the glory!

*Why is it so important that we give the glory
for our blessings and achievements to God?*

DON'T FORGET TO PRAY AND HAVE A GREAT DAY!

DAY 63

Today's Reading:
Numbers 21:1-9

I n this text, we find one of the great symbols of the Old Testament that points toward the cross of Christ as God's ultimate remedy for the world's sin problem. While the bronze serpent served as a means of salvation for Israel during this plague, its greater purpose is as an instructive symbol of God's saving grace toward us through Christ. You see, in a representative sense, the plague of serpents represents the deadly consequences of our sins while the bronze serpent is symbolic of God's mercy and grace shown to us through the cross of Christ. But remember that there was some effort required of the people in order to take advantage of the healing power of the bronze serpent. Unless they moved to within sight of it and looked upon it, they could not be saved. The mere fact that the bronze serpent existed was not enough to heal them. Neither was their simple belief in its power to heal them. They had to act in order to receive the healing. There was no power in their action but simply the obedience of having followed God's instructions. Thus it is with the cross and our salvation. While the power of God to save us from sins lies wholly in him and in the cross that he has set up, there is, nonetheless, some effort required on our part to take advantage of that power. Neither the cross's existence nor our simple belief in its power is sufficient to bring salvation. We must come to him in faith and obedience, following God's simple instructions for accessing his grace and forgiveness. May we come to the cross of Christ to find the healing and salvation that we so badly need.

Why do you think that God requires some
effort from us in receiving his salvation?

DON'T FORGET TO PRAY AND HAVE A GREAT DAY!

DAY 64

**Today's Reading:
Numbers 22:1-40**

The story of Balaam is a sad story of a man who was determined to go his own way despite the many urgings and warnings of God to the contrary. Though God had made it clear to him that Israel was a blessed people whom he would not be allowed to curse, Balaam continued to entertain the offers of Balak, in opposition to God's will. Even a conversation with his donkey and the presence of an angel could not convince Balaam to turn away from temptation. While the story of Balaam and his talking donkey is a favorite Bible story for children, what lessons does it hold for Christians who struggle with temptation and sin? Think of Balak as a representation of Satan in our lives. He clearly wanted Balaam to perform an act that was opposed to God's will, but he presented himself to Balaam as a friend. He was enticing and persistent. He offered gifts and honors as rewards for doing his bidding. Balaam, at least in today's text, does not commit any direct violations of God's commands, but he seems determined to put himself in the path of temptation, convinced that he was in no danger of disobeying God. Though he clearly understood the will of God regarding Israel, Balaam found himself in a position of compromise between completely submitting to that will and aligning himself with the enemies of God. In modern-day language, Balaam was straddling the fence, flirting with sin but comforting himself with the thought that he would not or could not defy God's command. As we will see in the example of Balaam, if allowed to remain in our way, temptation has a way of finding its way into our hearts and leading us into sin.

*What can we learn from Balaam's example
to help us in dealing with temptation?*

DON'T FORGET TO PRAY AND HAVE A GREAT DAY!

Day 65

Today's Reading:
Numbers 22:41-23:26

What is it about our sinful nature that causes us to continue to entertain temptation in spite of its inherent danger? At Balak's insistence, Balaam continued to look for ways to accomplish what God had already forbidden. Despite God's refusal to allow Balaam's mouth to speak a curse against Israel, Balak was undeterred in his attempts to find a way for Balaam's sin. Maybe the most important lesson to be found in this text is seen in the determined willingness of Balaam to do what God had refused to allow. As the evil king persisted in offering different perspectives and options, Balaam continued to prepare for the possibility of sin and to look for God's permission. One might argue that Balaam had yet to commit any wrongdoing, since he had not tried to force a curse contrary to God's command. After all, on each occasion he had asked for God's permission and had then spoken the words provided by God. But Balaam was in a dangerous cycle of allowing temptation to remain and looking for opportunities for that temptation to become sin. Motivated by pride and greed, and justified by the belief that he was ultimately safe from sin, Balaam continued to choose the recklessness of inviting temptation into his path over the refuge of righteous submission to God's will. The application of Balaam's example to our lives is obvious. We often find ourselves facing a similar situation to Balaam's. Understanding the will of God but wooed by pride, greed, or some other emotion, we flirt with temptation, looking for justification to do that which God has forbidden. It is a dangerous game that we cannot win.

Why do you think we so often look to justify sin?
What can we do to defeat this temptation?

DON'T FORGET TO PRAY AND HAVE A GREAT DAY!

Day 66

 Today's Reading:
Numbers 23:27-24:25

The story of Balaam and Balak seems to come to an anticlimactic end with this passage. Balak has failed to have Israel cursed through Balaam, and the two men go their separate ways. However, the oft-mentioned example of Balaam throughout the Biblical text implies that there is more for us to learn from this story. It would seem that the path that Balaam chose is one that hardened his heart and galvanized his desire for the honor and wealth that he had been promised in return for his disobedience. God prevented him from declaring a curse upon Israel, but it appears that Balaam found another way to turn his temptation into sin. According to Numbers 31, it was Balaam who advised the enemies of Israel to entice them with the false worship of Baal, causing God to withdraw his hand of protection from them. Consequently, the name of Balaam has gone down in Biblical history as being synonymous with greed and idolatry. What a powerful lesson his life provides for us. That lesson: resist temptation! While temptation may be an unavoidable challenge of life, we must not become comfortable with it. Don't invite it into your life or encourage it to continue. Don't minimize its negative influence or overestimate your ability to withstand it. If left unchecked, temptation can and will find a way to grow into sin. It will harden our hearts and destroy our relationship with God. So when it comes to temptation, fight against it. Watch out for it, avoid it, flee from it, and resist it. Choose the righteousness of God instead.

What are some practical things that
we can do to resist and defeat temptation?

DON'T FORGET TO PRAY AND HAVE A GREAT DAY!

DAY 67

 **Today's Reading:
Numbers 27:12-23**

As we saw earlier this week, Moses had failed to hold God up and declare him as holy before the people at the waters of Meribah. The penalty for that wrongdoing was that Moses would not be allowed to enter the land of Canaan. As the time drew near for the nation to cross over the river, Moses is invited by God to go up onto a mountain in order to peer across the river and see the Promised Land before dying. In an incredibly unselfish way, Moses' mind is immediately drawn to the nation of Israel and their need for a new leader, someone to provide earthly guidance and to keep them from being like sheep without a shepherd. Despite the many frustrations and aggravations that Israel had caused for Moses throughout the years, he had a deep love for this people—his people and the people of God. He had accepted his fate but wanted to make sure that Israel would be taken care of by a capable leader in his place. Joshua would be that leader. As I think about an application of this to our lives and to the people of God under the covenant of Christ, I am reminded that God saw the importance of providing a capable earthly leadership for his church. These men that God had designated to lead and watch over the church as elders are a vital part of his design for the body of Christ. But, as with Moses, there is always a need for capable men to take the place of those who are no longer able to lead. Where would Israel have been without Joshua and where would Christ's church be without the next generation of faithful leaders who are willing and ready to step into those positions when that time comes. Thank God for his wisdom and for faithful servants who are willing to lead.

Why is a strong and faithful earthly leadership important in the church?

DON'T FORGET TO PRAY AND HAVE A GREAT DAY!

DAY 68

Today's Reading:
Deuteronomy 1:1-8

To understand the book of Deuteronomy, it is important to place it within the proper context. It is the end of the forty years of wandering. The entire generation of Israelites who rebelled against God and refused to enter the Promised Land have died. Moses now stands before the children of that faithless and disobedient people, who are now a new generation of adult Israelites standing on the precipice of finally inheriting the land of Canaan. This final book of the Pentateuch records several speeches by Moses to the people in, what will be, his final days as their earthly leader. In this first address, which covers chapters 1-4, Moses' exhortations to the people can be summed up in one word: REMEMBER! He takes them back through their history since leaving Egypt to remind them of all that they have witnessed and experienced and to encourage them to learn from those experiences. As he details many of the events that have occurred during that time, he seems to focus on two primary themes. The first is the care, protection, and provision that God has provided for them. With his infinite power and goodness, he has shown kindness toward them and showered them with his manifold blessings. Secondly, they have been reminded of the shortcomings and failures of their fathers. This reminder was not for the purpose of rebuke but to encourage them to understand the importance of obedience and to learn from the mistakes of those who had gone before them. As I reflect on these exhortations of Moses, I am amazed at the timeliness of these ancient words. How vital it continues to be for us to constantly remember these same two lessons for our own lives. Thank God for his glorious word!

What are some things that God has done to
remind us of his goodness, love, and mercy?

DON'T FORGET TO PRAY AND HAVE A GREAT DAY!

Day 69

Today's Reading:
Deuteronomy 6:1-25

Verses 4-9 of this chapter, often called by its given Hebrew name, the Shema, is viewed by Jews as one of the most important and revered texts in the entire Old Testament. It is the central prayer in their prayer book and is often the first passage of Scripture that a Jewish child will commit to memory. It can still be found in many Jewish homes, written on small scrolls that are rolled up and placed in small boxes called mezuzahs that are attached to door frames. These important verses often become the central focus of this chapter, but it is important to realize that they are but a part of a beautiful passage that powerfully teaches the importance of keeping God ever before us as we journey through life. For us, as for the Israelites, life is full of temptation and enticement toward sin. We are surrounded on a daily basis by worldliness, immorality, and all manner of deception designed by the hand of Satan to draw our eyes, our minds, and our lives away from God. Only a purposeful and determined focus on God can protect us from being pulled into the world. As we continue to read through the Old Testament, we will see, through the example of the Israelites, a clear and sobering picture emerge of the disastrous consequences of allowing the world to capture our focus. From that perspective, it should certainly impress upon us the vital importance of this chapter's exhortations to remain centered on God and to not allow the world and its influence to rob us of that focus. May God help us to give our hearts, our minds, and our lives wholly and solely to him!

Why do you think that it is often difficult to remain focused on God? What can we do to help us to keep our focus on spiritual things?

DON'T FORGET TO PRAY AND HAVE A GREAT DAY!

DAY 70

Today's Reading:
Deuteronomy 7:1-26

The religious environment that exists in our culture today is one that is very much focused on the love that God has for us and the love that we are to feel toward him in return. There is no shortage of reminders concerning all the wonderful promises that God has made to those who believe in and love him, even if some of those suggested promises are based more on the thoughts and ideas of men than they are on the truth of God's word. However, what is often lacking in those discussions of the love between God and men is any real emphasis on the importance of obedience in that relationship. In fact, God's love, blessings, and salvation are often viewed by many to exist independent of any attitude or act of submission whatsoever on man's part. Yet, the message of both the Old and New Testaments is abundantly clear—the greatest blessings of God, especially the blessing of eternal salvation, are reserved for those who faithfully and humbly submit themselves to God in obedience. Certainly, God's love for mankind is universal and unconditional and to love God is vital and necessary to our relationship with him, but if that love does not produce within us an overwhelming desire to draw near to him through our own heartfelt obedience, then our love for him is not genuine or sincere. May we continue to have a love for God that causes us to grow more and more in our obedience to him!

What are some of the reasons that the importance of
our love for and obedience to God is so often overlooked?

DON'T FORGET TO PRAY AND HAVE A GREAT DAY!

DAY 71

Today's Reading:
Deuteronomy 10:12-22

Much of the book of Deuteronomy is devoted to a re-issuing of the laws of God. These laws and statutes that had originally been read in the hearing of the people at the foot of Mount Sinai are now read to this generation of Israel as they prepare to enter the Promised Land. Throughout the course of the giving of that law, the people are constantly reminded that, while the law is there for their governance and guidance and for the maintaining of their moral and religious purity, it is God, the divine Law-giver, who is to be the true object of their devotion. He is their God and they, above all others, are his chosen people, to receive his blessings and care. Their keeping of the law, while vital to their success, is ultimately secondary to their motivation for keeping the law—their devotion to God. Thus it is with us today as God's people in Christ. The New Testament, our covenant and law, serves as our pattern and guide in being faithful to God and in finding our way to the heavenly home that Christ has prepared for us. Our spiritual success is dependent upon our keeping of that law in a faithful and obedient way. But, ultimately it is our motivation for keeping that law that makes the difference. God doesn't just want an obligatory obedience; he wants the devotion of our hearts. While that devotion will necessarily motivate obedience, it will also more importantly define the reason for that obedience. May we always strive to give first our hearts and then our lives to God!

Why do you think that God is so concerned
with the devotion of our hearts to him?

DON'T FORGET TO PRAY AND HAVE A GREAT DAY!

Day 72

**Today's Reading:
Deuteronomy 30:1-20**

One of the unfortunate realities of humanity in our striving after God is the inevitability of our failure to be independently righteous. As determined as we might be in mind and as diligent as we might be in effort, the weakness of our flesh dictates that sin will find its way into our lives. But found within this regrettable state of mankind is a reminder of one of the greatest and most comforting aspects of God's character—his long-suffering, mercy, and forgiveness. It is remarkable to me that, as God spoke these promises to his people through Moses, He was well aware of the ungodly paths that they would take and the deplorable acts that he would be asked to forgive. God knew well the depths to which Israel would sink, and yet, he promised to forgive and restore them anyway. What an amazing God! But then I am reminded that Israel's story is our story. God tells us their story to teach us about ourselves. Those promises that he made to them—promises of forgiveness, restoration, and blessing to those who return to him—are the promises that he makes to us. God was so determined to forgive us, in fact, that he sent his Son to the cross to provide and seal that forgiveness. Because of that great sacrifice, there is no amount of sin and no distance from God that his love and his Son's blood cannot cover. If we are willing to return to him in faith and obedience, then his forgiveness, blessings, and salvation can be ours. It is hard to imagine that depth of love and yet, it is exactly that kind of love that makes our relationship with God possible.

*How can we show our appreciation and
gratitude for God's amazing grace and mercy?*

DON'T FORGET TO PRAY AND HAVE A GREAT DAY!

Day 73

 Today's Reading:
Deuteronomy 31:1-29

The death of Moses was imminent, and with that event, Joshua would become the leader of God's people. As Moses prepares the people for those things and for their crossing over the river into the Promised Land, and as he inaugurates Joshua as their new leader, he uses a phrase that will become an often repeated theme for the life of Joshua. Three times in this chapter, the Israelites and their new leader are told to "be strong and of good courage." They would face enemies and conflict as they sought to inhabit the land, but "be strong and of good courage." Joshua would be asked to take on the difficult task of leading this great nation of people into the Promised Land. "Be strong and of good courage." They are a stiff-necked and rebellious people who will not be faithful to God. "Be strong and of good courage." But if we focus too much on that one charge of God, we will miss the bigger point of what is being said to them. You see, the strength and courage that they are being called to exhibit is not one of their own making and self-confidence. With each command to "be strong and of good courage," there is the promise of God's abiding presence and help. Their strength and courage is in him, not in themselves. As God's people in today's world, we are still called to be strong and courageous, but just as in the case of the Israelites, those qualities are not to be found in ourselves apart from God. It is his presence and power in our lives that allows us to face our struggles and challenges with strength and courage. Let us, therefore, look to God for his help and guidance, and let us "be strong and of good courage."

Why is it important that we recognize God
as the source of our strength and success?

DON'T FORGET TO PRAY AND HAVE A GREAT DAY!

DAY 74

 Today's Reading:
Deuteronomy 34:1-12

O f all the great stories and lives of the Old Testament, Moses stands alone in the closeness of his relationship with God. Of Moses it was said that the Lord spoke to him "face to face as a man speaks to his friend" (Exodus 33:11). It is only fitting that this man, whose life was so unique, is also unique in the nature of his death. Due to his failure to give all the glory to God at Meribah, Moses would not be permitted to cross over into the Promised Land. However, as the time of Moses' death drew near, God called him up onto the top of Pisgah where he was allowed to view all the land of Canaan that had been promised to Abraham and that the nation of Israel was about to inherit. What a glorious sight that must have been to see the prize that lay at the end of their journey, even if he would not have the blessing of inhabiting it. After viewing the land, he died there on the mountain and God, himself, buried the body of Moses. However, Moses' story is not complete without considering one final scene. As Moses' physical eyes closed in death, his spiritual eyes were opened to reveal a promised land that far outshined the earthly land of Canaan. That land was one that Moses was welcomed into as a faithful servant of God, to receive the rest and reward of the redeemed. We may think it sad that Moses did not get to step foot in that land that he had worked so hard and travelled so far to inhabit, but while Moses' sin may have prevented him from having that land, God's forgiveness made it possible for him to have a much fairer land instead. What a beautiful story of redemption and salvation!

What lessons and encouragement for our own
lives can we gain from today's reading?

DON'T FORGET TO PRAY AND HAVE A GREAT DAY!

Day 75

 Today's Reading:
Joshua 1:1-18

A couple of days ago, we considered the statement that is certainly an important theme in this text: "Be strong and courageous." As Joshua becomes the leader of Israel, he has a great and challenging task before him—to lead God's chosen people into the land of promise. It is definitely a challenge that will require the strength and courage spoken of so often. But, interestingly, the strongest of those exhortations is devoted, not to their physical and military goals, but to their spiritual faithfulness. As formidable as their physical enemies were, Israel's victory was guaranteed with God's help, but when it came to their spiritual success, they faced a much greater challenge. Remembering that the story of Israel is told as a shadow of our own struggle to gain a heavenly promised land, this text has an important lesson for us. We often place so much of our emphasis on the physical—our struggles, our worries, our challenges. Those things occupy our minds and dominate our prayers as we fret over the hardship and struggle of overcoming them. But as difficult as those trials can be and as much courage as they require, they are not our greatest test in life. Just as with Joshua and the Israelites, our greatest strength and courage must be reserved for our efforts to remain faithful in our keeping of God's word. Not only does that spiritual goal represent our greatest challenge, but it is also our greatest key to success. Let us, then, devote ourselves to God and "be strong and very courageous."

What are some of the greatest spiritual challenges that you face?
What can you do, with God's help, to successfully face those challenges?

DON'T FORGET TO PRAY AND HAVE A GREAT DAY!

DAY 76

 Today's Reading:
Joshua 2:1-24

The Bible is filled with unlikely heroes—people who have flawed character and checkered pasts; people who would have been immediately rejected, had you and I been writing the story. Rahab is certainly one of those people. She was a foreigner—a resident of the city of Jericho. She was a harlot—a woman who lived her life and made her living in immorality. Surely God would not allow such a woman to find favor in his eyes. Yet, He did. Rahab believed in God and risked her own life to save the spies sent into Jericho. We read nothing more of Rahab after the destruction of Jericho, but that she and her family joined themselves to the Israelites and became faithful to God. The New Testament testifies to her faith and salvation. The Hebrews' writer reveals that it was by faith that she welcomed the spies and was saved (Hebrews 11:31). James tells us that she was justified by her works in receiving them (James 2:25). Matthew even reveals that this unlikely hero found a place in the lineage of the Messiah (Matthew 1:5). So, what is the lesson for us in all of this? Actually, there are at least two. First, we are reminded again of the grace and forgiveness of God. No matter where a person comes from or what their past might look like, God never closes the door. As long as there is a desire to turn to him and put away the life of sin, God is willing to offer cleansing and renewal through Christ. Secondly, we learn the important lesson that we should never reject or give up on people because of their past. God can use those people, and faith can change them. We must continue to work to show the love of Christ to them.

Why do you think that we are often so quick
to give up on people because of their past?

DON'T FORGET TO PRAY AND HAVE A GREAT DAY!

Day 77

 Today's Reading:
Joshua 5:1-15

Since the time of Abraham, circumcision had held a vitally important place within the lives of God's people. It had been a sign of their covenant with God and a constant reminder of their separation from the unbelieving world. It was a requirement of their relationship with God, and yet, during the years of wandering, this practice had been neglected, leaving an entire generation of adult Israelites uncircumcised. Before the conquest of the Promised Land could continue, it was imperative that this regretful oversight be corrected. God's people were about to begin a campaign that would take them into the midst of foreign nations and godless peoples. It was crucial that they be reminded of their unique relationship with God and that their covenant with him be sealed in their minds and bodies. Thus Joshua is instructed to circumcise all the men of the nation. While physical circumcision is not a requirement of the new covenant that we have with God through Christ, there is a form of spiritual circumcision that is still very much a part of our coming to him. This spiritual circumcision is achieved in the putting off of our sinful flesh through our baptism into Christ (see Colossians 2:11-12). Like the physical circumcision of the old law, this act that we participate in seals our covenant with God through Christ and sets us apart as his redeemed people. Though it is often downplayed and dismissed by our world today, the spiritual circumcision of baptism is just as crucial to our relationship with God today as physical circumcision was to the people of God under the old covenant.

Why is it so important that we have a reminder of our
covenant with God and separation from the world?

DON'T FORGET TO PRAY AND HAVE A GREAT DAY!

Day 78

**Today's Reading:
Joshua 6:1-27**

It was a battle plan that would have left military leaders of any time period shaking their heads and predicting certain defeat for Israel. It didn't involve sneak attacks or complicated strategies, just a silent march around the city following the Ark of the Covenant and seven priests carrying rams' horns. What must the soldiers and people of Jericho have thought as they watched this strange spectacle take place day after day for six days? And what about that seventh day? Was there an ominous feeling that arose within them as they watched the Israelite army march around the city, not one time but seven? Did they know that their doom was near as they heard the rams' horns sound and the army begin to shout with a mighty voice? One thing must have been for sure—as they saw the walls begin to crumble and fall inward on top of them, they knew beyond any doubt that this was not the doing of man. Yahweh, the God of Israel, had brought down those walls and had delivered destruction to the city of Jericho that day. Rahab had earlier revealed to the spies that the people of the city had seen what Israel had done to other cities and were fainthearted because of them. Now, Jericho knew the true source of Israel's strength. This battle also served as a great reminder to Israel that their hope and strength was not to be found in their own power and skill, but in the mighty hand of God. Their obedience and faithfulness to his commands would ensure their victory over any enemy. That same message rings forth for God's people today. Whatever obstacles or battles that we face in life, God's strength is our hope, and through him, we have the assurance of ultimate victory. Thanks be to God!

How has God worked to bring about spiritual victory in your life?

DON'T FORGET TO PRAY AND HAVE A GREAT DAY!

Day 79

 Today's Reading:
Joshua 7:1-26

I t is amazing how quickly the story of Israel can go from one of triumphant victory to one of crushing defeat. It is also amazing to see what a devastating effect one man's sin can have on an entire nation of people, but that is possibly the most important lesson to be drawn from this text. Just before the horns blew and the walls of Jericho fell, the people were warned not to take possession of any of the accursed things of that city. But Achan defied that command and took those very things for himself, thus bringing a curse and God's wrath upon the nation. His sin went undiscovered until the army of Israel suffered an unexpected defeat at the hands of Ai. This chapter serves as a grim reminder of the destructive effect that sin has, not only on the one committing the sin but also on those around him. As enticing and deceptively harmless as sin may seem, there is nothing good or harmless about it. It has the ability to destroy lives, relationships, families, churches, and even entire nations, and the innocent often suffer from its physical consequences as much as the guilty. Is it any wonder that God warns us so vehemently about guarding ourselves and the church against the influence of sin and protecting ourselves from those who are intent upon participating in it? His protective love desperately desires to keep us safe from sin's destructive power. May we share in that same desire!

Why do you think that sin has such a destructive effect on our lives?

DON'T FORGET TO PRAY AND HAVE A GREAT DAY!

Day 80

Today's Reading:
Joshua 14:6-15

Much of the middle portion of the book of Joshua is devoted to a description of the dividing out of the land to the tribes of Israel. Joshua oversaw the proceedings as each tribe received their inheritance. The highlight of this particular chapter is the request of Caleb. Remember that Caleb and Joshua were the only two of the spies to bring back a good report of the land and to encourage Israel to trust God and take the land according to his command. For that reason, they were also the only two Israelites of that generation who had lived to see the possession of the land. At the time of the reporting of the spies, Caleb had been promised the very land that he had spied out as an inheritance and reward for his faithfulness. Now, some 45 years later, at the age of 85, Caleb comes to ask for the land that he had been promised. That land, the land of Hebron, was a mountainous area with strongly fortified cities and large, powerful armies. It would not be an easy land to inhabit, but it was the land that Caleb had been promised by God, and it was the land that he wanted. It was precious to him because of that promise, and he was willing to do the work that it would take to inhabit it. What a great example Caleb is to us. He could have easily settled for another piece of land, one that would require less work and be more suitable for someone of his age, but he was as confident in God's promises and help at the age of 85 as he had been at the age of 40. Caleb reminds us that the promised inheritance of God is precious and is worth all of the effort and sacrifice that is required in order to possess it. That inheritance, for us, is Heaven, and there is nothing that we should want more.

Why do you think people sometimes struggle
to see Heaven as their most important goal?

DON'T FORGET TO PRAY AND HAVE A GREAT DAY!

Day 81

 Today's Reading:
Joshua 24:1-33

Much has happened during the leadership of Joshua. The land has been possessed and settled by the tribes of Israel. Enemies have been defeated and promises have been kept. The time of Joshua's death has come and, like his predecessor before him, Joshua takes one last opportunity to address the nation and to exhort them to faithfully follow God. What a powerful speech he delivers as he reminds the people of all that God has done for them to bring them into this land and to bless them in so many ways. He also calls attention to the fact that there are still enemies to face and battles to fight, and he admonishes them to continue to be faithful to God so that they will continue to be successful. He concludes his address with a powerful challenge to "choose this day whom you will serve." There was no place for half-hearted devotion or ambivalence in their faithfulness. They could not serve both Yahweh and any of the plurality of gods that they had been exposed to during their lifetimes. There had to be a clear and resolute choice made. As it was for them, so it is for us. Though we do not live in a society that is inundated with religious icons and false gods, there are certainly many objects that occupy the same place as those gods in the hearts and live of many people. Money, physical possessions, fame, honor, popularity, beauty, pleasure, and success would just name a few. Though these things may not be viewed as gods, they certainly demand the commitment, devotion, and even worship that are indicative of false religion. Joshua's challenge is, therefore, still very relevant for us today. We must choose whom we will serve, and if we choose to serve God, then we must give him all of our hearts and serve him and him alone.

What things occupy your life that could become gods to you if you allowed them to? How can you assure that that doesn't happen?

DON'T FORGET TO PRAY AND HAVE A GREAT DAY!

Day 82

**Today's Reading:
Judges 2:1-23**

J udges 2 provides somewhat of a summary for the entire book of Judges and for this particular period of Israel's history. In many ways, it is a very sad story of a nation that refused to remain faithful to God but that seemed determined, instead, to follow after other gods. With little discernment, time and time again, they became enamored with the false religions and idols of the Canaanite nations, only to feel the sting of God's punitive wrath and then, in desperation, to cry out to him for deliverance. At the same time, the book of Judges is also a beautiful story of the unconditional love and endless mercy of a longsuffering and forgiving God. Despite his anger and frustration over their sins and in spite of his perfect knowledge of their future transgressions, God continued to raise up judges who would deliver them from their captors and bring them back to faithfulness, if only for a short time. As I consider these things, I am reminded of the conversation between Jesus and Peter, recorded in Matthew 18, when Jesus teaches that we are to be willing to forgive someone who sins against us not seven times, but seventy times seven (or seventy-seven). That is a difficult principle for us to accept, even if it does come directly from the Lord. However, it is exactly the principle that God applies in his relationship with Israel in the Old Testament, and though we might not like to admit it, it is the very same principle that he applies to our lives as well. What a loving and forgiving God he is!

*Can you think of transgressions that you have committed
for which God has forgiven you multiple times?*

DON'T FORGET TO PRAY AND HAVE A GREAT DAY!

Day 83

 Today's Reading:
Judges 4:1-24

Among the judges, Deborah stands out as the only female judge. In a time when women rarely held positions of authority, this prophetess and woman of faith was chosen by God to free Israel from the oppression of Canaan and lead them back to faithfulness. Though we are not given any details as to why God chose Deborah to fill a position that in every other case was occupied by a man, we can clearly see the strength and faith with which she fulfilled her calling. By the direction of Deborah who was relaying the command of God, Barak led 10,000 men against an imposing force of Canaanite warriors and utterly destroyed them. But what is most striking to me about this text is Deborah's unwavering focus on God as the source of Israel's strength and the reason for their victory. Six times in this chapter, God is given the credit for Israel's victory over the Canaanites. She took no credit or glory for herself. Once again, Deborah reminds us of the great truth that our strength to overcome our spiritual enemies and to find salvation is found not in ourselves or our own strength and ability, but in the mighty power and wisdom of God that is at work within us. By his Son he has freed us from the tyranny of sin and led us to a life of peace and hope in Christ. May we, like Deborah, never cease to give God all the credit and praise for our spiritual victory in Christ!

Why do you think that God so often reminds us that
He is responsible for our strength and success?

DON'T FORGET TO PRAY AND HAVE A GREAT DAY!

Day 84

**Today's Reading:
Judges 7:1-25**

L ike so many battle stories of the Old Testament, the story of Gideon and his three hundred men is really a story of God's strength and power. Gideon was a great warrior and led a powerful force of fighting men 32,000 strong in number. As this army was preparing to go into battle against the Midianites, God gives Gideon what might have been seen as a surprising and somewhat troubling command—to decrease the number of his men so that they would not be tempted to believe that it was their own strength that had given them victory and forget that it was God who had fought for them. From a human point of view, that reasoning might seem selfish and arrogant, but we must understand the wisdom behind God's instructions. You see, God cared for his people and wanted them to be successful. He was willing to help them, protect them, and provide for all of their needs. But, if they began to think that they alone were responsible for their success, then they would inevitably quit depending on God and begin trusting in themselves. If that happened, then they would surely fail and eventually be defeated by their enemies. It was vital that they never forget that God was with them and responsible for their victories. Thus, he continuously set up scenarios to remind them of his presence and help. Remembering that these events are recorded for our learning, we are reminded that God is also with us to help us and to bless us with the things that we need. With him, we can overcome our enemies and be successful, but without him, we, too, would surely fail. In that truth is the great reminder that we must always trust him over our own strength.

Have you ever faced a battle that reminded you that you were not strong enough to win it alone? If so, how did you respond to that challenge?

DON'T FORGET TO PRAY AND HAVE A GREAT DAY!

Day 85

 **Today's Reading:
Judges 11:29-40**

H ave you ever made a promise to God? If he would only bless you with something that you considered a desperate need, then you would give him something in return, maybe more of your time, money, commitment, or faithfulness. There are several times in the Old Testament where such a statement is made to God. Jephthah's story is one of those examples. Jephthah's promise: in exchange for God's interceding hand to give him victory over the people of Ammon, he would give a burnt offering, but not just any burnt offering. He promised to offer the first thing that came out of his house to greet him when he returned home. What a heartbreaking turn this story takes when Jephthah's daughter and only child is the first one to come out to meet him. But the heartbreak quickly gives way to an incredible display of faith on the part of Jephthah. Though he is distraught over the thought of sacrificing his daughter to the Lord, he never entertains the thought of going back on his word. God had been faithful to him, and he must be faithful to God. Maybe even more impressive is the faith of Jephthah's daughter. When she realizes her fate, she does not beg for her life to be spared nor does she resent her father's oath; she simply recognizes the vital importance of his faithfulness to God and accepts her role as her father's sacrifice to him. This story, like many from the Old Testament, might seem heartless and cruel to us because of the much different world that we live in today, but it is intended to teach us an important and powerful lesson about the need to be faithful to God. Think about the things that we often promise to God and how petty those sacrifices are in comparison to what Jephthah gave. May we always consider our faithfulness to God to be more important than the things of this world.

*What is the greatest sacrifice that you have ever
made for the sake of your faithfulness to God?*

DON'T FORGET TO PRAY AND HAVE A GREAT DAY!

Day 86

 Today's Reading:
Judges 14:1-20

S amson is probably the best known of all the judges because of the extraordinary strength bestowed upon him by the Lord. He was a man that God had chosen even before his birth, to judge his people and to deliver them from the Philistines. Yet, for all of his physical strength, Samson was a man who was plagued by certain weaknesses. Though he was committed to the work of the Lord, it seems that Samson's ego, his temper, and his fleshly desires often interfered with his focus on God and his purposes. In the recorded events of Samson's life, we often find him in predicaments of his own making and depending on his God-given strength to save him from the trouble that he has brought on himself. While acknowledging the many great things that Samson did in God's service as a judge over Israel and in his defeat of the Philistines, it must also be noted that the most important lessons that we learn from this strong man's life are the ones that we learn from his weaknesses. When we place our own feelings and worldly desires above the will of God, we tread on dangerous ground, as we threaten to elevate ourselves above him in our hearts and minds. Like Samson and his strength, God has blessed each of us with abilities, talents, and opportunities that allow us to work and serve to his glory, but it is for us to decide how we will use those blessings and to, hopefully, commit to using them to accomplish his will above our own. Satan and the world certainly offer many things to distract us in hopes of drawing our focus away from God, but may we always commit to putting him first!

What talents or abilities has God blessed you with?
How are you using those things to his glory?

DON'T FORGET TO PRAY AND HAVE A GREAT DAY!

DAY 87

Today's Reading:
Judges 16:1-31

I t is one of the most famous, and tragic, love stories of all time—Samson and Delilah. Enamored by a woman who was used as a pawn by the Philistines to entice him into revealing the source of his great strength, Samson was lured into their trap and rendered helpless by Delilah's treachery. Once again, Samson had lost his focus on God and had allowed his own desires and feelings to lead him astray. The result, according to today's text, was that the Lord departed from him. No longer could he rely upon God's help to give him, as it were, superhuman strength to defeat his enemies. Blinded by the Philistines and made to be a slave in their prison, Samson had become nothing more than a source of his enemies' mockery of God. But, as you know, this would not be the end of Samson's story. In one great final act of courage and sacrifice, Samson shows a reliance upon God that has seldom been recorded in the telling of his life. That last, desperate plea of Samson's began with the words, "O Lord God, remember me, I pray!" Though the Lord had departed from him for a season, Samson trusted in the mercy and grace of God to forgive him and to help him in this final act of vengeance against his enemies. If Samson's life teaches us about the danger of giving into our human wants and feelings (as we noticed yesterday), then it also teaches us of the power of repentance and the constant willingness of God to return to us as we return to him. Thank you, God, for giving us hope and reminding us of your great love!

What can we learn about sin and repentance from the life of Samson?

DON'T FORGET TO PRAY AND HAVE A GREAT DAY!

Day 88

 Today's Reading:
Judges 17:1-13

This chapter in the book of Judges is not about a judge, but rather it is about a man who commits great wrongs against God and, as a result, causes a great deal of trouble for Israel. Though we are not told the background of this story, it is enough to know that Micah was guilty of making carved images and offering worship to those idols. He further enhanced his wrongdoing by then hiring a Levite to be his personal priest, thinking that having this man from the priestly tribe in his service would cause God to condone and bless his idolatry. While we easily see the absurdity of Micah's logic, we are often blind to the same reasoning in our own religious world and fail to heed the warning that this text provides. How often do we see people and groups who, in the name of Christianity, offer worship and devotion to "idols" such as self, flamboyant personalities, or worldly things, just to name a few. Then, in an effort to legitimize that worship, they cloak it in something akin to God-ordained activities? It is, in fact, happening all around us, and it is no more pleasing to God today than it was in Micah's day. When we consider our worship to God, we must first recognize that our worship is to and for God, not for ourselves. That being the case, we must offer true and genuine worship to him according to his will. If our only desire is to please ourselves or to gain personal benefit from our worship activities, then that worship is no longer directed to God but rather to the idol of self. May we never allow our own desires to interfere with our true, genuine, and obedient worship to God.

How can our worship become more about us than about God?
What can we do to avoid this danger?

DON'T FORGET TO PRAY AND HAVE A GREAT DAY!

DAY 89

Today's Reading:
Ruth 1:1-22

The story of Ruth takes place within the larger, historical context of the period of judges. As we have seen over the last few days, it was a particularly dark time in Israel's history, but through the story of Ruth, God reminds us that even in such circumstances there is room for hope and redemption. It is a story that begins with a great deal of sadness and loss as an Israelite family leaves their homeland and travels to a foreign land to escape a famine. While dwelling in that land, the husband and head of the family dies followed by the death of his two sons, leaving three widows to find their way in a harsh and unfriendly world. But within this story of sorrow and loss, we find a hidden jewel—a heartwarming statement of love and devotion from Ruth, a young Moabite widow, to her mother-in-law, Naomi. Despite Naomi's pleas for Ruth to return to her father's house in hopes of finding another husband, Ruth chooses to stay with Naomi, leaving her own homeland and returning to the land of Judah with her mother-in-law. Broken and empty, these two women returned to Bethlehem having nothing in this world except each other. Among the greatest blessings that God has given us in this life is the companionship of special people that stand faithfully with us and share in our joys and our sorrows. These special people can come in the form of a spouse, parents, children, siblings, or the closest of friends. What a wonderful blessing it is to be able to share our lives with those who make our good days even better and our bad days bearable. Thank God for those wonderful companions!

Who are the companions in your life who are a great help and encouragement to you? Have you told them lately how much they mean to you?

DON'T FORGET TO PRAY AND HAVE A GREAT DAY!

Day 90

Today's Reading:
Ruth 2:1-23

As we read the second chapter of the story of Ruth, it would appear that Ruth is the benefactor of much good fortune and happy coincidences. She happens to wander upon the field of a relative of her dead husband. Boaz happens to come by while she is there to check on his workers. He happens to take notice of her and asks a servant who happens to know who she is. That is a lot of fortuitous happenings for one day! Or is it? You see, this chapter and, in fact, this entire story, is not about the good fortune of a couple of women who were down on their luck. It is the story of the gracious and providential hand of God that was working behind the scenes to bring about good in the life of a woman (and a man) who were unknowingly part of a very important story within God's overall plan and purpose. In many ways, the providence of God is a mysterious thing. Though we understand it to be "the working of God through natural means," exactly when or how God works is often unknown and unseen, at least in the here and now. However, as the story of Ruth unfolds, we clearly see God's hand at work in amazing ways to bring about Ruth's good and his purposes. The same is true in our lives. Though, from our vantage point, we may not be able to see the overall plan and how the circumstances of our lives fit into that plan, we can be sure that God does. If we will trust him and submit our lives to him, he can still work in our lives through his amazing providence to bring about good and to accomplish his perfect will. Praise be to God for his power, wisdom, and love!

*Can you look back over your life and see circumstances
where God was working to bring about good?
In what ways did God bless your life during those times?*

DON'T FORGET TO PRAY AND HAVE A GREAT DAY!

Day 91

Today's Reading:
Ruth 3:1-18

This chapter is often difficult for us because it largely revolves around obscure Hebrew laws and odd cultural traditions that we know little about. In our struggle to make sense of those things, we can overlook what may be the most important element of this portion of the story. While this certainly is the story of Ruth and the incredible love and devotion that she shows for Naomi, her mother-in-law, it is also the story of Boaz. We learn of a man of impeccable character and wonderful compassion and his magnanimous kindness and generosity toward Ruth. In a time of moral and spiritual darkness in Israel, Boaz represents a shining light of integrity and goodness. The actions of Ruth in chapter three, performed at the direction of Naomi, were physically risky and, in the minds of some, morally questionable. Boaz could have easily taken advantage of her, humiliated her, or had her punished for her behavior, but instead, he graciously accepted, cared for, and protected her, both in terms of her safety and her reputation. Through his actions, he proved himself to be a man of honor and one who feared God and, in all likelihood, secured a place for himself within the genealogy of David and of Christ. From Boaz, we learn a great and important lesson about our own actions and responses, especially in difficult circumstances. While Boaz was determined and insistent on doing the right thing, his actions were also motivated by compassion and kindness. So often, we seem to be of the mindset that we must choose one or the other as if we cannot act righteously and compassionately at the same time. Yet, the truth is that these two vital components of our character and conduct are mutually dependent upon one another. May we learn to value and practice both!

Can you remember a time in your life when someone went out of his way to show you kindness? If so, what effect did that act have on you and your life?

DON'T FORGET TO PRAY AND HAVE A GREAT DAY!

Day 92

 Today's Reading:
Ruth 4:1-22

The story of Ruth ends the way that any good love story should end: with our hero and heroine living happily ever after. Surprisingly, however, much of the focus of the final chapter of this book is focused on Naomi instead of Ruth. The son that was born to Ruth and Boaz was a great blessing to Naomi because he would perpetuate the family name. This woman who had come back to Bethlehem empty and broken is now full and satisfied. The God that she had thought was set against her was, in actuality, working in her best interest all along and had, in the end, blessed her mightily. In Naomi, we see a snapshot of our own lives for we are sometimes plagued with hardship, loss, and sorrow. There are times when we may feel that God is set against us, punishing us for some unrecognized wrong in our lives. There may be times when we feel empty and broken, our lives shattered by circumstances beyond our control. But what we see and learn from the life of Naomi is that God had not forsaken her. He was always there, working in unseen ways to bring about her good. He blessed her life with people who would care for her, provide for her, and stand faithfully by her side during the most difficult days of her life. Her plight and anguish had not gone unnoticed by a loving and compassionate God who blessed her with more than she could have ever hoped for. Can there be any doubt that God cares for us in the same way, watching over us, providing for us, and blessing us in greater ways than we can fathom through his providential care? What a wonderful God he is!

Have you ever gone through a period in your life
when you felt as if God had forsaken you?
Looking back, how did God care for you during that time?

DON'T FORGET TO PRAY AND HAVE A GREAT DAY!

DAY 93

 Today's Reading:
1 Samuel 1:1-28

The book of 1 Samuel opens with another example of a faithful and godly woman who finds herself in very difficult circumstances. With a strong faith and a loving husband, it seems that Hannah had a good life, except for the fact that she was childless and, in the world and time in which she lived, to be a childless woman was a great source of shame and sorrow. To make matters worse, Elkanah's other wife, who the text calls Hannah's rival, constantly antagonized her because of her barrenness. In her greatest hour of need and desperation, Hannah becomes a wonderful example to us of faith and faithfulness. She takes her sorrow and need to God in prayer and looks to him for help. What better or more effective action could she have taken? She put her problem, her heartache, and her life in the hands of an almighty and compassionate God, but her commitment and faith in God did not stop there. She also committed the life of the precious son that she was pleading for to his hands. If God would only answer her prayer and grant her request, then she would give that son back to him to be his servant. What a great act of faithfulness! But Hannah's prayer was only the beginning of her faith and the easiest part of her commitment to God. You see, the real challenge to Hannah's faith came when God granted her a son, and she was faced with the reality of following through with her promise. But, with no recorded hint of hesitation or turning back, she took Samuel, as soon as he was old enough, and left him to serve in the temple of the Lord. What a wonderful example she is of faith and commitment!

What are some ways in which we can demonstrate our faith and faithfulness to God during difficult circumstances in our lives?

DON'T FORGET TO PRAY AND HAVE A GREAT DAY!

Day 94

 **Today's Reading:**
1 Samuel 3:1-21

As a young man growing up in the tabernacle under the tutelage of Eli, Samuel's training and service was probably fairly uneventful for the most part. He likely spent much time learning the ins and outs of tabernacle service, carrying out the priestly duties, and serving in small and menial ways at the behest of the elderly priest, Eli. But Samuel's life changed drastically on the night that is recorded in 1 Samuel 3. As God called him and revealed his prophetic word to him, Samuel's status changed from lowly servant to respected prophet. Notice that the first message revealed to Samuel was a difficult one that left him in a quandary. God had judged the house of Eli and would punish him because of the blasphemy of his sons and his own failure to correct them. Despite the fear and angst that Samuel felt, he revealed the message of God to Eli, his earthly master and teacher. Have you ever wondered what would have happened if Samuel had not spoken the word of God? What if he had decided to spare Eli's feelings and save himself the trouble and kept God's word to himself? No doubt, the story of Samuel would be a much different one than what is recorded in our Bibles. It occurs to me that though we are not called in a vocal way today as Samuel was, we are called through Christ to come to God in faith and obedience and to share his word with others. The sharing of that word is not always convenient or comfortable, and we are often tempted to spare the feelings of others or save ourselves the trouble by keeping it to ourselves. Maybe this scene from Samuel's life teaches us of the importance of being more committed to the word of God than we are to our own comfort and convenience.

What circumstances can make sharing the gospel uncomfortable?
How can we deal with those circumstances in a positive way?

DON'T FORGET TO PRAY AND HAVE A GREAT DAY!

DAY 95

Today's Reading:
1 Samuel 4:1-22

The Ark of the Covenant was Israel's most prized possession, but it was far more than just a physical relic. It represented to them the very presence of God among them. In many ways, it was their protection and source of strength because when it was with them, then God was with them. The Ark was often taken with them into battle as a symbol and reminder that God was fighting for them. But what Israel failed to realize was that it was their own faithfulness and not the mere presence of the Ark that guaranteed God's presence and help. Without the faithfulness of the nation, the Ark became of no more power or importance than any other artifact. In this text, as a result of the sins of Hophni and Phinehas, God gave Israel into the hands of their enemies, the Philistines. When the Israelites brought the Ark to the battlefield thinking that it would assure God's help and their victory, it was promptly captured and taken. According to God's word to Samuel, Hophni and Phinehas along with their father, Eli, died that day, and as an even greater tragedy, the Ark of the Covenant was lost to their enemies. In a similar way today, many people feel that as long as they have some representation of religion present in their lives, such as attendance at worship or giving to the church, then the faithfulness of their daily lives is not necessary. This event should teach us that that theory is a false one, and that our daily faithfulness is essential to our relationship with God. May we always be committed to God and strive to be faithful to him in all things.

In what ways should we demonstrate our faithfulness
and commitment to God on a daily basis?

DON'T FORGET TO PRAY AND HAVE A GREAT DAY!

Day 96

 Today's Reading:
1 Samuel 8:1-22

Israel wanted a king so that they could be "like all the nations." They wanted someone to sit on a throne and to rule over them; someone who could demand the respect of their rival nations; someone to be a symbol of power and prominence to their enemies. In a true monarchy, the king has absolute power and authority. His word is final in all matters, and no one has the right to question or overrule him. This is the government that Israel sought. Samuel, who was serving as judge over Israel at the time, was understandably upset by their demand. He felt rejected as their leader, but God's words to Samuel in response to his prayer reveal the truth of Israel's attitude and actions. As they had done many times before in choosing to chase after false gods, Israel had again rejected God and his rule over them. You see, what the Israelites failed to realize was that they already had a king—God, the King of kings. He was the one who ruled them with absolute power and authority. It was his word that was final in all things. He went before them into battle to lead them in victory over their enemies. He may not have been a physical man who occupied a physical throne, but God was King over Israel in every sense of the word. The only problem was that Israel had rejected God's rule over them. His authority and form of government was no longer acceptable to them. To be like all the other nations was more important to them than to faithfully exist under God's rule. All of this causes me to wonder—who is the "king" of our lives? Have we allowed God to hold that position of rule and authority, or have we demanded another king such as the world or even ourselves? May we always submit ourselves to God as king!

What are some things that we can do to
ensure that God remains the king of our lives?

DON'T FORGET TO PRAY AND HAVE A GREAT DAY!

DAY 97

 Today's Reading:
1 Samuel 10:1-27

The Israelites were a stubborn nation of people. Despite God's condemnation of their rebellion and his warnings about the problems associated with a having an earthly king, the people remained resolute in their demand. So, God instructed Samuel to give them what they wanted and chose Saul to be the first king over Israel. Saul was everything that could be asked for in a king. He was tall, handsome, and even seemed to have an endearing humility to his character. He was the perfect king, except that he would soon become jealous, paranoid, and defiant. But despite Saul being the centerpiece of this text, it is God, as always, who steals the show. It is impossible to read the Old Testament without being amazed by the mercy and longsuffering of God toward his people. Israel has, once again, rejected him and demanded their own way. Yet God still treats them with kindness and love. He has heard their cries and instructs Samuel to anoint Saul as king so that he might save Israel from the Philistines. While there will certainly be a price to pay for their rebellion, God, in his infinite wisdom and power, uses the imperfect path of their choosing to bring about his perfect will. Thus it is with God in our lives as well. We often make unwise choices in our paths of life—sometimes due to rebellion, other times in ignorance. Nevertheless, God is merciful and longsuffering toward us. He will not prevent our freewill and allows us to make our own choices. Whether those choices are right or wrong, he is still able to use our imperfect paths to accomplish his perfect will. To God be the glory!

Why is it so important that God allows us
to have free will in choosing our own paths in life?

DON'T FORGET TO PRAY AND HAVE A GREAT DAY!

Day 98

 **Today's Reading:
1 Samuel 13:1-15**

One of the dangers associated with a position of great authority, such as king, is in coming to believe that the rules do not apply to you. It may be that Saul fell victim to this mentality in the scene described in this text. Surely no one under his rule had any authority or permission that he, as king, did not have. Certainly, not just anyone could offer sacrifices but, in an emergency such as they faced here, surely God would allow him to make the sacrifice instead of Samuel. What Saul failed to remember is that God's laws are unchanging and non-negotiable. Under the Law of Moses, only the priests were allowed to offer sacrifices, and even King Saul, who was from the tribe of Benjamin, did not have that authority. Though this scene might seem to have no practical lesson to teach us, I think that there is at least one thing that we desperately need to learn from it. Though we may not be kings or have positions of great authority, it is possible, and sometimes quite easy, for us to develop that same attitude of entitlement in which rules do not apply to us. It may be because of who our parents or other relatives are, or because of all the hard work that we have done in the past, or simply because of the good moral lives that we live that we become somewhat arrogant in our faith and become convinced that God does not expect the same things of us that he expects of others. But, like Saul, we would do well to keep in mind that God's law is still unchanging and non-negotiable. What he has commanded, he expects us to obey, regardless of who we are or where we have come from. We must remember that at our core, we are all nothing more than lowly sinners in need of the saving grace of a merciful God.

*What are some things that we can do to help us
to remain humble as children and servants of God?*

DON'T FORGET TO PRAY AND HAVE A GREAT DAY!

DAY 99

 Today's Reading:
1 Samuel 15:1-35

In yesterday's reading, we saw one dire mistake by Saul that threatened his throne. In today's text, we see the action that sealed his fate as king. It was a simple command: utterly destroy the Amalekites and do not leave anyone or anything alive. However instead of applying submissive obedience, Saul chose to apply human logic. How wasteful it would be to destroy all the flocks and herds and other things of value. Wouldn't it be better for Israel to keep those things for herself? They could even sacrifice some of the animals to God. And concerning King Agag, what a prize it would be to take him alive. Verse 9 of this chapter pretty well sums up the mindset of Saul and his army: they spared the best of all that was good and would not utterly destroy it, but they did not hesitate to destroy those things that were despised and worthless. How often are we guilty of using our human logic and reasoning in order to justify our disobedience to God's commands? We tell ourselves that this is what God would want us to do or that God wants us to be happy or that he wouldn't condemn us for this. I don't have any doubt that had we been able to be among the Israelite armies on that fateful day when they defeated the Amalekites, we would have heard very similar statements made. It is so easy to justify the things that we want and make excuses for the times when we are not obedient to God's word. But, as Samuel reminded Saul, "to obey is better than sacrifice, and to listen than the fat of rams." May we ever be committed to obeying God, no matter what.

Why do you think that is it so tempting for us
to use our own logic instead of simply obeying God?

DON'T FORGET TO PRAY AND HAVE A GREAT DAY!

DAY 100

Today's Reading:
1 Samuel 16:1-13

One of the difficulties of human relationships is that when it comes to knowing people, we must largely depend on what we see on the outside—their appearance, their actions, their words. This limitation often leads us to snap judgments and first impressions that are not indicative of a person's true character and heart. There are times when we might judge people to be immoral, unacceptable, or even dangerous based only on their outward appearance when they might be none of those things. At other times, we might judge a person to be trustworthy, kind, or even a faithful Christian based on his appearance only to learn that he is the complete opposite. God, however, is not hindered by the limitations that we struggle with. As Samuel stands before the sons of Jesse to anoint a new king, Samuel has only the appearance of the young men to judge them by, but God directs him away from the one that "looks the part." David may not have been Samuel's first choice for king based on his outward appearance, but God knew his heart and that he was "a man after God's own heart." Thus it is with us. God knows us, and not just the outward things, the appearances and the image that we project to people. God knows our hearts. He knows the good and the bad, our strengths and our weaknesses. He knows our motivations and desires. If we are showing people an image of ourselves that is not consistent with our true character, then God's perfect knowledge can be a frightening thought. However, if we are pure of heart and motive, God's knowledge of us should be a comfort. It matters not what men think or say because our God knows us. Let us, therefore, work to have a pure heart and then allow that heart to be reflected in our lives.

How can we ensure that our lives accurately reflect pure hearts?

DON'T FORGET TO PRAY AND HAVE A GREAT DAY!

Day 101

 Today's Reading:
1 Samuel 17:1-30

The story of David and Goliath is a favorite of children and Bible class teachers. It is a wonderful story of faith and courage in the face of overwhelming odds. However, some of our ideas and images of this event may be a little inaccurate. There is no doubt that Goliath was every bit as powerful and intimidating as the Scriptures and our Bible class stories describe. He was tall (over nine feet tall) and strong, and when he spoke his challenge to Israel, an entire army was made to be afraid. Our view of David, on the other hand, might need some adjustment. David was the youngest son of Jesse and was not part of the armies of Israel. We often depict David as being a young boy (maybe a teenager) who was small and frail. Yet, it seems that David was none of these things. In chapter 16, David is called "a mighty man of valor" and "a man of war" (verse 18). David, himself, will later say that he had fought and defeated both a lion and a bear (17:34-35). He was no weak little child. He was a warrior. He was not part of the armies of Israel, probably because he held the special position of armor-bearer to King Saul (16:21). But despite David's strength and experience, his reaction to Goliath is impressive. When all of the fighting men of Israel shrank back in fear and dismay, David became irate at the idea of this man mocking God and defying His people. There was too much faith and love for God in the heart of David for fear to find a place. His only desire was to silence the enemy and demonstrate the power of God. It would be a defining moment in David's life.

Are there times when faith and fear compete for control of your mind and actions? What can we do in those times to help faith win out?

DON'T FORGET TO PRAY AND HAVE A GREAT DAY!

DAY 102

Today's Reading:
1 Samuel 17:31-58

No armor, no shield, no sword. David stepped onto the battlefield with nothing in his hand but his shepherd's staff, a sling, and five smooth stones. To the Israelites, it seemed to be a suicide mission, and to Goliath, it was an insulting act of disdain. But David had a purpose. He was going on to the battlefield, armed not with the weapons of men, but with the power of God to fight for him. David's approach to this battle was not simply a demonstration of faith, although it was certainly that. He had seen God's armies cower in the shadow of one mighty warrior and knew that they had forgotten the true source of their strength and victory. His purpose was to demonstrate, not only to the Philistines but even to his own people, that God did not require the swords and spears of men to defeat his enemies. God would defeat this mighty Philistine warrior with a shepherd and the crudest of weapons. David leaves no room for doubt as to the source of his strength. His trust is in God. Over and over again, he declares that God will deliver Goliath into his hands. Believe it or not, there is a great lesson for us to learn from this event in the life of David. When is the last time that you went into battle against a giant? Never? Think again. Our giants don't come in the form of a nine foot tall warrior; they come in the form of family crises, financial emergencies, health scares, and other difficulties that we encounter throughout life. Each one of these things can cause us to cower in fear and forget that God is the source of our strength and victory. David's example teaches us that we can face these enemies with courage and faith, and we can trust God to help us to overcome!

What "giants" have you faced in your life?
How did God help you to overcome them?

DON'T FORGET TO PRAY AND HAVE A GREAT DAY!

Day 103

 Today's Reading:
1 Samuel 19:1-24

As David grew in fame and popularity, so did Saul's jealousy and desire to do away with him. While it may not have been unusual in that day and time for kings to eliminate their rivals, it certainly should not have been an attitude or desire that occupied the heart of the king of God's people, Israel. Surely Saul should have had a different spirit, one more in line with God's character and will for his people. It seems that in moments of clarity, such as we see in this text, he understood that his ill-will toward David was not deserved nor was it acceptable. Yet, Saul could not overcome the negative thoughts and feelings that he had toward David. His actions were ruled by pride and emotion rather than by integrity and sound reasoning. Saul's example reminds us of the power that emotions have in our minds and hearts and of the need to control them lest they cloud our judgment. As condemning as we may be of Saul's attitudes and actions, we must not forget that we are often prone to the same weaknesses. While our actions may not be as extreme as his, it is often easy to let our emotions drive us, causing us to do and say things that are ungodly and hurtful to those around us. Jealousy, envy, and pride are still dangerous attitudes that can lead us to act irrationally and in ways that are opposed to what God has called us to be. Often, our greatest weakness can be our own feelings, and we must constantly work to keep them in check. May we always look to God for guidance and direction.

Why are our emotions so powerful in dictating our attitudes and actions?
What can we do to make sure that our emotions do not overrule God's will?

DON'T FORGET TO PRAY AND HAVE A GREAT DAY!

Day 104

 **Today's Reading:**
1 Samuel 20:1-42

The friendship that existed between David and Jonathan is one that is unique in the pages of Scripture. David's son, Solomon, would later write that "there is a friend who sticks closer than a brother" (Proverbs 18:24), and surely Jonathan was that type of friend to David. His devotion to his friend was one that transcended blood and was greater than any personal aspiration that he might have had for his own future. This text reveals that Jonathan loved David "as his own soul." What grief it must have caused him to learn of his father's deep hatred and murderous intentions toward David! As we think about this beautiful friendship, we are reminded of the great blessing that is found in the ability to love and to enjoy human relationships. God has blessed each of us with people in our lives who encourage and strengthen us and who want nothing but the very best for us. Sometimes, those people take the form of family members—parents, grandparents, siblings, and others who are part of the family that we are born or adopted into. At other times, there are special people of our own choosing—friends or spouses with whom we, through the course of time and experience, develop a special relationship of mutual respect, love, and devotion. What a lonely and difficult life it would be without those special people! Thanks be to God, the God of love, who has taught us how to love and has given us family and friends to walk through this world with.

What special people has God blessed your life with?
How can you show those people your love and appreciation?

DON'T FORGET TO PRAY AND HAVE A GREAT DAY!

Day 105

 Today's Reading:
1 Samuel 22:1-23

King Saul is a sad and powerful testament to the depths to which jealousy, greed, and pride can lead a person. He has become extremely paranoid, accusing everyone around him of conspiring against him. There is no one, from his closest advisors to the priests of the Lord, that Saul trusts. So desperate is he to retain his power and position (a position, by the way, that God has already told him has been taken from him) that he orders the execution of the priests of the Lord. Saul was certainly a man on the brink, but why and what can we learn from him? It seems to me that Saul finds himself in this position because he has become wholly focused on himself and on worldly things and has forgotten about God. Protecting his position and title appears to be the only thing that matters to Saul, and he seems willing to do so at any cost. He has forgotten that it was God who made him king, and because of his sins, God has now rejected him as king. Though it may not seem so at first glance, our lives and circumstances are not that much different than Saul's. Everything that we are and have is by the grace of God. As Paul states in Acts 17:28, "In Him we live and move and have our being." But like Saul, we often meet with the temptation to become focused on ourselves and worldly things and forget God's role in providing those things. We make plans, set goals, and chase dreams without including God or considering his will for our lives. The example of Saul stands to remind us of the danger of such a mindset. May we never allow the world or our own desires to take the place of God.

Why do you think that the world and
worldly things are such a temptation for us?
What can we do to protect ourselves from giving in to that temptation?

DON'T FORGET TO PRAY AND HAVE A GREAT DAY!

Day 106

Today's Reading:
1 Samuel 24:1-22

In sharp contrast to the hateful and violent spirit of Saul, in this text we find the humble submission and gracious respect of David toward the king. Despite Saul's sinfulness and malice toward David, he was God's anointed king and, in David's eyes, that was reason enough to treat him with reverence and respect. He would not lift his hand against him even when he was given the perfect opportunity. Even the cutting off of the corner of Saul's robe caused David to be filled with sorrow and remorse, having committed an act of disrespect toward his king. David is a prime example of an admittedly difficult and often neglected principle that Jesus and the New Testament writers would later teach—to love your enemies and to not return evil for evil. David could have easily justified killing Saul in that cave. After all, Saul was pursuing him with nothing but murderous intentions, but David knew that Saul's sinful attitude and actions did not justify his own sinful response. From a human nature point of view, there are few things that are more difficult than for us to love our enemies and to be kind to those who are nothing but unkind to us. That mentality often seems to go against everything that we feel, but the fact remains that wrong does not justify wrong. Regardless of how others may treat us, we must strive to be what God has called us to be in our thoughts, attitudes, words, and actions. How difficult must it have been for David, a mighty and seasoned warrior, to do no harm to Saul when his every instinct was surely telling him to kill the man who was trying to kill him? But David was a man after God's own heart and gives us a great example of restraint and submission to God's will.

Why do you think that humility is such a difficult quality to master?

DON'T FORGET TO PRAY AND HAVE A GREAT DAY!

DAY 107

 Today's Reading:
1 Samuel 26:1-25

A gain, David is presented with an opportunity to kill Saul, and again, he refuses to. What stands out most to me in this passage is what seems to be at the forefront of David's mind (and life) — the Lord. Fifteen times in the recorded words of David in this chapter, he invokes the name of the Lord. He acknowledges His will and working and submits himself to God, he gives God the credit and praise for the blessings of his life and even the current circumstances, and he expresses a desire to be pleasing to God and in a faithful relationship with him. David shows an exceptional ability to keep the first things first and to not become distracted by the difficulty of his circumstances or the emotional highs or lows that he may have felt at times. This man who would give us so many of the psalms demonstrates in his life the very qualities and attitudes that he so often wrote about. In our lives, it is often such a challenge to keep our minds and hearts focused on God. If we are not careful, we can allow the circumstances of life and the world to distract us and cause us to lose that focus. The answer to this dilemma is found in the example of David—so devoted was his heart to God and so engrained into his life was the will of God that he could not act without considering God nor could he speak with acknowledging him. What a humbling experience it is to compare my own relationship with God to that of David, but oh what a wonderful mark his example sets for me to aspire to.

What can we do to help us stay focused
on God despite the circumstances of our lives?

DON'T FORGET TO PRAY AND HAVE A GREAT DAY!

Day 108

Today's Reading:
1 Samuel 28:1-25

G od had chosen him to be king. He had been with him and given him victory over his enemies. But now Saul finds himself alone, facing a powerful enemy, and frightened. As is often the case when faced with difficult circumstances, Saul desired the counsel and help of God, but God was not there. He had rejected Saul as king and severed his relationship with him, but remember that it was, in reality, Saul who had rejected God. He had disobeyed God's commands. He had disregarded God and followed his own ways. He had even killed the Lord's priests and sought to kill the man that God had chosen to replace him as king. No, God had not so much abandoned Saul as he had simply allowed Saul to follow the path that he had chosen for himself—a path that led him down a road of sin and far away from God's presence. Now, desperate for guidance from God concerning the Philistines, Saul employs the help of a medium (one of the very mediums that he had once banned from the land because of the ungodly nature of their beliefs and work) to conjure up the spirit of Samuel. To the shock and alarm of the medium, the spirit of Samuel actually appeared before Saul, but his message was not the one that Saul had hoped for: Israel's armies would be defeated by the Philistines, and Saul and his sons would meet their death. The fate of both Israel and King Saul were sealed.

What can we learn about our relationship
with God from this scene in Saul's life?

DON'T FORGET TO PRAY AND HAVE A GREAT DAY!

Day 109

Today's Reading:
1 Samuel 31:1-13

O ne week ago, we were reading about David's courageous facing of the Philistine champion, Goliath. On that day because of David's faith and courage, Israel won a great victory over the Philistines. How different are the circumstances of today's reading. The armies of Israel are fleeing in defeat from the Philistines just as Samuel's spirit had prophesied. The three sons of Saul have been killed in the battle, and Saul, afraid to face the harsh treatment of his enemies, takes his own life. When all is said and done, Saul's entire army is dead and his body is taken by the Philistines to be treated with reproach. What a tragic end to a life that had such promise at one time. Though God was not pleased with Israel's demand for a king, he had allowed it and had chosen Saul to be that leader. Surely, if Saul had remained faithful to God, he and the nation would have been blessed. He could have enjoyed all the success that came with the faithful adherence to God's law, but instead, much of his reign had been plagued by the fear and paranoia of knowing that God had rejected him, only to end in shameful defeat to an ungodly enemy. There is a correlation for us in Saul's story. You see, we have been chosen by God—chosen to be redeemed to him through Christ and chosen to be his children and heirs of Heaven. We have the opportunity to enjoy the peace, hope, and blessings of the wonderful promises and care of God. But if we, like Saul, choose the path of disobedience and sin instead, we, too, can find ourselves facing sorrow, defeat, and, ultimately, destruction. May we always choose God!

What is involved in "choosing God" in our lives?

DON'T FORGET TO PRAY AND HAVE A GREAT DAY!

Day 110

 **Today's Reading:
2 Samuel 5:1-25**

It has been a turbulent time in Israel since the death of Saul; a time characterized by division, betrayal, murder, and war. But this chapter sees a positive turn in Israel's circumstances and the beginning of a much brighter time in Israel's history. With the death of Ishbosheth, Saul's son and David's biggest rival, the division that had plagued the nation since Saul's death comes to an end, and God's people are once again united under the leadership of David. In addition, the city of Jerusalem was taken by David and his men and became the City of David and the most important city in Israel. This chapter and this period of Israel's history can be summed up in the words of verse 10: "And David became greater and greater for the Lord, the God of hosts, was with him." In Saul, we have seen the consequences of forsaking God and being left without his help and protection. However, in David, we see a renewed sense of hope for the nation because of David's faithfulness to God. I am reminded that, though our times and circumstances may be much different than those of ancient Israel, this principle of faithfulness remains true. If we in our lives will be faithful to God, he will certainly be faithful to us in the blessings and care that he provides. So often, we can be tempted to follow the path of Saul in deciding that we can manage our lives without God, but that path is sure to fail just as Saul's did. May we ever follow the path of faithfulness and depend upon God's strength and care to sustain us.

What are some of the blessings that come with our faithfulness to God?

DON'T FORGET TO PRAY AND HAVE A GREAT DAY!

DAY 111

 Today's Reading:
2 Samuel 6:1-19

The story of Uzzah's tragic death is one of those powerful reminders that when God gives a command, he means for it to be kept. At first glance, it may seem that God's wrath toward Uzzah was extreme and un-called for, seeing that Uzzah's wrongdoing was committed in an effort to protect the Ark of God. Shouldn't his good intentions count for something? But before we begin to criticize God's judgment, let's take another look at this scenario. The failure of Uzzah (and others) was not only in his touching the Ark. Rather, the touching of the Ark was the result of circumstances set in motion by an earlier impropriety. Just as God had commanded that the Ark not be touched by the hands of those who transported it (Numbers 4:15), he had also commanded that the Ark be transported by being carried by the priests. God had never authorized the use of a cart to transport the Ark. Ironically, a "new" cart (meaning one that had never been used for any common or profane purpose) was used out of respect for the Ark, yet the entire process represented a disregard of God's will and prescribed method. Uzzah and his cohorts were looking for a shortcut—an easier and more convenient way to accomplish their task, maybe thinking that a show of respect toward God in using this unapproved method would cause God to accept their change to his design. How often do we see the same thinking in today's religious world? Using our own reasoning and ingenuity, we alter God's prescribed plan for the sake of ease, convenience, or acceptability and then claim that because we do it to honor God, he will surely accept us. May we heed the warning given to us through the example of Uzzah.

In what ways does our world often alter
God's plan for the sake of convenience?

DON'T FORGET TO PRAY AND HAVE A GREAT DAY!

DAY 112

Today's Reading:
2 Samuel 7:1-29

This is one of the most beautiful chapters of the Bible as it expresses the very special relationship that existed between God and David. The chapter begins with David's desire to honor God by building a house for him, a permanent structure to replace the tent that housed the Ark of God. While that house would have to wait to be built by his son Solomon, David's love and devotion to God was rewarded by the great promise of God to build David a house by blessing him, his seed, and the nation on his behalf. God's show of love and devotion to David would be immeasurably greater than anything that David could offer to God. While David has nothing to offer God that matches the generosity or magnitude of God's promises, David gives to God what he does have—his humble and heartfelt praise and thanksgiving. The last half of this chapter is devoted to the overflowing gratitude and worship of David's heart. Even as the king of Israel, David feels unworthy of God's favor and blessings and is amazed by his grace. As I consider the sentiments expressed in this chapter, I am reminded that in many ways it ought to be a reflection of our own relationship with God. No doubt, each one of us could freely admit that God has blessed us in ways and to a degree that is far above and beyond what we deserve or could have asked for. In addition to those manifold blessings, he has made great and precious promises of a spiritual future beyond anything that this life has to offer. In return, we have nothing to offer but our lives and our praise, and while those things cannot compare to what God gives, they are all that God asks of us. What a wonderful and gracious God he is!

Why does God desire our worship and praise?
What should our attitude be as we worship him?

DON'T FORGET TO PRAY AND HAVE A GREAT DAY!

Day 113

 Today's Reading:
2 Samuel 11:1-27

As familiar as I am with the story of David and Bathsheba, it seems that I can never read it without asking the question, "How?" How could a man with the devotion to God that David had possibly allow himself to go down such a dark path? How could a man so focused on spiritual things get so caught up in worldly desires? While this text gives us an account of the events that made up David's downward spiral of sin, we are not given insight into the attitude or state of mind that motivated his decisions and actions. Was it pride? Arrogance? Worldliness? We do not know. What we do know is that David put himself into a very dangerous and compromising position, and it cost him dearly. You see, before David lusted after Bathsheba, committed adultery with her, attempted to deceive Uriah, or had him killed, he made a pivotal decision that set all of those actions into motion. That decision is found in the simple phrase, "But David remained at Jerusalem." The chapter opens by telling us that it was the time of year "when kings go out to battle." Though David was a warrior king and accustomed to the battlefield, he sent his army into the fray while he stayed in Jerusalem. Doing so gave him the opportunity to be tempted and provided few deterrents to his giving in to those temptations. This sad series of events in the life of David is a powerful example not only of the snowballing effect of sin, but also of the danger of placing ourselves in compromising positions. To truly understand the destructive nature of sin is to understand the importance of protecting ourselves against the very appearance of evil and the presence of temptation. May we be diligent in doing just that.

How can we protect ourselves from dangerous and compromising situations?

DON'T FORGET TO PRAY AND HAVE A GREAT DAY!

Day 114

**Today's Reading:
2 Samuel 12:1-14**

"You are the man!" Oh, how those words must have stung the heart of David. His adultery with Bathsheba had been about nothing more than his own weakness and physical desires, but upon learning that Bathsheba was with child, David panicked and went into damage-control mode. From that point, David's actions seemed to be motivated by nothing more than his desire to hide his indiscretions and escape any negative effects that they may have caused. It is interesting to see how one can be so consumed with self-preservation that he is blinded to his own sins and the devastation that those sins are causing in the lives of others. It can happen in the life of any person, given the right circumstances. But if we are going to learn from David's failure, we also need to learn from his reaction to that failure. Through Nathan the prophet, David was reminded that nothing escapes the eyes of God and that there is a price that must be paid for sin. When made aware of his sins, David responded in the only way that was appropriate—with a broken heart and humble confession of guilt: "I have sinned against the Lord." There was no attempt to avoid guilt or justify his actions. There were no excuses and no more lies. David had sinned. Though his actions had been shameful and had demonstrated the weakness of his flesh, David's words of confession and repentance (see Psalm 51) were a beautiful expression of his desire for God and sorrow over sin. As we learn about the danger and destructiveness of sin from David's example, let us also learn from his humble admission of guilt and desire for forgiveness.

Why is it often difficult for us to admit guilt and ask for forgiveness?

DON'T FORGET TO PRAY AND HAVE A GREAT DAY!

DAY 115

Today's Reading:
2 Samuel 12:15-25

How do we react to the negative physical consequences that often accompany our sins? So often, it is with resentment, bitterness, or anger. If God has forgiven me, then why am I being made to suffer? You see, we often perceive forgiveness to come with the removal of all consequences whether they be spiritual or physical. However, the truth of the matter is that while God's forgiveness does bring the removal of the spiritual punishment that sin deserves, our sinful actions often bring about natural physical results that we must continue to endure, though we have been forgiven. In the case of David, though God had "put away" his sin there would still be a physical price to pay, a part of which would be that that his son, the child that was conceived in adultery, would die. What a devastating blow this must have been to the heart of David! Yet, David's reaction to this tragedy was not one of resentment or bitterness. David humbly accepted God's judgment while continuing to mournfully plead with God for mercy and grace on behalf of his ill son. Still, through the illness and eventual death of the boy, David never blamed or turned against God. Instead, his first action after learning of the death of his son was to worship the Lord. Come what may, David trusted the Lord and humbly submitted himself to his will. As is so often the case, David's attitudes and actions stand as an example to all who read of them. May we be willing to accept the Lord's will whatever it may be.

Have you ever had to deal with the physical
consequences of sin even though you were forgiven?
What can we learn from David about dealing with those circumstances?

DON'T FORGET TO PRAY AND HAVE A GREAT DAY!

DAY 116

**Today's Reading:
2 Samuel 15:1-37**

As we move forward in the life of David, we find that the relationship between him and his son Absalom has been a strained and difficult one. After years of being estranged, the two are finally reunited (at the end of chapter 14), only for Absalom to begin to conspire against his father with a plot to take his throne. Absalom's skillful and devious maneuvering was so effective in building his conspiracy that David was forced to flee from Jerusalem for fear of his life. Absalom's bitterness toward David and his desire for the honor and power of the throne motivated him to work aggressively to dethrone his father and become king in his place. It is amazing to see the depths that one can be driven to by bitterness and envy. How often it continues to happen in today's world. Ungodly attitudes and motives so often cause relationships to be broken and people to be hurt. When we consider the character and conduct that God calls us to have, it is easy to see that these attributes are not only for our spiritual well-being but for our physical good as well. How much happier and more content are our lives when we treat people with the love and respect that God desires! May God help us to conduct our lives in a way that fulfills his will and calling.

Why do you think envy and ambition are such strong motivators for people? How can we control those attitudes so that we remain faithful to God?

DON'T FORGET TO PRAY AND HAVE A GREAT DAY!

DAY 117

 **Today's Reading:**
2 Samuel 18:1-33

David's son, Absalom, had become a dangerous foe to the king, having been successful in drawing most of Israel away from David. As he marched his enormous fighting force toward David's stronghold, arrogantly confident that his father's small army would not put up much of a fight, they were caught unprepared in a surprise attack by David's men. The result was a slaughter of Absalom's army and victory for David. In the course of this battle, Absalom's head becomes caught in a tree, and against the direct command of David that Absalom be spared, he is eventually killed by Joab and his men. What should have been a triumphant day because of David's great victory quickly becomes one of sorrow and mourning in the heart of David over the death of his son. We may wonder why David was so distraught over the death of someone, even a son, who had treated him so reproachfully, but it is important to remember that much of David's sorrow was over the fact that this situation existed because of his sins. God, through Nathan, had told David that because of his sins regarding Bathsheba and Uriah he would "raise up evil against [him] out of his own house" (see 2 Sam. 12:11). David understood that by his own sinful choices, he was at least partially responsible for Absalom's sins and his death. His mourning was not only over Absalom's death but for the guilt and consequences of his own sins. David was again reminded, as are we through God's word, of the terrible cost of sin and the toll that it can take in our lives.

Why is sin such a powerfully destructive force in our lives and world?

DON'T FORGET TO PRAY AND HAVE A GREAT DAY!

Day 118

Today's Reading:
2 Samuel 19:1-23

As the commander of David's entire army, Joab was a faithful and trusted confidant of the king, but he was also a loyal soldier in the service of his nation. Joab had disobeyed David's command in the killing of Absalom, not as a matter of disrespect toward the king but as an act of loyalty to the nation. Now, as David openly mourns for the loss of Absalom, Joab makes another bold move in defense of his nation. There comes a time when even kings need to be set straight and awakened to the effect of their actions upon their people. David had become so distracted by his own sorrow and guilt that he had forgotten that an entire nation was looking to him for leadership. They had fought valiantly in defense of their king, and their victory—a great victory for the nation—needed to be celebrated and commended. Joab reminds David of this fact and of his responsibility to be a faithful king and leader to his people. It occurs to me that, like David, we can often become preoccupied with our own problems or lives and, in the process, fail to acknowledge the successes and service of those around us. One of the great challenges of the Christian life is to be less self-focused and more concerned with the needs and well-being of others. Whether it be our own children or others who seek to do good on our behalf, it should always be our goal and diligent striving to acknowledge and encourage them lest they become discouraged and lose heart. May God help us to accomplish this mindset.

Who has worked on your behalf to bring about good in your life?
What can you do to encourage and acknowledge them?

DON'T FORGET TO PRAY AND HAVE A GREAT DAY!

Day 119

 **Today's Reading:
2 Samuel 22:1-25**

Even during his own day, David was known as the psalmist of Israel. Among his many talents was the ability to produce beautiful words to describe the praise, thanksgiving, heaviness, or despair that at different times filled his heart. So timeless are many of those verses, that they still impact our worship today. The words of this chapter are repeated with only a little variation in Psalm 18. It is a beautiful psalm of praise to God for his constant presence in the life of David and for his mighty hand of deliverance from all of David's enemies. The years preceding the writing of this psalm had been turbulent and trying ones for David and for the kingdom. Not only was Israel constantly faced with enemies from outside her borders, but for the second time in his tenure, David had seen his kingship challenged and the nation divided by an internal struggle for power; this time at the hands of his own son Absalom. But with the defeat of Absalom's rebellious army, the nation was once again unified and had been victorious over their external enemies as well under David's leadership. Looking back over all that the nation had been through during his rule, David could see clearly that God's mighty hand had been with him and had delivered him from his enemies. From a heart overflowing with gratitude and praise for God's mercy and kindness, David pens the words of this beautiful psalm. May we be able to see and acknowledge God's love and care in our lives as David did in his.

*How can we be sure that our worship adequately
expresses our love and thankfulness toward God?*

DON'T FORGET TO PRAY AND HAVE A GREAT DAY!

Day 120

Today's Reading:
2 Samuel 22:26-51

As we continue to consider this beautiful psalm of praise to God, let's think about some of the things that David acknowledges concerning God. First, he acknowledges God's attentive ear. As David cried unto the Lord in times of trouble, God heard his pleas and responded with power to be his strength and salvation (verses 1-7). David then paints an awe-inspiring picture of God's overwhelming power as He acts to deliver His people from the hand of evil. This metaphorical image of God's power shows him to be above every other power that exists and to have at his disposal every element of nature to use as he wills (verses 8-16). The result of God's attentive ear, along with his irresistible power, is the deliverance of his servant. Though the enemy was strong, too strong for David to defeat, God had given him victory (verses 17-21). The next section might seem curious to us as David discusses his righteousness and faithfulness in keeping God's laws. He is not claiming in these verses to have never failed, for certainly he had. These words are more a testament to God's mercy and forgiveness than they are to David's righteousness. Despite his failures, God had been gracious to him and cleansed him of his sins (verses 21-28). Much of the remainder of this psalm repeats the same themes already mentioned, but notice that the audience of the verses has changed. In the first half of the psalm, David was talking about God ("He") as though he were telling others about God's greatness. In the second half of the psalm, David is addressing God directly ("You") with his praise and worship. What a beautiful psalm of praise to God!

What types of themes do you think should be at the center of our worship?

DON'T FORGET TO PRAY AND HAVE A GREAT DAY!

Day 121

Today's Reading:
2 Samuel 23:1-7

Chapter 23 begins with the declaration: "Now these are the last words of David." This certainly does not mean that these were the last words that David ever spoke but rather, most likely, that this was the last psalm that David penned. Though it is not as clear and unambiguous as many others, this psalm is believed by many to be a Messianic prophecy. Thinking back to the covenant that God formed with David in the beautiful words of chapter 7, God had promised to establish David's seed forever. In the words of this psalm, David considers the justness and purity of that One who would rule over God's people (Christ); then he acknowledges that though his own house is not without wrongdoing, God's covenant was sure and would surely be fulfilled. And what of those who would rebel and rise up against God's anointed? They would be punished and destroyed. Centuries later, that perfect and just descendent from the line of David would come in the person of Jesus Christ. He would not be an earthly king but would rule in a much greater sense over God's people as Savior and Lord. With the word of God and with his own blood, he would put down the rebellious enemies of God's redemptive plan and be victorious over sin and death. God had been faithful to the covenant that he formed with David and, in doing so, had secured salvation for all who would come to him through Christ. Hallelujah! What a Savior!

How does it make you feel to know that
God is faithful to his word and covenant?

DON'T FORGET TO PRAY AND HAVE A GREAT DAY!

Day 122

Today's Reading:
2 Samuel 23:8-23

This text, extending through the end of chapter 23, can be tedious to read with many names that are difficult to pronounce. However, it sheds light on an interesting and important aspect of David's life. As king, David ruled over a massive army made up of thousands of well-trained and very capable soldiers. But this chapter names some very special men surrounding David and describes some of their amazing exploits. Think of these thirty-seven men as Israel's special forces unit and David's personal protection force. (By the way, notice the last name on this list in verse 39: Uriah the Hittite, adding another interesting wrinkle to the story of David and Bathsheba.) The feats of strength, courage, and warfare accomplished by these men were truly amazing, but do not make the mistake of assuming that they were successful in their ventures simply by their own skill and might. No doubt, they were incredibly skilled warriors, but on more than one occasion in this chapter, we are reminded that the Lord gave them victory. You see, all the skill and strength in the world is not enough to allow us to be victorious over every enemy on every occasion, but when God fights for us, there is no enemy that can defeat us. In our lives today, we may not be involved in hand-to-hand combat, but we are engaged in a war nonetheless. If we try to fight those battles alone, we will eventually fail. Ultimate victory can only be ours through the power of Christ. Thanks be to God who gives us the victory!

What battles have you had to fight recently? How did God help you?

DON'T FORGET TO PRAY AND HAVE A GREAT DAY!

DAY 123

Today's Reading:
2 Samuel 24:1-25

While there is much that could be considered about this chapter, there are a couple of questions that quickly arise in the mind of the observant reader that we will consider and try to answer. First, many wonder why God commanded David to take a census of the people and then became angry with him for doing so. On this point, it might be very helpful to look at 1 Chronicles 21, a parallel text that describes the same event as 2 Samuel 24. While our text says that God commanded the census, the text in 1 Chronicles says that Satan moved David to take the census. This apparent contradiction is cleared up by understanding a principle that is used often in Old Testament literature. While it is understood that God is all-powerful and in ultimate control of every force and event that takes place in the world, he never violates man's free will. Often the Biblical writers will attribute an event to God because God allowed it to happen, recognizing his universal power and authority. This principle is seen in the hardening of Pharaoh's heart, the harmful spirit sent to Saul (1 Samuel 18:10), and in several other instances. In this case, it should be understood that Satan induced David into taking the census while God was responsible for it only in the sense that he allowed it. Secondly, many wonder why taking the census was sinful at all? While we are not given a clear answer to this question, it is suggested by many, and seems logical, that David wanted to count the people (probably just the fighting men) out of a sense of pride in a desire to boast of the size and might of his army. In doing this, David had forgotten that regardless of the size of his army, God was their source of strength and victory. Therefore, the census was an exercise in self-sufficiency. Hopefully, these thoughts will help to answer some of your questions.

In what ways do we sometimes "count our forces,"
that is, rely on our own strength and resources?

DON'T FORGET TO PRAY AND HAVE A GREAT DAY!

Day 124

**Today's Reading:
1 Kings 1:28-53**

U nder David's rule and with God's blessings, the nation of Israel had become a mighty force in its world. For that reason and many more, the allure of the throne of Israel was a powerful motivator for those who saw some claim to it. We have already seen the actions of one son of David, Absalom, attempting to overthrow his father and claim the throne. Now, in David's old age, another son, Adonijah has plans of his own. With little regard for the wishes of his father or for the will of God, Adonijah goes about the process of making himself king in the eyes of the people. However, it was not to be so, for David (and God) had other plans. Solomon, the son of David who was "the beloved of the Lord" (see 2 Samuel 12:24-25) was the one who had, long ago, been chosen to succeed David as king. So immediately upon hearing the news of Adonijah's actions, David sets into motion the process of anointing Solomon as the true king over Israel. What is the lesson to be learned from this event in Israel's history? Maybe it is simply the reminder that we must always seek God's will instead of our own. David had many sons, any one of which could have presumed the throne to be his, but there was only one that God had chosen to be the next king. When we put our own will above God's, as Adonijah did, we set ourselves up for failure. May we always have a heart that desires to be faithful to God and that seeks out his will in all things.

*What attitudes or actions are necessary
in order to seek and submit to God's will?*

DON'T FORGET TO PRAY AND HAVE A GREAT DAY!

Day 125

 Today's Reading:
1 Kings 2:1-12

David's life has been one that was filled with great demonstrations of his own faith and of God's power. Even before he was king, he proved himself to be a man who was unique in his love and devotion toward God. During his forty years as king over Israel, David, in his faithfulness, had accomplished many things through the mighty hand of God and had seen the nation grow to unparalleled heights in her power and renown. He had also experienced, firsthand, the pain and loss that come as a result of sin. It is on this basis of experience that David gives these final exhortations to his son, Solomon. His advice: be faithful to God. Keep his commandments. Do not turn away from him or put your own desires above his will. God had made great promises to David about his lineage and their place in the nation, but the fulfillment of those promises was dependent upon the faithfulness of each generation. Though the time, circumstances, covenant, and promises are all different, David's advice still rings very true in our own lives today. Our gracious and faithful God has made great promises to us concerning our lives in this world and especially about our future in Heaven. However, those promises, while available to all men, are dependent upon our own faithfulness and obedience to God. If we are content to live apart from God in this world, then we cannot hope to spend eternity with him in the next. But if we are diligent to keep his word and to submit to his will in this life, then eternal life will surely be ours because of the wonderful saving grace of God!

What spiritual advice would or have you given to your children?

DON'T FORGET TO PRAY AND HAVE A GREAT DAY!

Day 126

 Today's Reading:
1 Kings 3:1-15

If you only had one request and could have anything that you asked for, what would it be? Money? Success? Fame? These are just a few of the things that are most sought after by the world and would probably be at the top of most people's lists. Not surprisingly, those same things would have been at the top of the list in Solomon's day, too. Therefore, it is truly amazing to see what Solomon does when placed in that exact situation. Solomon saw himself as a young and inexperienced man with the humbling responsibility of ruling over God's chosen people. It was a task for which he considered himself unworthy and ill-equipped. When offered the opportunity to have anything that his heart desired, Solomon very wisely chose to ask for wisdom and understanding, but notice that his request is not just for wisdom in general. His desire is to have the wisdom to rightly discern between good and evil and to thus properly judge God's people. More valuable than great riches and more coveted than the honor of men in the heart of Solomon was the understanding of God's will. His selfless request found favor in the eyes of God, and he was granted his request plus all of the things that he had not asked for—riches, honor, success, and fame. This scene from the life of Solomon causes me to stop and consider what I ask God for. Do I focus on the physical things that would make my life happier, easier, or more comfortable? Or do I focus on the things that will bring me closer to God and help me to be more pleasing to him? So often, we tend to focus more on physical things than spiritual. May we learn to value the spiritual things of God above all else.

In addition to your physical needs, what spiritual
things would you add to your petitions of God?

DON'T FORGET TO PRAY AND HAVE A GREAT DAY!

DAY 127

 Today's Reading:
1 Kings 4:20-34

This reading gives us a glimpse into the unmatched wealth, glory, and wisdom of Solomon. God had truly blessed him and the kingdom of Israel far beyond any nation of his time. So renowned was the wealth and wisdom of Solomon that kings and diplomats from surrounding lands came to witness the wonder of Israel's greatness. Remember that Solomon had not asked God for riches or fame or honor. He had simply asked for wisdom to rule God's people, but because Solomon had put God first in his heart and life, God had blessed him far beyond his simple request. I am reminded by this situation of two different New Testament passages that speak directly to our lives. First, the words of Jesus in Matthew 6:33— "But seek first the kingdom of God and his righteousness, and all these things will be added to you." Like Solomon, if we will put God and the things concerning his kingdom first in our hearts and lives, God will surely care for us and bless us with all that we need in a physical way. Also, the inspired words of Paul in Ephesians 3:20— "Now to him who is able to do far more abundantly than all that we ask or think, according to the power at work within us…" God's ability to bless us has no limits, and our faithfulness certainly brings God's blessings. Neither of these passages promise us that God will cause the faithful to be exceedingly wealthy, famous, or honored by men. What they do tell us, however, is that we serve a God who cares for his people, is aware of their every need, and is capable of blessing them in ways that are beyond their comprehension. What a great God he is!

What are some of the things that God has blessed you with in this life?

DON'T FORGET TO PRAY AND HAVE A GREAT DAY!

Day 128

 Today's Reading:
1 Kings 6:1-38

Many years earlier, Solomon's father had wanted to build a house to honor God and to serve as a permanent place for the presence of God to dwell among them. Because of the amount of blood that was on David's hands, God did not allow him to pursue that goal but promised that his son would achieve it. This chapter records the seven-year long task of building the temple. No detail was overlooked and no expense was spared in providing a house for God. This text gives us some idea of the size, appearance, and adornment of that spectacular building. What a marvelous and beautiful structure it must have been to behold. Yet, when we consider the transcendent glory and holiness of God, we quickly realize that no physical building, no matter how costly or beautiful, is worthy to be a dwelling place for God. Instead, God has chosen a spiritual building as his dwelling place—the church, through the hearts and lives of his people (see Ephesians 2:22). Since that is the case, it begs the question: what type of "building" are we providing for God? Understanding the greatness and glory of God, Solomon desired to build the greatest and most beautiful building possible. Are we doing the same with our spiritual lives? In our individual lives and in our combined life in the church, are we presenting God with the purest, most beautiful (spiritually speaking), most sincere, and most lovingly constructed "house" possible? Certainly, God is worthy of no less than the best that we have to offer.

What can we do to make our hearts and lives
a beautiful dwelling place for God?

DON'T FORGET TO PRAY AND HAVE A GREAT DAY!

Day 129

 Today's Reading:
1 Kings 8:1-21

This reading, along with the remainder of this chapter, records a very special occasion for the nation of Israel. After seven years of constant labor, the temple is complete and now their most precious possession, the Ark of the Covenant, is being put into place. What a wonderful and joyous event it must have been, and what a positive and jubilant mood must have filled the gathering. But the thing that strikes me most about this scene is that it is not so much a celebration of the house of God as it is a celebration of the God of Israel. Solomon's words of dedication and prayer to God are wholly focused on God. It is a reverent and devoted time of worship, remembering all that God has done for them and all that he has promised to do. It is a time for praising God and thanking him for his many blessings. It is not a time for Solomon to boast of all that he has done for God but rather to acknowledge all that God has done for him. Again, Solomon provides a wonderful example to us of the attitude and heart that we should have as we approach God. In our world today, worship has very often become so much about us—about what we want, what we like, and what makes us feel good. But while we certainly benefit from our time before the throne of God, we must remember that our worship is not about us. It is to be completely and totally about God. It should be a time of reflecting on God's goodness, grace, and mercy and praising him for his love, care, and blessings. It should be a time of humbling ourselves while lifting him up. It should be joyous, yet reverent; thoughtful, yet heartfelt. Above all, our worship to God should be a reminder to us of the great privilege it is to be his children and a sacrifice of praise and devotion to him.

What could you do to make your worship more about God?

DON'T FORGET TO PRAY AND HAVE A GREAT DAY!

Day 130

 Today's Reading:
1 Kings 9:1-9

For the second time during his reign over Israel, God comes to Solomon in a dream. This time it is not to give him a request but rather to speak to Solomon about his future and that of the nation. God has been pleased with the devotion that Solomon has shown to him in the building and dedicating of the temple. His promise to him is the same as it was to his father, David: "Follow Me with a faithful heart and I will be with you and your lineage so that you will never be without a man on the throne." But there is also a somber warning of foreshadowing in God's words to Solomon. If Solomon and the people decided to forsake God and go after other gods, then Israel would be put away and become nothing more than a grim reminder of the consequences of turning away from God. God, knowing what would take place in Israel's future, devoted much more of his communication to Solomon on the consequences of his wrongdoing than on the rewards of his faithfulness. Solomon, and those who would come after him, would make the unfortunate choice to chase after other gods, and the nation, divided by greed and worldliness, would spend much of the next few centuries being punished by God for their sins. True to God's word, their story has become a vivid reminder to all who read it of the consequences of disobeying and rejecting God. Oh, that we might learn from their mistakes and devote ourselves to faithfully serving God!

What can we learn from the story of Israel
about the consequences of rejecting God?

DON'T FORGET TO PRAY AND HAVE A GREAT DAY!

DAY 131

 Today's Reading:
1 Kings 10:1-10

The visit that Solomon receives from the queen of Sheba is one of those stories that is often the subject of children's Bible classes, and it is another great proof of the overwhelming wisdom of Solomon and the glory of Israel under his rule. But there is another aspect to this story that may often be overlooked. Notice again what is said in the beginning of this text: "Now when the queen of Sheba heard of the fame of Solomon concerning the name of the Lord ..." Did you catch it? Solomon's fame was "concerning the name of the Lord." Solomon owed all of the sources of his fame—his wisdom, riches, power, etc.—to God and, through his renown, God was glorified. Whenever people from a foreign land would speak of Solomon, they would acknowledge the God of Israel as his benefactor. When the queen of Sheba sees with her own eyes the glory of Solomon's kingdom and hears with her own ears the wonder of his wisdom, she gives God the credit and glory. When I consider this aspect of Solomon's story, I am reminded of Jesus' words concerning our own lives as his followers: "In the same way, let your light shine before others, so that they may see your good works and give glory to your Father who is in heaven" (Matthew 5:16). Solomon credited God with his successes and allowed him to receive all the glory. Are we not called to do the same? Does Jesus not tell us to live our lives in such a way that people see our conduct, attitudes, service, and compassion, and give God the glory? You see, God did not bless Solomon in such great ways as just a means of rewarding his faithfulness. His blessings had the intent and purpose of exalting his own name throughout the world. The same is true for us. God blesses us with abilities and opportunities, not only for our own good, but also for the purpose of exalting his name and bringing glory to him. May we always strive to fulfill that purpose!

Think about the abilities, talents, and opportunities of your life.
How can you use those things to bring glory to God?

DON'T FORGET TO PRAY AND HAVE A GREAT DAY!

Day 132

**Today's Reading:
1 Kings 11:1-43**

To this point in Solomon's time as king over Israel, his rule has been characterized by peace and prosperity. Israel has flourished as never before and Solomon is renowned throughout the world for his wisdom and riches. All of this has been possible and achieved through God's blessings and because of Solomon's faithfulness to God, but in this chapter, we see a very sad and unfortunate turn of events. Among the many extravagances that Solomon had surrounded himself with were many foreign women whom the text says he loved. He did this in opposition to the continual warnings and commands that God had given to Israel to not inter-marry with people of other nations, lest they turn his people's hearts against him. Solomon fell into this very trap. In his old age and in his desire to please these wives, Solomon turned his heart against God and began to worship and set up high places devoted to the false gods of his wives. This critical error on Solomon's part obviously angered God and led to his reproach upon the nation. Almost immediately, enemies began to rise up against Israel and events were set into motion that would cause the nation to be divided after Solomon's death. What a sad end to such a great and blessed life as Solomon had enjoyed! It is amazing to see how powerful the influences can be that we surround ourselves with, and how quickly a life can be devastated by the choice to turn away from God. May we always remember that there is nothing in this world that matters more than a faithful relationship with God.

Why do you think that people often forsake God to pursue worldly things?

DON'T FORGET TO PRAY AND HAVE A GREAT DAY!

Day 133

 Today's Reading:
1 Kings 12:1-33

With the death of Solomon begins a great struggle for power between Solomon's son, Rehoboam, and Solomon's servant, Jeroboam. As the son of the king, Rehoboam assumes that he is the rightful heir to the throne, but because of Solomon's sins, God has other plans. While Rehoboam will be allowed to lead two tribes (Judah and Benjamin), the nation would be divided, and the remaining ten tribes would follow after Jeroboam according to the word of the Lord. In the process of accomplishing this outcome, God would take the opportunity to provide powerful lessons to us. In the case of Rehoboam, we learn of the consequences of ignoring the wise counsel of experience and following after the inexperienced ideas of one's contemporaries. In modern day terms, you might say that Rehoboam (and his friends) were on a power trip. Assert your authority, they advised him; show them who is in charge, they said. Following that bad advice proved to be disastrous for the nation as it caused ten tribes to revolt and follow after Jeroboam. In a very real and practical sense, there is much for us to learn from this scene. In the church, there is often far too little intergenerational support. Lost in that "gap" is often a great deal of the experience and wisdom of seasoned Christians. How profitable would it have been for Rehoboam to listen to the counsel of the older advisors, and how profitable would it be for us to value the wisdom of those more experienced Christians among us? May we learn the lessons that God has so richly blessed us with.

*Why do you think we are often so hesitant to heed
the advice of older, more experienced Christians?*

DON'T FORGET TO PRAY AND HAVE A GREAT DAY!

Day 134

 Today's Reading:
1 Kings 14:1-20

Jeroboam had been given a large portion of the tribes of Israel to rule over as king. He had also been given the promise of God that if he would be faithful to God and follow his laws that God would bless him and the nation for his sake. But instead of heeding the word of God, Jeroboam quickly followed the path of self-reliance and preservation, prompted by fear and faithlessness. In an effort to keep the people from going to Jerusalem where he feared they would be persuaded to return to Rehoboam, Jeroboam set up two high places, one in the south at Bethel and one in the north at Dan, complete with golden calves for the people to worship. Ironically, his attempts to maintain his position and success put him in direct opposition to God, the very source of his position and success. It occurs to me that people are often guilty of that same mistake today. In their desire to be successful financially, socially, or in some other arena in life, some will sacrifice their worship, their giving, or their faithfulness. They will do so in order to devote all of their time, energy, or resources to achieving their goals, but they do not realize that in their pursuit of worldly blessings, they have abandoned the very source of blessing. There was nothing wrong with Jeroboam being king. After all, God had placed him there. But when being king became more important than obeying God, Jeroboam sinned. In the same way, there is nothing wrong with physical things or success. God created and grants those things. But when worldly things become more important than obeying God in our lives, we sin. May we always keep our focus clear and our priorities straight, and always put God first!

What can we do to help us maintain
a proper attitude toward worldly things?

DON'T FORGET TO PRAY AND HAVE A GREAT DAY!

Day 135

 Today's Reading:
1 Kings 14:21-31

The seventeen years of Rehoboam's reign over Judah were difficult ones. The kingdom spiraled quickly downward into an abyss of idolatry and abomination. The land was filled with sinful practices that aroused the anger and jealousy of God. As a result, the kingdom was attacked and looted by the Egyptian army, and many of the treasures and riches that Solomon had accumulated, including those things belonging to the king's house and the temple, were taken. But maybe the saddest testament of all to the depths to which Judah had sunk is the statement made concerning their relationship with the tribes of Israel. "And there was war between Rehoboam and Jeroboam continually." These brethren from the seed of Abraham, the tribes that God had chosen as his own special people and had blessed and brought to this land of promise, were now engaged in a bitter and unending war. Sin had driven a wedge between these two kingdoms that were once one and had destroyed what was once a great nation. Thus is the nature of sin. It is divisive and destructive. If left unchecked it destroys lives, families, friendships, churches, and even entire societies. Ultimately, of course, sin destroys the most important relationship of all—the relationship between man and God. If there is only one lesson to be learned from the Old Testament and a study of the Israelites, it is likely the dangerous and destructive nature of sin, both spiritually and physically. No wonder God so adamantly warns us to avoid and fight against sin in our own lives. No wonder he was willing to pay such a great price to free us from its deadly grip. Thanks be to God who has delivered us from the destruction of sin!

Why is sin such a destructive force in our world and lives?

DON'T FORGET TO PRAY AND HAVE A GREAT DAY!

Day 136

**Today's Reading:
1 Kings 15:25-16:7**

When God is forgotten and man is ruled by nothing more than his base desires and emotions, there can be no result except that of confusion, lawlessness, and sin. Jeroboam, for his own selfish purposes, had led the kingdom of Israel away from God and into the practice of idol worship, and the kings who came after him followed the same path. What this text shows us is that, though Israel and her kings had forgotten about God, God had not forgotten about them. As disobedient and hard-hearted as they were, they were still his people. Though he was very disappointed and even angry with them, he still loved them. Therefore, God's righteous indignation was kindled against these kings who continued to follow in the ways of Jeroboam and led his people further and further away from him. They would be punished and destroyed for their rebellion. But don't make the mistake of believing that, in his punishment of Israel or her kings, God was ever acting out of hatred or malice. He is not capable of such emotions or motives toward mankind. Rather, it was a sense of love and concern that prompted God to act. His only desire was to have them forsake their foreign gods and sinful ways and return to a faithful relationship with him. So it is with God today. Regardless of how far we might wander away from God and into sin, he never stops feeling love and concern for us. Man can deny him, mock him, curse him, and turn others against him, but God never stops loving. His only desire for all of humanity is that we escape sin and its eternal consequences and find the safety and security of a faithful relationship with him through Christ. Oh, that our world might be convinced of that truth!

*What do you think it is that allows God to continue
to show love and concern despite man's sinfulness?*

DON'T FORGET TO PRAY AND HAVE A GREAT DAY!

Day 137

 Today's Reading:
1 Kings 16:8-34

The history of the ten northern tribes sees one bad and godless king after another. In fact, in the history of this kingdom as recorded in the Old Testament, there was never a king who sought to restore the nation to faithfulness. Considering that history, it is quite remarkable to read that Ahab "did evil in the sight of the Lord, more than all who were before him" (16:30), and that he "did more to provoke the Lord, the God of Israel, to anger than all the kings of Israel who were before him" (16:33). As we will see in the coming days, Ahab with the encouragement of his evil wife, Jezebel, will exalt Baal as the god of Israel and, as a result, will bring more hardship and suffering upon the northern kingdom than had been known in its short history. As has already been stated in an earlier reading from this week, one of the great lessons of the Old Testament is to understand the dangerous and destructive nature of sin. We also see in the history of Israel the progressive nature of sin. The longer the nation stays away from God, the further it wanders from him. As you read today's text, the kingdom that you read of is one that is unrecognizable as the people that God brought out of Egypt and gave his law to. There is no mention of the law or worship or anything that resembles what God had called and commanded them to be. Thus is the nature of sin. It is a cancer that eats away at our sense of right and wrong and will eventually destroy any desire we might have for a relationship with God. Oh, that we might avoid that slippery slope of sin!

How would you describe the progressive nature of sin?
What examples can you think of?

DON'T FORGET TO PRAY AND HAVE A GREAT DAY!

DAY 138

 Today's Reading:
1 Kings 17:1-24

In opposition to Israel's most evil king, God sends his greatest prophet— Elijah. At a time when Israel was at its lowest and most defiled point, this man of God bursts onto the scene with the devastating proclamation of a famine that would cripple the nation. But despite the need and deprivation that is associated with a famine, this chapter is really about the care and provision of God for those who are faithful to him. It is interesting that Elijah proclaims this famine on the land, but then nothing is recorded about its devastating effects. Rather, the focus of the entire chapter is on God's miraculous provision for Elijah, with special emphasis on the words of God: "I have commanded." First, at the Brook Cherith, God not only provided the water of the brook but says, "I have commanded the ravens to feed you there." When the brook dried up due to the famine, Elijah was instructed to go to Zarephath, God saying to him, "I have commanded a widow there to feed you." With a miraculously unending supply of flour and oil, she fed Elijah, her son, and herself for many days. Don't miss the meaning or the power of that little phrase, "I have commanded." Elijah having food and water during a terrible famine was not a coincidence or bout of good luck. It was by the divine command of God. God was mindful of his circumstances and attentive to his needs. In a time when Israel was suffering the consequences of their rejection of God, Elijah was safe in his care. What an amazing lesson of hope and comfort to God's faithful people today!

Can you think of some things that God has
commanded concerning our care and well-being?

DON'T FORGET TO PRAY AND HAVE A GREAT DAY!

Day 139

Today's Reading:
1 Kings 18:20-46

This scene represents one of the most overt confrontations recorded in the Bible between God and a false god. In dramatic fashion, Elijah challenges the prophets of Baal to a demonstration that would prove once and for all who was the true God. With supreme confidence in God, Elijah taunts and provokes the prophets of Baal, calling for them to entice their god to act, but their desperate attempts throughout the day produced nothing. Then as the time of the evening sacrifice drew near, Elijah called all the people near and began to carefully rebuild the altar to the Lord that had been torn down in that place. The people must have been filled with confusion when Elijah instructed them to soak the altar and sacrifice with water until the trench that he had dug around the altar was filled. In response to Elijah's prayer, and in an amazing demonstration of his mighty power, God sent fire from heaven to consume the sacrifice, the stones, the dust, and the water. There was no doubt—there was only one true and living God, and it was the Lord, Jehovah. Our world today is filled with skeptics and unbelievers who scoff at the idea of God. They lift up many other things into his place and call them gods, but it is still true that there is only one God! The God of Elijah, the God who demonstrated his power on Mount Carmel, is still God. He is my God and yours. Though he may interact with us in different ways today, he is still just as powerful as he ever was. What a blessing and honor it is to be called his children and to know that we belong to the God of Elijah!

How can God's presence and power be known in our world today?

DON'T FORGET TO PRAY AND HAVE A GREAT DAY!

DAY 140

Today's Reading:
1 Kings 19:1-21

I can't help but think about the euphoric feeling of victory that Elijah must have experienced on Mount Carmel. God had proven himself, the prophets of Baal had been executed, there seemed to be some degree of reconciliation between him and Ahab, and the three and a half year drought had come to an end. Everything was good. But how quickly that euphoria turned to hopelessness. With the determined threat of Jezebel, Elijah found himself running for his life, eventually hiding in a cave. At the center of this text is the burning question that God asks of Elijah, not once but twice: "What are you doing here?" You see, God has a habit of asking questions, not because he needs to know the answer, but because he wants the one to whom the question is asked to examine his own heart and consider the answer. Elijah's presence in that cave showed that he had allowed his own fear and discouragement to overwhelm his faith in God. He was not relying on the God that had preserved him through the drought and given him victory over the prophets of Baal to protect him from Jezebel's threats. Instead of courageously standing for God as his prophet, Elijah was cowering in fear and wallowing in self-pity. Hiding out in that cave betrayed everything that Elijah knew about God and everything that God had called him to stand for. God's answer, given to Elijah in a beautiful way, was that whether in big ways or small he was always there. At times, his presence could be seen in all-consuming fire sent from heaven. At other times, he was to be found in the smallest of whispers, but regardless of the nature of his presence, he was always there. What a wonderful encouragement to Elijah, and what a wonderful lesson for us.

What encouragement can we gain from this scene from Elijah's life?

DON'T FORGET TO PRAY AND HAVE A GREAT DAY!

Day 141

 Today's Reading:
1 Kings 21:1-29

The New Testament warns us that "Bad company ruins good morals" (1 Corinthians 15:33). I am not sure that Ahab could ever be described as a person of good moral character, but I am convinced that he was made worse by the influence of his wife, Jezebel. This text provides just one example of the evil nature and unscrupulous ways of this wicked woman. When it came to the plot of land at the center of this text, Ahab wanted it, but it seems that it never crossed his mind that, as king, he could just take it by force without reason or justification. Maybe, in his heart of hearts, he knew this to be immoral and sinful. Jezebel, on the other hand, had no such concerns. Through deception and plotting, she had Naboth killed and took the land in her husband's name. Ahab played the role of accomplice after the fact by, without hesitation, taking possession of the land after Naboth's death. Who would Ahab have been, and how would his story have changed had it not been for the evil influence of Jezebel? We will never know. All of this brings to mind the question: does the company I keep make me better or worse in terms of my morals and character? It can become very easy for us to find ourselves surrounded by people who do not have the same concerns for a pure and godly life that we do. In that situation, we can inadvertently fall under their influence and be made to share in their sins. For that reason, it is vitally important that we choose our companions carefully, knowing that they will have a part in making us who we are. May God help us to make good choices.

Why do you think that our companions
are such a powerful influence on our lives?

DON'T FORGET TO PRAY AND HAVE A GREAT DAY!

Day 142

Today's Reading:
2 Kings 2:1-25

Elijah's life and work had been extraordinary. In the midst of one of Israel's darkest spiritual hours, Elijah had served faithfully and valiantly as a prophet of the Lord. Now, with his work complete and Elisha appointed to take his place, Elijah is taken to be with God in a way that is even more extraordinary than the nature of his life. With a chariot of fire to separate him from Elisha and a whirlwind to receive him up to Heaven, Elijah becomes one of only two individuals recorded in the Scriptures to not see death. This story may seem so outside of normal circumstances that there is no possible lesson for us to learn from it that applies to our lives, but it seems to me that the lesson may very well be one of God's love, care, and reward toward his faithful children. Elijah had been a faithful servant to the Lord, and though the text doesn't necessarily highlight it, his life must have been one of many hardships and trials. He had sacrificed and endured much because of his commitment to the Lord, and when his work was done, God rewarded him with the rest that he so badly desired. There is great hope for us in recognizing that God continues to love and care for his people in this same way. He is aware of the struggles and sacrifices of our lives and knows every fear and sorrow of our hearts. If we will remain faithful to him and committed to his cause, we will surely find a place of rest and reward at the end of this life, provided for us by a loving and gracious Father. What a wonderful hope!

*What promises has God made to us concerning
the rest and reward of faithfulness?*

DON'T FORGET TO PRAY AND HAVE A GREAT DAY!

DAY 143

 Today's Reading:
2 Kings 3:1-27

God often has a very interesting and colorful way of demonstrating his power while meeting the needs of his people. The armies of Israel, Judah, and Edom are facing a fierce enemy in the Moabites and have been severely weakened by days without water. Through the words of Elisha, God reveals to them that out of regard for Judah's king Jehoshaphat, he will give them victory over the Moabites, and to demonstrate his willingness and ability to help them, God fills a dry valley with water in what Elisha calls, "a light [that is, an easy] thing in the sight of the Lord." Not only did God use that water-filled valley to provide for the needs of the armies, but he also used it as a means of confusing the Moabite armies, leading to their defeat. Have you ever felt completely overwhelmed by the circumstances of your life? Have you ever wondered if God has forgotten about you? Have you ever prayed for God's help and then wondered why he answered in the way that he did? Well, Old Testament texts like this remind us of the amazing wisdom and incredible power of God to know our needs and meet those needs in ways that we can't even imagine. There are no circumstances that we find ourselves in and no struggle that we encounter that God is not capable of helping us to endure and overcome. We must only learn to trust and rely upon him.

In what ways have you seen the power and
wisdom of God displayed in your own life?

DON'T FORGET TO PRAY AND HAVE A GREAT DAY!

Day 144

 Today's Reading:
2 Kings 4:1-44

Shortly before Elijah was taken up into Heaven in the whirlwind, he asked Elisha to request of him something that Elijah might do for him. Elisha's request was not a small one—a double portion of Elijah's spirit. The "double portion" was the part of a man's inheritance reserved for the firstborn son. Elisha was asking to be placed in that position of advantage and be treated as the firstborn among the "sons of the prophet." He was not asking for worldly gain but rather for an endowment of Elijah's spirit to enable him to carry out his spiritual duties as prophet. The result of this granted request was the great power that Elisha displayed from the Lord. This chapter gives us a sampling of that miraculous ability granted to Elisha from God—a degree of power that would not be seen again by the hands of a single man until the appearance of Jesus himself. However, power is not the only attribute of Elisha's life that is pointed out in this chapter. If you look carefully, you will also see a compassion and concern that reflects that of the God that he served. All of the miracles that are recorded here are done to meet the needs of people or to help someone who was in distress of some kind. Elisha had been given a great gift by the Lord, and he used that gift in a powerful way to demonstrate the love of God. We may not have the miraculous abilities that Elisha had, but we can certainly use the talents and abilities that God has blessed us with to show the love of God to those around us through our compassion and service. May we always strive to do just that.

In what ways can we demonstrate the love of God to those around us?

DON'T FORGET TO PRAY AND HAVE A GREAT DAY!

Day 145

 Today's Reading:
2 Kings 5:1-27

The story of Naaman's healing is a great example of the faith and obedience that God asks of those who come to him for spiritual healing and life. In his human way of thinking, Naaman saw no reason to obey the senseless instructions given to him by Elisha for the healing of his leprosy. If not for the concerned pleading of his servants, Naaman might never have known the saving power of God. Certainly, God could have healed Naaman by any means that He wanted or without requiring anything of Naaman at all, but God required what He required. There was no special power or medicinal advantage in the waters of the Jordan; they were simply the waters that God had commanded. The power was in God and in Naaman's willingness to obey. The lesson for us is clear. So often in today's world when we read or hear of God's commands for us regarding our forgiveness and salvation, we, like Naaman, fail to see the importance of following those simple instructions. We rationalize that God is all-powerful and does not need our "help" in providing salvation. But as in the example of Naaman, the power of forgiveness is not in the actions or elements themselves or in anything that we can do of our own power; the power of forgiveness and spiritual healing is in God and in our willingness to submit to his will and become obedient to his word. May we find the strength to put our own ideas aside and simply obey God!

Why do you think that God asks for our obedience
in receiving his forgiveness and salvation?

DON'T FORGET TO PRAY AND HAVE A GREAT DAY!

Day 146

 Today's Reading:
2 Kings 6:1-23

I love this story about Elisha and his servant. Facing seemingly insurmountable odds, Elisha's servant reacts in a typical and expected way—with fear and panic. "Alas, my master! what shall we do?" But, by faith, Elisha understood something that his servant did not—that, though God may have been unseen, he was there and was supplying all the help that Elisha needed to overcome his enemies. Elisha's response to the servant's concern was one that probably seemed absurd at first: "Do not be afraid, for those who are with us are more than those who are with them." Through the prayerful request of Elisha, his servant was miraculously allowed to see the help of God in the form of an army of fiery chariots all around. What a revelation! How often do we find ourselves facing what seems like insurmountable odds, surrounded by circumstances that leave us fearful and wondering how we will ever survive? While we may not have the advantage of an Elisha to help us miraculously see the help of God, we have something even better—the faithful promises of a loving and all-powerful God revealed to us through his holy word. Regardless of our circumstances, we, through the eye of faith, can see and know that God is with us to help us and to see us through. No matter what we may be up against, we, too, can know that "those who are with us are more than those who are with them." To God be the glory!

What examples can you give of times when God,
though unseen, has helped you?

DON'T FORGET TO PRAY AND HAVE A GREAT DAY!

Day 147

 Today's Reading:
2 Kings 9:1-37

There are times when we are shocked by the violence and treachery of the Old Testament, and to an even greater degree, we are troubled at the fact that God seems to be behind much of that bloodshed. It is often very difficult for us to consolidate these acts of death and destruction with the God that we know and serve. Why would a God of righteousness, mercy, and love command such violence? As you read these types of texts, keep two things in mind: First, this was a very different time and world than the one in which we live. Those things that are foreign to us were not that unusual in that day and time. Secondly, we must maintain a focus on the overall goal and purpose of God. In this chapter, for instance, God is bringing judgment upon Jezebel for all of her evil ways. He had foretold this punishment in the days of Elijah, and the word of the Lord is always faithful. Then there is one more thing that we must remember as we read the Old Testament: it is written for our learning (Romans 15:4). Texts such as this remind us of the terribleness of sin and of the destruction that inevitably comes as a result of it. God has warned us that judgment is coming and that there is a price that must be paid for a life of rebellion and sinfulness, and as has already been stated, the word of the Lord is always faithful. May we learn the lessons that God teaches us and allow those lessons to motivate lives of faithfulness.

Why do you think that our world often minimizes the destructiveness of sin?

DON'T FORGET TO PRAY AND HAVE A GREAT DAY!

DAY 148

Today's Reading:
2 Kings 20:1-21

Many of the events of Hezekiah's life will be discussed as we read through the Chronicles, but for now, consider this extraordinary event in his life. Hezekiah was sick and "at the point of death." He was one of the few good kings of Judah and had done much to restore godly worship in the land. Now, as Isaiah tells him of his impending death, Hezekiah cries out to God in fervent prayer. His plea for mercy was heard, and God granted him fifteen more years. We have seen through our study that God is faithful in bringing judgment upon the ungodly, according to his word. It is also important to understand that God is a faithful and merciful God to those who fear and faithfully obey him. Through his word, God has made many great and precious promises to those who are faithful and obedient to him. He cares for us, provides for us, protects us, and hears and answers our prayers in ways that are in keeping with his perfect will. As God's people, we are called to have faith in him and to trust in his wisdom, power, and love to meet our needs. Events such as this one in the life of Hezekiah serve to remind us not only of God's ability to meet our needs and answer our prayers, but also of his desire to bless his people and do good toward them. Thank God for his marvelous love and care and for the confidence that we gain through his holy word.

In what ways does God show his love and
care toward his faithful people today?

DON'T FORGET TO PRAY AND HAVE A GREAT DAY!

Day 149

 Today's Reading:
2 Kings 22:1-20

Among the kings of Judah, Josiah stands out as extraordinary for several reasons, including his young age when becoming king, his unyielding devotion to God, and the amazing courage that he displays in ridding the land of idol worship. Much of this will be discussed with tomorrow's reading, but for now, let's think about another element of Josiah's life and rule that is important to appreciating the extraordinary nature of his life. Consider the condition of the nation when Josiah became king. In this chapter, we read of the efforts to repair the Temple, during which the Book of the Law was found. Think about that—so far had Judah wandered from God that his law had literally been lost along with any knowledge that they may have had of it. They had forgotten about the covenant that God had formed with them at Mount Sinai and had gone their own way. How can God's people wander so far away from him that they no longer have any knowledge of his word? Unfortunately, it is not difficult to see how many, even today, are in the same position. The word of God, given to us for the purpose of teaching, guiding, and correcting us, has in many cases been totally forgotten and left behind. Man has followed his own way with little regard for the covenant that we have with Christ. May God help us to learn from the example of Josiah and Judah and find our way back to him.

In what ways has our world lost and forgotten the word of God?

DON'T FORGET TO PRAY AND HAVE A GREAT DAY!

Day 150

Today's Reading:
2 Kings 23:1-25

While the nation of Judah had rebelled against God and forgotten his law, Josiah is described with the following words: "And he did what was right in the eyes of the Lord and walked in all the way of David his father, and he did not turn aside to the right or to the left" (2 Kings 22:1). When the Book of the Law was found and read in his presence, Josiah tore his clothes in his distress over how neglected the law had been. Then, at the still young age of 26, Josiah began a sweeping plan of reform in the kingdom of Judah in order to bring the nation back to faithfulness. He tore down the altars and high places devoted to the worship of false gods. He removed the priests that worked in the service of those false gods. He defiled the places that were sacred to the false religions. Imagine the courage, faith, and devotion to God that was required for this young man to stand up against an entire nation of idol worshippers to defy their gods and destroy everything that was sacred and holy to them. Josiah teaches us a valuable lesson about the commitment that faithfulness often requires. There are times in our lives when standing up for God may mean standing alone. There are times when doing right means going against the majority. Being faithful to God is not always easy or convenient, but it is always the right thing. In a very dark period in Judah's history, Josiah was a very bright light. May God help us to follow his example of courage and commitment to God.

What are some things that we can do to help us have the courage and commitment to stand up for God despite the circumstances or consequences?

DON'T FORGET TO PRAY AND HAVE A GREAT DAY!

Day 151

 Today's Reading:
2 Kings 25:1-21

Despite all of Josiah's efforts to reform the nation and restore godliness, God's anger continued to burn hot against Judah because of all the evil that Manasseh, Josiah's grandfather, had done. Through the actions of a foreign king, Nebuchadnezzar, God would bring Judah into captivity and punish her for her ungodliness. One might wonder why God would allow his people to be taken into captivity and the city of Jerusalem to be destroyed. How could these events possibly exalt or bring glory to the name of God? In our human thinking, it just does not make sense, but as the Lord would later say through the prophet Isaiah, "For my thoughts are not your thoughts, neither are your ways my ways, declares the LORD. For as the heavens are higher than the earth, so are my ways higher than your ways and my thoughts than your thoughts" (Isaiah 55:8-9). Over and over again in the Old Testament story, God uses godless leaders and nations to bring about his will, resulting in the exalting of his name. What was true then continues to be true today. God does not require people or even nations to believe in him and be devoted to him in order for him to use them to accomplish his will. He is above all and his will reigns supreme. The God that we serve is the God of the universe and of this world. All praise and glory be given to him!

What hope and encouragement can we gain today
in the knowledge that God and his will reigns supreme?

DON'T FORGET TO PRAY AND HAVE A GREAT DAY!

Day 152

Today's Reading:
1 Chronicles 15:1-29

Much of what is recorded in the Chronicles is parallel to what is recorded in the books of Samuel and Kings. In 2 Samuel 6, we saw the tragic death of Uzzah as a result of the inappropriate handling of the Ark of the Covenant (this is also recorded in 1 Chronicles 13). Because of that earlier error, King David was very diligent in making sure that the ark was transported in the appropriate way as it was carried into the tabernacle. With careful preparation, the priests and Levites took on the role of carrying the Ark according to the instructions of God's law. It is impressive to see, in this passage, the care and respect with which the Ark of the Covenant is treated. It was the most treasured and significant of all of Israel's possessions, representing their covenant with God and his constant presence with them. David had prepared a special place for it, and with jubilant celebration, it is carefully relocated to that location. Maybe the lesson in this text is found in remembering what the Ark represented—the presence of God—and in realizing how precious and important that presence was to his people. We—our lives and bodies—are the temple of God under the covenant of Christ, but how much do we appreciate and treasure his presence in our lives? Are we careful to treat his temple in a way that brings glory and honor to him or do we carelessly neglect and abuse the temple of God? Do we remember and rejoice in his constant presence in our lives, or do we live as if he is nowhere to be found? May God help us to live with all the respect, love, and honor that is due our great God!

In what ways might we bring honor and
glory to God in the treatment and use of our lives?

DON'T FORGET TO PRAY AND HAVE A GREAT DAY!

DAY 153

 Today's Reading:
1 Chronicles 21:1-30

This chapter begins with a very interesting statement: "Then Satan stood against Israel and incited David to number Israel." There are two quick lessons to be learned from this sentence. First, Satan is the ultimate source of our temptation and disobedience, stopping at nothing to deceive us and lure us into sin. Secondly, even a man after God's own heart, like David, is not immune to the traps of Satan. If David can sin against God in this way, then certainly, I am able to as well. But as much as this chapter is about sin, it is also about repentance and forgiveness. When David recognized his error, he quickly admitted his fault and asked for God's forgiveness and mercy. As a condition of his repentance, David was commanded to erect an altar and offer a sacrifice to God on the threshing floor of Ornan the Jebusite. Though he was the king and was offered the sacrificial items as a gift, David refused to offer a sacrifice to God that had cost him nothing. David was determined to be right with God, and he understood that a sacrifice is only a sacrifice if it costs something. In our lives today, God does not require sacrifices of burnt offerings but rather a living sacrifice of our own lives given in commitment and service to him (Romans 12:1). So often, however, we want to "commit" our lives to Christ in order to gain his forgiveness, yet we are not willing to give up anything or make any changes to the way we live. We must understand, just as David did, that our lives cannot truly be considered sacrifices unless our commitment costs us something.

What has your living sacrifice cost you?

DON'T FORGET TO PRAY AND HAVE A GREAT DAY!

Day 154

Today's Reading:
1 Chronicles 29:1-30

I n the New Testament, we read: "Each one must give as he has decided in his heart, not reluctantly or under compulsion, for God loves a cheerful giver" (2 Corinthians 9:6). Among the biblical examples of willing and cheerful giving, this Old Testament scene stands out. Though David had wanted and planned to build a temple for the Lord, God did not allow him that honor but did give him the promise that his son, Solomon, would build that magnificent structure. Still, David desired to do something for the Lord and be part of the process, so he went about the task of taking up a collection of materials to be used in the temple's construction. It is amazing to see the generosity of the Israelites in this free-will offering that is a picture-perfect example of the type of giving that Paul would later exhort the New Testament church to practice. As David offers a prayer of praise and thanksgiving following the collection, we see the attitude that made their generous giving possible. "But who am I, and what is my people, that we should be able thus to offer willingly? For all things come from you, and of your own have we given you." One of the most difficult truths for us to grasp concerning our physical possessions is that everything that we have is actually God's and has been given to us as a gift of his love for us to use to his glory. We tend to think of all that we have done to earn or to gain all the things that we have and, therefore, to believe that those things are ours and ours alone. But only when we develop the attitude that David and Israel displays in this passage will we truly be able to give freely and cheerfully to God.

Why do you think that it is important to
God that we be willful and cheerful givers?

DON'T FORGET TO PRAY AND HAVE A GREAT DAY!

DAY 155

Today's Reading:
2 Chronicles 3:1-17

I t is hard to imagine the beauty and grandeur of the temple that Solomon constructed. This magnificent structure would represent to the Jews the dwelling place of God and the defining center of their religious lives. As such, it merited the very best that Israel had to offer—no detail was too small and no effort was too great; no metal was too costly and no stone was too precious. After all, this building was a reflection not only of the love and devotion of Israel to God, but also of the greatness and majesty of God himself. Consider a modern day Christian equivalent to this concept. We have buildings that serve as a place of meeting for the church today, but we understand that those buildings do not represent God's dwelling place. Instead, God inhabits a spiritual building, his church, made up of the hearts and lives of his people. As part of that spiritual temple, you and I are responsible for determining what kind of building it will be. The example of God's people under the old covenant is that they gave the very best that they had to God with willing and joyful hearts and worked diligently to create a building that would bring honor and glory to God in the sight of all who witnessed it. Does God not deserve the same from us? By building lives of holiness, faithfulness, love, and service, we offer God the very best that we have and create lives that shine as lights in the world to the glory of God. In so doing, we help to make his church a holy temple that outshines even the temple of Solomon!

In what ways can we give our very best
to God as part of his spiritual temple?

DON'T FORGET TO PRAY AND HAVE A GREAT DAY!

Day 156

**Today's Reading:
2 Chronicles 13:1-22**

When reading through the kings, we considered many of the kings of Israel after the kingdom was divided. You might have noticed that none of those kings was faithful to God, and the nation of Israel continued to wander farther and farther away from him. The story of Judah was not quite so bad. While some kings did not follow God's ways, others did, and the nation typically followed the king's lead. Abijah was the second king of Judah after Solomon, and he found himself at war with his estranged brethren in Israel. Possibly the most crucial and telling statement of this account, and the one that offers the greatest lesson for us, is found in verse 18: "Thus the men of Israel were subdued at that time, and the men of Judah prevailed, because they relied on the Lord, the God of their fathers." Judah's victory was not due to their overwhelming strength or strategic advantage. They were victorious because they trusted in God instead of their own power. Theirs was a victory of faith. In our lives today, we face many battles, though they may not be in the form of army versus army. Family problems, financial crises, sickness, temptation, worry, guilt, discouragement—these and many other daily struggles make up the battles that we fight. But despite that difference, the same thing is true for us that was true for the army of Judah. We will overcome and be victorious in our battles, not by our own strength but rather by our reliance upon God. If we will trust in him, he will care for us and give us the help we need to be victorious. Thanks be to God!

In what battles are you currently engaged?
In what ways have you put your trust in the Lord to give you victory?

DON'T FORGET TO PRAY AND HAVE A GREAT DAY!

Day 157

 Today's Reading:
2 Chronicles 14:1-15

Following his death, Abijah's son Asa became king over Judah. It is said of Asa that he "did what was good and right in the eyes of the Lord his God." He removed the altars and false gods from the land, restored true worship, and sacrificed to the Lord. Because of his faithfulness, God blessed him and the kingdom for his sake. Found within the story of Asa's reign is an admonition given to him that stands as a continual lesson for God's people today. Through the prophet Azariah, Asa is told, "The Lord is with you while you are with him. If you seek him, he will be found by you, but if you forsake him, he will forsake you." How true are those words for people of any age. The New Testament is full of statements like "seek and you will find" (Matthew 7:7) and "draw near to God and He will draw near to you" (James 4:8). You see, God is not a God who desires to be separated from his people and to rule from afar. He does not isolate himself from those who desire a relationship with him, but rather allows himself to be found. As long as we are willing to be close to God, submitting to his will in faith and obedience, he will be with us to bless and care for us as our heavenly Father. What a wonderful assurance it is, to know that we serve a faithful God who promises to be with us for as long as we are with him!

What are some of the attributes of a life that is "with God?"

DON'T FORGET TO PRAY AND HAVE A GREAT DAY!

Day 158

 Today's Reading:
2 Chronicles 19:1-11

Asa's son, Jehoshaphat was the next to sit on the throne of Judah. He was also a good and righteous king, following in the ways of his father and of King David. While Asa had done well in removing false gods and altars from the land, he had failed to completely rid the nation of unacceptable worship in that he allowed the high places to remain. Jehoshaphat accomplished what his father had failed to do. He removed the high places and turned the hearts of the people back toward God. He also set up judges to handle civil matters and Levite priests to handle religious matters with the intent that all that was done would be according to God's law and pleasing to him. In considering the lives of Asa and Jehoshaphat, there is a thought that comes to mind about our own lives and relationship with God. It seems that, on occasion, we become determined to rid our lives of evil influences and sin, and so we do some cleaning out and straightening up in our hearts, our minds, and our lives. However, it can be very easy for us to, like Asa, overlook some small fragments of the temptation and sinfulness that has polluted our lives. The problem is that those small, maybe seemingly harmless fragments become seeds of temptation and influence that can grow into full-blown unfaithfulness if not removed. Like Jehoshaphat, we must be determined to be thorough in the removal of sinful influences in our lives. Our faithfulness and salvation is too important to allow any worldly desire or temptation to take us away from God.

What steps have you taken to rid your life of sinfulness and temptation?
Are there any fragments that remain to be taken care of?

DON'T FORGET TO PRAY AND HAVE A GREAT DAY!

DAY 159

 Today's Reading:
2 Chronicles 21:1-20

Following Jehoshaphat, the kings of Judah were less than diligent in maintaining their faithfulness to God. Jehoshaphat's son Jehoram followed in the ways of Israel and specifically after the gods of his father-in-law, Ahab. He brought the worship of Baal to the land of Judah and set a dangerous precedent for the kings that would follow him. Jehoram offers us a powerful example of the importance of the paths that we choose and the consequences of choosing the wrong path. His father and grandfather had both been good kings, doing what was right in the sight of the Lord. Jehoram was raised in a God-fearing home and was, no doubt, taught to love and revere God by his father. In stark contrast to that background, his wife was the daughter of Israel's wicked King Ahab and his even more wicked wife Jezebel. She had been raised to recognize and worship Baal as her god. Jehoram was faced with the choosing of his life's path—to follow in the footsteps of his father or to walk in the way of his wife's family. He chose poorly, and that choice brought devastating consequences on his life and on the nation of Judah. Consider our lives. Jesus tells us that these same two paths stand before each of us today (Matthew 7:13-14). One leads to destruction and the other to eternal life. We will all have opportunities to make that choice and will, no doubt, be encouraged and influenced by people in both directions. The good news is that the right and wise choice is obvious; we must only have the commitment and courage to make it. May God help us to always choose him!

*Where can we find guidance and encouragement
in choosing the right path in life?*

DON'T FORGET TO PRAY AND HAVE A GREAT DAY!

Day 160

 Today's Reading:
2 Chronicles 23:1-21

Beginning with Jehoram, the nation of Judah was in a state of moral and spiritual decline. His son, Ahaziah, had formed an alliance with the son of Ahab and was eventually killed by Jehu. With none of Ahaziah's sons being of age to take the throne, there was no one to assume power over Judah. Seeing this situation, Ahaziah's mother, Athaliah, killed all of Ahaziah's sons (her grandsons), and she ruled over Judah for a period of six years. However, one son, Joash, was saved by his sister and hidden away until he was old enough to become king. Joash was a good king, at least as long as he had the guidance of Jehoida the priest. He repaired the temple and restored right worship, but he could not restore godly devotion to the hearts of the people. After Jehoida's death, the people came before the king, and in order to find favor with them, Joash forsook the Lord and began to worship idols. The examples of both Joash and Jehoram remind us of the danger of evil influences. In both cases, these kings allowed the people surrounding them to draw them away from God and into sin. Their error serves to remind us all of the need to guard ourselves against the undue influence of those around us. As the New Testament warns us: "Do not be deceived: 'Bad company ruins good morals'" (1 Corinthians 15:33). While it may be impossible to avoid contact with some who have chosen sinful paths (in fact, our Christian mission demands that we have contact with the world in order to be lights and to lead them to Christ), we would do well to carefully choose those who are closest to us and who have the most influence over our lives. We want to be sure that they will strengthen our faith instead of weakening it and lead us closer to God instead of away from him.

Who are the greatest influences in your life?
Is their influence positive or negative?

DON'T FORGET TO PRAY AND HAVE A GREAT DAY!

Day 161

 Today's Reading:
2 Chronicles 26:1-23

L ife is full of spiritual dangers and pitfalls. As we have read through the lives of the kings of Judah, we have seen many of these dangers and the devastation that they can cause. Uzziah provides another powerful example. His reign began in a good way. He followed after the Lord and was rewarded for his faithfulness. The text tells us that "as long as he sought the Lord, God made him prosper." Under Uzziah's leadership and with God's help, Judah had a powerful army and was very successful in conquering their enemies, so much so that he was known among the nations for his great strength. But it was in this great strength and success, given to him by the Lord, that Uzziah was confronted with his greatest weakness—pride. In his arrogance and pride, Uzziah took it upon himself to do what only the priests were allowed to do—offer incense to the Lord. Surely, with all of his strength and authority, no one would withstand him and prevent him from performing this ritual himself. Yet, Uzziah found out quickly that God would not be mocked and that His commands were applicable to all, regardless of name or position. Even while he stood in the temple arguing with the priests who were trying to prevent him from committing this sinful act, Uzziah, the mighty king of Judah, was struck with leprosy by the Lord. His life was instantly reduced to one of humble isolation and illness. In the world and church today, many people continue to be drawn into sinful attitudes and practices by pride. The idea that "I can do anything that I want to do and no one can stop me" is a dangerous and ungodly one that ignores the boundaries and requirements that God has put into place regarding his church. Just as with God's law in the Old Testament, certain roles, positions, and duties within the church are limited to those who meet specific criteria determined by God. Our responsibility is to simply humble ourselves before him and submit to his will in all things.

Why do you think that pride is such a dangerous attitude?

DON'T FORGET TO PRAY AND HAVE A GREAT DAY!

Day 162

 Today's Reading:
2 Chronicles 28:1-21

Often times, in life there is a watershed moment—that event or moment that provides the opportunity to make a life-shaping decision. In many cases, that moment is brought about by a tragedy or very difficult set of circumstances that causes one to contemplate his course and consider making a change. Ahaz was arguably the worst and most evil king of Judah, even going so far as to sacrifice his own children to false gods. Because of his evil ways, God caused the nation to suffer great defeats at the hands of their enemies, including Israel. It is this set of circumstances that brought about the watershed moment in Ahaz's life. In similar circumstances, other kings had realized their sinful ways and turned back to God in repentance, which was always God's intent and desire in bringing defeat and suffering to his people. Ahaz, however, made the opposite choice. The text tells us that "in the time of his distress King Ahaz became increasingly unfaithful to the Lord." His rebellion and idolatry were multiplied, as if he were angrily lashing out at God. Ahaz's story causes me to wonder about how we often react in stressful and distressing times. Though we may not realize it, those times could be providing a watershed moment for us wherein we have the opportunity to return and draw nearer to God, or to push God away in rejection of his love. May we always choose to trust in God and to give ourselves to him in faith and obedience.

How can these difficult moments in our
lives serve to strengthen our faith in God?

DON'T FORGET TO PRAY AND HAVE A GREAT DAY!

DAY 163

Today's Reading:
2 Chronicles 29:1-36

As I read of these kings, I often wonder about the influences that led them to live the way that they did. Sometimes, those influences are clearly revealed, while in other cases there is nothing said at all. While Ahaz was one of the worst and most evil kings of Judah, his son Hezekiah was one of the best of the divided kingdom. We are not told who it was that taught Hezekiah about God and instilled in him the determination to restore the kingdom to faithfulness, but there is no doubt that someone or something had a powerful effect on this young man's heart. As soon as Ahaz died and Hezekiah was made king, he began to reverse many of the things that his father had done to take the nation away from God. The temple was re-opened and restored, the idols and all that was related to them were torn down and destroyed, and proper worship was reinstated. As a result of these reforms, Judah was blessed by God and saved from her enemies. One of the great lessons of the Old Testament is surely that God is a patient, merciful, and forgiving God. When you consider the depths to which Judah had sunk in her evil and idolatrous ways, it is truly amazing to see how quickly God relents from his punishment and returns to blessing them when they turn back to him. That same God is still patient, merciful, and forgiving toward us today. We are all sinners, deserving of God's wrath and condemnation, and yet, God continues to be loving toward us, giving us opportunity after opportunity to repent of our sins and enjoy the blessings of fellowship with him. What an awesome God he is!

Why do you think that God is so quick to forgive and restore?

DON'T FORGET TO PRAY AND HAVE A GREAT DAY!

Day 164

 Today's Reading:
2 Chronicles 33:1-25

T hough Hezekiah was a good king who followed the Lord, his love for God was not passed on to his son, Manasseh. After becoming king, Manasseh reverted back to the ways of his grandfather, Ahaz. He set up idols and high places, even placing an idol in the temple. Like his grandfather, he offered his sons as burnt offerings to the gods, and he took part in all forms of evil and godless practices. However, Manasseh was not like Ahaz in every way. When faced with the wrath of God by the hand of the Assyrians, Manasseh, unlike Ahaz, humbled himself, repented of his wickedness, and turned back to God. He removed the idolatrous images and altars, made sacrifices to God, and commanded the people to worship the Lord. The lives of these kings continue to teach and remind us of valuable lessons that are vital to our own spiritual lives. Manasseh had fallen far from God's favor and had allowed a great deal of wickedness and sin to invade his life. He had done horrible things in the name of a false religion, and yet God still pursued him with a desire to bring him and the nation back to faithfulness. There are times in our lives when we may think that we have gone too far and done too much to ever be back in a faithful relationship with God again. We may see forgiveness and salvation as an impossibility based on the great amount of sin in our lives, but Manasseh reminds us that there is always a way back. God never gives up on us. If we desire forgiveness and are willing to repent of our sins, God is always willing to forgive us and accept us back into his fold. Thanks be to God for his amazing love and mercy!

What advice would you give to a person who
was far away from God but wanted to come back?

DON'T FORGET TO PRAY AND HAVE A GREAT DAY!

Day 165

 Today's Reading:
2 Chronicles 29:1-36

We have read previously about King Josiah and the restoration of Judah that he brought about. Unfortunately, that restoration was short lived. Four different kings of Judah are named in this chapter, but none of them are really the true focus of the text. At the center of this chapter is the striving of God against the rebellion and hard-heartedness of his people. I am struck by the statement found in verse 15 of this chapter: "The Lord, the God of their fathers, sent persistently to them by his messengers, because he had compassion on his people and on his dwelling place." Despite all that they had done to reject the Lord, he still cared for them and desired to do good toward them. Though they would spend seventy years in Babylonian captivity, God never quit loving them, and though they did not always acknowledge him, he never quit being their God. Thus is the nature of God. He is longsuffering and merciful, full of love and grace. The Old Testament story of God and his people is largely a very sad story of rejection and sin on the part of Israel and Judah toward God, but it is also a story of hope, forgiveness, and restoration because of a God who is ever ready to love and forgive. Though set in a much different time and in very different circumstances, our story is much the same. Far too often, ours is a story of rejection and sin as we choose to follow our own paths and reject God's guidance. But as long as time and life remains, there is always hope because of the never ending love of God and his wonderful grace shown to us through his Son. Thanks be to God!

How have you experienced the love and forgiveness of God in your own life?

DON'T FORGET TO PRAY AND HAVE A GREAT DAY!

Day 166

 Today's Reading:
Ezra 1:1-11

The book of Ezra picks up right where 2 Chronicles left off—with the proclamation of Cyrus, king of Persia, allowing some of the captive Israelites to return to Jerusalem and rebuild the temple. There are many events that took place during those seventy years of captivity that are recorded in the books of prophecy. We will consider some of those things as we read through those books, but for now, we move ahead in time to the beginning of the end of the period of captivity. At the center of this chapter is Cyrus, the newly enthroned king of Persia. It is remarkable to read the words of respect and honor that Cyrus, a Gentile king, gives to God. However, these words do not necessarily prove that Cyrus was a believer. In fact, the evidence suggests that Cyrus was a polytheist whose normal practice was to return captured peoples to their homeland to restore their gods. He did this in hopes that he would find favor in the eyes of all the gods and would therefore be blessed by them. Still, in the case of the Jewish captives, the text clearly states that "the Lord stirred up the spirit of Cyrus." Ultimately, the return of the Jews to Jerusalem was the Lord's doing. In fact, both Isaiah and Jeremiah had prophesied about Cyrus and his release of the Jews for the purpose of rebuilding the temple. What a marvelous demonstration of the providential working of God! Cyrus did not have to be a believer in order for God to use him. Long before Cyrus was a king in control of God's people, God had chosen him and set in motion a series of events that would lead to the return of his people to Jerusalem. What a blessing it is to belong to and serve such an awesome God!

Could the Lord still use unbelievers to accomplish his will today? How?

DON'T FORGET TO PRAY AND HAVE A GREAT DAY!

DAY 167

 Today's Reading:
Ezra 3:1-13

C an you imagine the emotion that filled the people's hearts as the foundation of the temple was laid? The glorious temple of Solomon that many of the older generation had known had been destroyed by Nebuchadnezzar's army, and for seventy years, God's people had no sacred place to meet for worship, no place to come into God's presence, no place to sacrifice to him or to seek atonement for sin. For seventy years, they had had no way of keeping their covenant with God. What joy and satisfaction they must have felt when they were finally able to return to Jerusalem, offer sacrifices to God, and begin the process of rebuilding the temple. The old men wept while the younger men shouted for joy. What a scene it must have been! It occurs to me that this is the same nation of people who had been sent into captivity because of their rejection of God. They had not valued him or faithfully served him in the years leading up to the destruction of Jerusalem. This fact makes their reaction to the laying of the temple's foundation even more remarkable. Their years of separation from God and from their land had obviously caused a change of heart in them. They had recognized their desperate need for God and now understood the great blessing of being able to worship and serve him freely. It causes me to wonder if we don't sometimes take God for granted in our lives today. We have the opportunity to worship and serve God without hindrance, but does the ease of our Christian lives lead us to not appreciate those opportunities as we should? Oh, that God would help us to be filled with joy and praise with every opportunity to go before him in worship!

What are some things that we can to do to help
us to truly worship God with joy and gladness?

DON'T FORGET TO PRAY AND HAVE A GREAT DAY!

Day 168

 Today's Reading:
Ezra 6:1-22

The return of the Jews to Jerusalem was not without opposition. There were those who did not want to see that nation return to its former glory and desired to keep them from rebuilding their holy city. But as we have already seen in the case of Cyrus, God had providentially placed people in positions of authority who would bring about his will. Darius is another one of those men. Although Darius had not been the ruler who allowed the first convoy of Jews to return to Jerusalem, he was a fair-minded king who was interested in doing what was just and right. When presented with an objection to the rebuilding of the temple, Darius looked into the matter to determine what his predecessor had decreed. Upon finding that the Jews were being truthful, Darius not only upheld the decree of Cyrus but further commanded that monetary assistance was to be given to the Jews in completing the temple reconstruction. Thus, by the hands of God's people and with the help of a godless nation, the work on the temple was complete, and the Jews once again had a special and sacred place in which to offer worship and sacrifices to the Lord. Though we have stated it before, this great truth of God's Word cannot be repeated too often: our God is an awesome God! He is the ruler of the universe and of this world, and his will reigns supreme. Whether by the hand of his chosen people or by the hand of unwitting and unbelieving accomplices, God works in and through mankind to accomplish his will and to bring his plan and purposes to fruition. What a blessing it is to call him "Father" and to know that he cares for us in such a great way!

In what ways have you experienced
the providential care of God in your life?

DON'T FORGET TO PRAY AND HAVE A GREAT DAY!

DAY 169

 Today's Reading:
Ezra 8:15-36

This chapter tells of the return of Ezra to Jerusalem along with many families of the tribes of Israel. They are, no doubt, anxious to leave the land of captivity and return to their homeland and to the holy city of Jerusalem. They are anxious to restore the temple and, with it, proper worship to God. They are anxious to seek a renewed relationship with God and to return the nation to its former glory. But notice what happens before they begin to pursue all of those desires and goals—they take time to fast and pray. Understanding the great importance of what they were about to do, and recognizing the challenges involved in the task, Ezra dares not begin that journey without first seeking the help and blessings of God upon their travel and work. What a great lesson for us! How often do we embark on works or journeys, intending to do great things to the glory of God, without properly beseeching his help and blessings? We plan, prepare, recruit, budget, and advertise all for the purpose of giving our effort the very best chance of success, but then we often fail to do the one thing that has the most power to give us success—sincerely and fervently seek God's guidance, help, and blessings. As Christians and as those who believe in the power of our awesome God, should we not make prayer our first, last, and continually most important strategy for success in any effort for his sake? May we learn from Ezra's example and make prayer a vital part of our Christian lives and work.

Why do you think that we often neglect to pray when faced with challenges?

DON'T FORGET TO PRAY AND HAVE A GREAT DAY!

Day 170

 Today's Reading:
Ezra 9:1-15

Even while God's people were in the process of re-establishing their place in Jerusalem and their relationship with God, they found themselves caught up in one of the primary prohibitions that God had placed on them when their forefathers initially entered the Promised Land. At that time, God had commanded them not to intermarry with the peoples of those lands. This was a vitally important command, given to ensure both the physical and the spiritual purity of the nation of Israel. All these many years later, that prohibition was still in place and important for the same reasons. So as Ezra learns of their disobedience in this regard, he is "appalled" and seemingly overwhelmed with both anger and sorrow. His prayer to God is not so much a pleading for God's mercy and forgiveness as it is a simple admission of guilt and shame before a just and holy God. While it can surely be assumed that Ezra desired the mercy and forgiveness of God, he also understood that their sin was great and that there was no action or attitude that Israel could have to make them worthy or deserving of that forgiveness. They were guilty sinners, nothing more, and they were entirely at the mercy of God's righteousness and grace. I think that there is certainly an important lesson for us to learn here. While we surely recognize God's goodness and grace shown to us through Christ, we must also never forget that we, too, are nothing more than guilty sinners. We stand before a just and holy God, completely unworthy of his love or forgiveness, and yet, we have the beautiful promise of his mercy and salvation because of Christ. What an amazing God!

Why is it important to our spiritual well-being
that we be willing to admit our sinfulness?

DON'T FORGET TO PRAY AND HAVE A GREAT DAY!

DAY 171

**Today's Reading:
Nehemiah 1:1-11**

M any families of the Israelites had already returned to Jerusalem. They had rebuilt homes and begun the work of restoring the temple, but the city, including its walls, was still largely in ruins. Without walls, a city of that world was defenseless and vulnerable to attack, but more importantly, at least in the mind of Nehemiah, it was a city that had no regard or respect from its neighbors. An unwalled city was a source of mockery to its enemies and a source of shame to its residents. When Nehemiah heard this report from Jerusalem, his heart was broken for the circumstances of his people and their holy city. He was overcome with emotion and poured out his heart to God. But Nehemiah was not only a man of prayer; he was a man of action. His desire was not only for God to do something to help his people in the rebuilding of Jerusalem; his desire was for God to help him to have the opportunity to be involved in God's work of rebuilding the city (as we will see in tomorrow's reading). Notice that he not only prays for God's blessings upon the nation, but also that God might be with him and grant him favor before the king. Nehemiah's prayer brings to mind this thought: how often do we see something that needs to be done—some work, service, encouragement, or task—and desire to see it done. Maybe we tell others about the need, complain about it not being done, and certainly we pray about it, that God will allow and help it to be accomplished. But how often do we have the desire that Nehemiah had to personally be involved in that effort? How often do we pray that God will bless us with that opportunity? May God help us to have the spirit of Nehemiah in doing His work.

*Why do you think that people are often slow
to take on the responsibility of doing work?*

DON'T FORGET TO PRAY AND HAVE A GREAT DAY!

Day 172

 Today's Reading:
Nehemiah 2:1-20

It was a task of monumental proportions. As Nehemiah viewed the ruins of the walls first-hand, he must have been overwhelmed by the devastation that spread out before him and by the massive challenge of re-building them. But, if Nehemiah felt unequal to the task, he did not show it. As he stood before the leaders of the people, his message was a simple one: "...let us build the wall of Jerusalem..." In the words that follow that challenge, we learn the source of Nehemiah's confidence—God! God had been kind to him and was with him, and if God would continue to be with them, there was no reason to believe that they could not achieve this goal. Nehemiah did not trust in his own ability but in the mighty power of God. What about you? Have you ever felt overwhelmed by a task or challenge that you faced? Have you ever considered the circumstances that surrounded you and thought to yourself, "I just can't do it"? Well, if you have, then learn from the example of Nehemiah. The truth of the matter is that we all face circumstances on a daily basis that we cannot overcome alone. But we are not alone! Just like Nehemiah, we have the constant presence and help of a loving and all-powerful God who hears our prayers and knows exactly what we need. It is by his strength that we are able to be successful in meeting our challenges. Consider the words of Paul in the New Testament: "I can do all things through him who strengthens me" (Philippians 4:13). So, whatever you may face today, know that it is nothing that you and God cannot handle!

In what ways has God helped you to accomplish overwhelming challenges?

DON'T FORGET TO PRAY AND HAVE A GREAT DAY!

Day 173

Today's Reading:
Nehemiah 3:1-32

This chapter, like much of the book of Nehemiah, offers a tedious listing of names and details concerning the efforts to rebuild the walls of Jerusalem. Why did Nehemiah labor to record and God see fit to preserve such details for modern readers? Beyond the obvious desire of Nehemiah to preserve a record of this historic task and the names of those who were involved in it for posterity, there is an important lesson to be found in this account. Remember that the work of rebuilding this wall was a task of monumental proportions. Estimates vary but suggest that the length of this wall was as much as two and a half miles. It was not going to be a job that was completed easily or by Nehemiah alone. As it takes us for a tour of the wall around Jerusalem, this chapter reveals a spirit of cooperation and mutual determination to see the completion of this important work. While the dream to rebuild the wall was initially Nehemiah's, it became a shared goal of many who joined together in their efforts. In the modern-day church, we are not involved in building a wall. Instead, we are concerned with the winning of souls and the building up of Christ's kingdom. This, too, is a monumental task that will require the mutual desire, prayers, and effort of many if we are to be successful. As Christians, we must firmly believe in the work that we have been called to do and fervently labor in the Lord's service. If we do, we can be successful like Nehemiah in achieving the work that we have set out to do. May God help us to have a heart and hands that are ready to work!

What are some of the lessons that we can
learn from the rebuilding of the walls?

DON'T FORGET TO PRAY AND HAVE A GREAT DAY!

DAY 174

**Today's Reading:
Nehemiah 4:1-23**

The work of rebuilding the wall was not an easy one. The broken stones and burnt rubble that remained from the wall's destruction had to be removed, and a new structure had to be built. It was difficult, back-breaking work that was made even more difficult by the constant interference of Jerusalem's neighbors. Seeing the refurbished city of Jerusalem as a threat to their own power and security, the leaders of these cities made plans to attack and destroy the inhabitants of Jerusalem before they could fortify the city. But God was with his people, and their efforts would not be thwarted. Just imagine the nerve and determination it must have taken for the people to work on the wall with one hand while holding a weapon with the other! But, as Nehemiah says about the people, they "had a mind to work." Because of that desire and determination, and with the help of God Almighty, this group of people accomplished what was considered to be impossible. Again, I see in this account a reflection of our own lives and circumstances. We live in a world that, in many cases, is declaring Christianity to be dead, or at least dying. They tell us that we have outgrown God and the Bible, that people aren't interested in "church" anymore, and that our efforts to reach people with the gospel are a waste of time. But what the naysayers and opponents of Christianity do not understand is the same thing that Sanballat, Tobiah, and the other conspirators against Jerusalem did not understand—that we, as God's people, do not work alone. We have his help and his promises, and as long as we have a mind to work, there is no task that cannot be accomplished to the glory of God.

*Why do you think that God and Christianity
are viewed so negatively by so many in our world?
What can we do to help our world come to know and love God?*

DON'T FORGET TO PRAY AND HAVE A GREAT DAY!

Day 175

 Today's Reading:
Nehemiah 5:1-19

As I read chapter four, I get the impression that, despite some discouragement because of their enemies, those who are working on the reconstruction of the wall are united in cooperation and purpose with a great sense of camaraderie. But as we learn in this chapter, there is an undercurrent of frustration and discontentment among the people because of some oppression and unfair treatment that is taking place at the hands of some of the nobles. When Nehemiah is made aware of these offenses, he is indignant and immediately calls an assembly to deal with the problem. In his rebuke of their unjust actions, Nehemiah poses this rhetorical question: "Ought you not to walk in the fear of our God to prevent the taunts of the nations our enemies?" What a great question and what a powerful statement about the influence of one's life! You see, when considered in the broader context of our daily lives, it becomes clear that our everyday words, attitudes, and conduct have a significant effect on those who are living in the world. By the way that I choose to live my life, interact with others, and treat those around me, I can either cause people to have a positive impression of Christ and his church, or I can cause them to view Christianity in a negative light. The apostle Paul would later write: "Show yourself in all respects to be a model of good works, and in your teaching show integrity, dignity, and sound speech that cannot be condemned, so that an opponent may be put to shame, having nothing evil to say about us" (Titus 2:7-8). May God help us to understand the power of our influence and to live our lives "in the fear of God."

How can our lives be a positive or negative influence on others for Christ?

DON'T FORGET TO PRAY AND HAVE A GREAT DAY!

Day 176

 Today's Reading:
Nehemiah 6:1-19

Have you ever been distracted by something? You have an important task to complete and are working diligently at it when something comes up—maybe it's a phone call, an unexpected visit, or a reminder of some other job that needs to be done. It can be so easy to become distracted and to allow our progress on that important task to be hindered. The goal of Nehemiah's enemies was not only to distract him, but they even wanted to do harm to him. However, Nehemiah refused to be taken away from the important work of rebuilding the wall. In his mind, there was nothing that was more important or pressing than the completion of that job and the restoration of Jerusalem to its former glory. No matter the urgings or threats that were sent to him, Nehemiah remained completely focused on and committed to his work. The results of that determined focus were amazing—in just fifty-two days, a brief period of time by any standard, the wall of Jerusalem was completed, the enemies of God's people were put to shame, and God was glorified! In our lives today, it is important for us to remember that Satan does not have to completely turn us against God in order to win. If he can only distract us from doing the Lord's work, then he can successfully defeat God's purposes in us. Through the use of trials, temptations, our emotions, and even people in our lives, Satan is constantly trying to turn us away from serving the Lord, even if for just a moment. But if, like Nehemiah, we can remain firmly focused on God and his will, then we can also do amazing things with the help of the Lord.

Why do you think that it is often so easy for us to become distracted from the Lord's work? How can we avoid or defeat that temptation?

DON'T FORGET TO PRAY AND HAVE A GREAT DAY!

DAY 177

 Today's Reading:
Nehemiah 8:1-18

Have you ever been moved to tears by the reading of God's word? We often think of the Old Testament in terms of example after example of unfaithfulness, hard-heartedness, and rebellion, but there were moments when God's people demonstrated a remarkable appreciation and reverence for God and his word. In this text as Ezra read the word of God aloud in the people's hearing, they stood with their heads bowed and wept, presumably in recognition of their shortcomings in keeping God's law. Though Ezra instructs them to rejoice instead of mourn at the reading of God's word, their reaction certainly shows that they were deeply moved by this momentous occasion. It causes me to wonder—how are we affected by our times before the throne of God in worship? As we are involved in the reading and consideration of his word, singing of praises to his name, coming before his throne in prayer, and gathering around the table of remembrance, are we filled to overflowing with an appreciation and reverence for the God that we are worshipping? Are we confronted with our own sinfulness and, at the same time, overwhelmed by the amazing love and mercy of God? If we are not careful, it can be very easy to find ourselves in a routine of worshipping God with no thought or feeling. But, as Christians, every opportunity to worship should be a special occasion, understanding the great privilege that we have to approach God. May those times never become anything less than extraordinary!

What are some things that we can do to ensure
that our worship is heartfelt and genuine?

DON'T FORGET TO PRAY AND HAVE A GREAT DAY!

Day 178

 Today's Reading:
Nehemiah 9:1-38

God is good! That is one of the defining themes of these beautiful words voiced to God by the people as they confess their sins. God has blessed them, cared for them, protected them, and provided for them in great and marvelous ways. In contrast to that goodness, they and their ancestors have become stiff-necked and have rebelled against him time and time again. But God's goodness is not dependent upon man's obedience, and his mercy is great and never-ending. In view of the goodness of God, the people are consumed with sorrow and guilt over their own sinfulness and throw themselves on the mercy of God, vowing their commitment and faithfulness to him. As I think about this powerful scene, I am made aware of two important truths in my own life and, I believe, in the lives of many Christians. First, there is far too little recognition and sorrow over sin. So often, we are very nonchalant toward our sinfulness, thinking "sure I make some mistakes but, over all, I'm a pretty good person." Unfortunately, that attitude does little to motivate godly sorrow and repentance. We must recognize that as we come before God, we are nothing more than unworthy sinners in search of his mercy and grace. That brings us to the second truth: there is far too little recognition of the goodness and mercy of God. Oh, we know that God is good. We give him thanks and sing songs of praise in our worship, but are we truly overwhelmed when we consider the undeserved grace and mercy that he continually showers upon us? Consider how it would transform our worship and our lives if we were constantly and humbly aware of our own unworthiness in the presence of the overwhelming goodness of God!

How would you explain God's overwhelming
goodness to someone who didn't know him?

DON'T FORGET TO PRAY AND HAVE A GREAT DAY!

Day 179

 **Today's Reading:**
Nehemiah 13:1-31

It is amazing to see the change that can take place when people honestly and sincerely seek the word of God. This chapter chronicles many of the reforms that Nehemiah brought to Jerusalem in order to bring them into conformity with the law of God, but notice how the chapter begins: "On that day they read from the Book of Moses in the hearing of the people." Having been in foreign bondage, the people had lost touch with the law and found themselves ignorant of God's commands with regard to the house of God. Under Nehemiah's guidance, they corrected many of their errors and found their way back to God. I am convinced that much of the religious error and confusion in our world today is due to a very similar ignorance of God's word. We have neglected it to the point that we do not know what God expects or desires with regard to our worship, our teaching, and our lives. What if we could step away from all of the thoughts, ideas, and traditions of men and honestly and sincerely seek the word of God? What if we were willing to submit to God's will, even if it differed from what we had always believed or practiced? What would be the result of such attitudes and actions? First and foremost, obedience would be the result. We would find ourselves in conformity with God's word and faithful to his will. Secondly, unity would be the result. If we were all obedient to the same word, then we would all believe and practice the same things, bringing us into unity with one another. What a wonderful situation that would be! May God help us to truly seek him and his word.

Why do you think that there is so little knowledge of or desire for the word of God today?

DON'T FORGET TO PRAY AND HAVE A GREAT DAY!

Day 180

 Today's Reading:
Esther 2:1-23

Esther should not have been there. She was a Jew—a member of a captive nation living in a foreign land. She had no right to be among those who were vying for the queen's throne, much less to be the one chosen to occupy that position. Yet there she was, in a position of favor and prominence. But why? How did this happen? As you read through this chapter, there are several factors that are clearly seen: she did not reveal her Jewish nationality, although I'm sure that could have been discovered without too much effort. There was also the fact that Esther was, apparently, a woman of great physical beauty. She also benefitted from the wise counsel of Mordecai on how she should conduct herself before the king. While these factors all played a role in Esther's becoming the queen, there was one other, more important and powerful force at work to influence this situation—God! You see, even though the name of God is never used in the book of Esther, it is a beautiful story of the magnificent providence of God, played out in the life of one unassuming woman who was given the opportunity to save her nation. As I think about these things, I am struck by the fact that many of us are often guilty of underestimating our own abilities and potential to make a difference in the lives of those around us. However, we must never forget that God is able to use us to accomplish his will. Through his power and providence, we may be placed in a situation where we can make a difference, but it is up to us to take advantage of those opportunities and fulfill God's purpose. May he help us to have the strength, courage, and faith to do just that.

What can you do today to allow God to use you to accomplish his will?

DON'T FORGET TO PRAY AND HAVE A GREAT DAY!

DAY 181

Today's Reading:
Esther 3:1-15

N ot only does this chapter not mention God, it also does not mention the book's namesake, Esther. Nonetheless, it is an important text that teaches us at least two very important lessons. First, we are confronted with the fact that the predicament of the Jews, that is, their impending doom, was brought on by the faithfulness of Mordecai. His refusal to bow down to Haman was the catalyst for the series of events that brought about the decree allowing the annihilation of the Jews. With these events, we are reminded that faithfulness to God in the midst of an unbelieving world often brings hardship and persecution. We must, therefore, have courage and faith as we live our lives before God. The second lesson that we learn from this text has to do with the perfect knowledge and providential purposes of God. You see, Esther was placed in a position to save the Jews before the Jews even needed saving. When Esther became queen, though the Jews were captives and foreigners in the land, there was no significant animosity toward them on the part of the king or any of his nobles. They were allowed to exist in relative peace, but God knew that those circumstances were going to change and that they were going to have to be saved. So even before that need arose, God was already working to provide salvation for them through Esther. In our lives, there are often things that happen that we did not anticipate and were not expecting, but we can trust that long before those circumstances arose, God knew what we would go through and was preparing a way for us to endure. What a wonderful God he is!

As we look at the sometimes difficult circumstances of our lives,
how can we know that God is there to care for and help us?

DON'T FORGET TO PRAY AND HAVE A GREAT DAY!

Day 182

 Today's Reading:
Esther 4:1-17

C ontained within this chapter is what might be one of the most profound and powerful statements made by any character in the Bible except for Jesus Christ. In response to Esther's fearful reluctance to act on behalf of her people, Mordecai says to her: "And who knows whether you have not come to the kingdom for such a time as this?" While he was not pretending to know the mind or purposes of God, Mordecai was acknowledging the ability of God to work in the affairs of men and to use those whom he chooses, to accomplish his purposes. Facing dire circumstances, this man of faith was confident in God's desire and power to save His people, and he was willing to see the possibility of Esther playing an important role in God's plan. What about us? Do we trust God to care for us and work in our best interest, providing the help that we need in any situation? Are we willing to acknowledge the providence of God and see his hand at work in the circumstances of our lives? Better yet, are we willing to allow God to use us to accomplish his will and purposes? With the encouragement of Mordecai, Esther made the decision to make the bold move of going before the king on behalf of her people. Doing so required a great deal of faith that God was with her and that she was doing his will. And so it is with us. When you find yourself in a situation in which you have the opportunity to make a difference for good, remember the encouragement of Mordecai: who knows whether you have not come to this place and set of circumstances for such a time as this?

Have you ever had the opportunity to make a difference is some situation?
How did you react to that opportunity?

DON'T FORGET TO PRAY AND HAVE A GREAT DAY!

DAY 183

 **Today's Reading:
Esther 5:1-14**

I n this chapter, we find two plots running simultaneously. On one hand we have the unselfish plan of Esther to gain the favor of the king for the saving of her people. At great personal risk, Esther dares to go before the king without being summoned in order to seek his mercy and intercession on behalf of the Jews. To do so, she will be forced to reveal her nationality, jeopardizing not only her position but also her very life. On the other hand, we see the plot of Haman, motivated by pride and anger. He had already secured, from the king, permission to destroy the Jews, but it was not enough. So overcome with rage was Haman at the refusal of Mordecai to bow down before him that he commanded, with the urging of his wife and friends, to have preparations made immediately for the execution of Mordecai. This great contrast of motives and plots can serve as a metaphor for the conflict that often exists in our own hearts and lives. The apostle Paul would later write about this great conflict that was constantly raging in his own life between the flesh and spirit (if you have time, read Romans 7:7-25). The fleshly side, driven by pride and lustful desire, is constantly pulling us toward sin, while the spiritual side, motivated by a humble desire to do the will of God, pulls us toward righteousness. As this battle is waged for our hearts, lives, and souls, we must each choose to go the way of Haman, selfishly bowing to our own desires and prideful lusts; or we can choose the way of Esther, selflessly giving ourselves to the will and the work of God. Which way will you choose?

What are some things that we can do to help us in making the right choice?

DON'T FORGET TO PRAY AND HAVE A GREAT DAY!

DAY 184

 Today's Reading:
Esther 6:1-14

In many ways, the book of Esther centers around the story of Mordecai as much as it does Esther. Though he is in the background of the story, Mordecai provides many of the great teaching points of this study. His humble spirit, his wise counsel, his unwavering faith, and his firm commitment to God—these attributes of Mordecai's character combine to create a model of faithfulness that is worthy of emulation. As this chapter opens, the stage is set for Mordecai's execution, but Haman's plan was not to be. While there is no indication in the text of the direct, miraculous intervention of God, there can be no doubt that God's providential care was at work in the events that took place on the night recorded. Because of an act of kindness on the part of Mordecai that was recorded, and then seemingly, forgotten, the tables are turned, and in a great stroke of irony, Mordecai receives the honor that Haman desired for himself while Haman is hanged on the gallows intended for Mordecai. What insight and encouragement can we gain from this text? Certainly, we can know that God is with his people. Do not make the mistake of attributing the good things that came to Mordecai to coincidence or luck. Through the eyes of faith, we can clearly see the hand of God at work in these events. We are also reminded of the blessings that often come to those who do good. Mordecai's act of revealing the plot against Ahasuerus brought no immediate reward, but it motivated great future blessings. Likewise, we may never know how God can use our good and faithful works today to bless us in the future. Thank God for his great love and for the wonderful example of Mordecai.

What encouragement do you find in the example of Mordecai?

DON'T FORGET TO PRAY AND HAVE A GREAT DAY!

Day 185

 Today's Reading:
Esther 7:1-10

While this chapter is largely about Haman and the penalty that he pays for his pride and selfish acts, do not overlook the great act of courage that is performed by Esther. As she goes before the king, she cannot ask for the lives of her people without revealing her true heritage. Remember that from the beginning, she has withheld this information from the king. Certainly, he could have been very angered with her over this deception and removed her from her position or even had her killed. His heart could have been hardened against the Jews, strengthening his resolve to carry out the decree issued by Haman. With so much on the line, Esther displays an enormous amount of courage in her plea to the king. But, consider this question: what was the source of her courage? You see, we often think of courage as a personal quality stemming from our own confidence, strength, or boldness. While courage is certainly a commendable quality, we must not forget that true courage must be rooted in something else. In Esther's case, her courage was a byproduct of her faith. She was not courageous based on her own ability, confidence, or strength. Rather, she found her courage in God and in her confidence that God was with her and working on her behalf. The risks that Esther faced paled in comparison to the power of God to work in her favor and to deliver her and her people from their enemies. I am reminded by these things that we may often be called to stand up for what is right, and when those times come and we need the courage to act, where will that courage be found? May our faith in God give us strength and courage!

What can we do to increase our faith and, thus, to increase our courage?

DON'T FORGET TO PRAY AND HAVE A GREAT DAY!

Day 186

 Today's Reading:
Esther 8:1-17

T o truly appreciate this text, it is helpful to be reminded of the seriousness of the circumstances in which the Jewish captives find themselves. In all of their history, this scenario must be ranked among their most perilous of times. Although Haman has been executed, his decree is still in force, and through its carrying out, the Jews face complete annihilation. Not only do God's people face extinction, but his plan for redemption hangs in the balance as well. In such a precarious situation, we might expect God to raise up a great warrior or mighty king to save the day and rescue his people. Therefore, it may seem ironic, at such a pivotal moment in Jewish history, that he would choose a quiet and humble young lady with a gentle spirit to be the savior of his people. But, as the prophet Isaiah recorded, the Lord's thoughts are not our thoughts and his ways are not our ways (see Isaiah 55:8-9). Esther is a great example of God's perfect wisdom in providing for his people and accomplishing his will. I am very thankful for Esther because of the great lesson that she reminds us of. How often do we look at ourselves in the mirror and think, "What can I do?" We do not see ourselves as having the talent, personality, influence, or power to truly make a difference in the world. May I remind you that Esther didn't see those things in herself either? But God knows us better than we know ourselves, and if we are willing to give our lives to him, he can use us to accomplish his will and do great things to his glory. May we always be willing to be humble servants in God's service.

In what ways can you use your talents and abilities to serve God?

DON'T FORGET TO PRAY AND HAVE A GREAT DAY!

DAY 187

 Today's Reading:
Job 1:1-22

H ave you considered my servant Job?" The story of Job begins with an amazing statement concerning the faith and integrity of Job from none other than God himself. In his query to Satan, God essentially challenges his adversary to find any fault in his servant, Job. In the events that follow that debate over Job's faithfulness, God demonstrates an incredible amount of confidence in Job's devotion and commitment to him. We will read many things about Job over the next few days and see a myriad of emotions and struggles in this suffering man's heart, but it is important to remember that he never gave up on God! Though he mourned, suffered, and questioned, Job's hope was always in God to deliver him. Whenever I read this first chapter of Job, one of the questions that comes to mind is, "What would God say about me?" Job was not a sinless man, but God held him in high regard because of his unwavering devotion and impeccable character. How do I measure up? Certainly, I, like Job, have my share of shortcomings and failures, but can God possibly look on me with the type of regard and confidence with which he viewed Job? By his grace, I hope so, but when I read the story of this great patriarch of faith, there is one lesson that stands out very clearly: regardless of the trials and sufferings that Job encountered, and though his presence was not always obvious, God was with Job every step of the way. He saw every tragic event and heard every agonizing word, and in the end, God appeared to give comfort and provide relief. What a wonderful reminder that is for us as we face the trials and sufferings of life!

What evidence could be given of your
faithfulness and commitment to God?

DON'T FORGET TO PRAY AND HAVE A GREAT DAY!

DAY 188

 Today's Reading:
Job 2:1-13

Much can be learned about the character and faith of a person's life by witnessing how he reacts to adversity. Job has lost almost everything from a physical perspective—his possessions and wealth, his children, his health and vitality, and even the support of his wife. But, he has not lost his hope or his overwhelming respect for God. When faced with the incredulous verbal attack of his wife, Job responds with all of the strength and contentment of a man who truly understands that his life does not consist only of worldly things. "Shall we receive good from God, and shall we not receive evil?" What a beautiful statement of trust and confidence in God! Job understood a great truth that very few in our world seem to grasp. Many are typically very quick to ask, and seemingly expect, God to bless them with good things. They want good health, monetary blessings, care and provision for their families, protection from harm, and many other things that they trust God to provide. However, when trials come, many of those same people are quick to question, blame, and become angry with God for the difficulties that have come their way. In other words, they desire the good things but are unwilling to accept the bad. Compare this mentality with the words of Job. Though he had been greatly blessed by God in his physical life, he was also mindful that life had its struggles, and he refused to turn on God during those difficult times after accepting so many good things from him. What a wonderful reminder to us that, though life is filled with ups and downs, good things and bad, God is always God, he is always good, and he always deserves our devotion, thanks, and praise.

How can you help to encourage someone who is
struggling with life to continue to trust God?

DON'T FORGET TO PRAY AND HAVE A GREAT DAY!

Day 189

 Today's Reading:
Job 3:1-26

With this chapter begins the arduous task of reading through the many poetic speeches of this book. There is nothing pleasant or enjoyable about chapter 3. It is difficult, painful, and at times, shocking to read the anguished cries of a man so despondent. Nevertheless, this is an important chapter in understanding the mindset of Job as he struggles under the weight of unbearable suffering. It also provides some valuable lessons for those who can relate to Job's feelings. The island of suffering and despair is a lonely place. Even while surrounded by friends who, at the time, were empathizing and compassionate, Job was alone in the agonizing grief that overwhelmed him. Without the benefit of the "backstage view" that we are provided in the first two chapters, Job struggles to attach some kind of meaning and understanding to the tragic events that have come upon him, but he finds none. The only relief that Job can fathom is in the longing that his life had never been or, in the very least, that it were no more. If you have ever spent time on the dark island of suffering and despair, then you can take solace in knowing that it is not as lonely a place as it feels. There are many others, Job included, who have inhabited that place at some point in their lives and they know what it is like. We can also learn from Job that to question, grieve, and struggle with hopelessness is not an indictment of our faith in God. So often, on top of all of the other things that we struggle with, we also feel guilt over the thoughts and feelings that we have, but to grieve and to question is simply to be human. Finally, Job teaches us about perseverance. You see, despite his anguish and his despair, Job did not curse God, and he did not give up. May we find comfort and companionship in Job during our times of suffering.

Have you ever felt all alone in your suffering?
What were some things that helped you to persevere in those times?

DON'T FORGET TO PRAY AND HAVE A GREAT DAY!

DAY 190

 Today's Reading:
Job 4:1-21

Eliphaz is the first of Job's friends to speak, which probably indicates that he was the oldest and most respected of the three men. His words reflect a common belief of the day and one that has persisted throughout the ages. "Remember: who that was innocent ever perished? Or where were the upright ever cut off?" Eliphaz believed, as we often do, that good things happen to good people while bad things happen to bad people. If you have ever had the thought that you (or someone you love) are a good person trying to live a good life, and so it is not fair that some tragedy has overtaken you then you have espoused a version of this philosophy. The problem is that under the slightest scrutiny this belief falls apart. After all, we can all think of examples of people who live godless and immoral lives and yet prosper while others, who are faithful servants of God, suffer. The fact of the matter is that a good and faithful life will not shelter us from all physical hardships, and a sinful life does not guarantee a physical life of suffering. Jesus would later remind us that God "makes his sun rise on the evil and on the good, and sends rain on the just and on the unjust" (Matthew 5:45). Both good and bad, blessing and suffering, are part of the human experience, and everyone who lives very long on this earth will experience both. Additionally, there are many times when we do not and cannot understand the reason behind the trials that we encounter. But that is precisely the purpose of the great book of Job—to remind us that, though we cannot always know or understand the reasons why, God always does and his wisdom, purpose, and will are always perfect. So, trust him and persevere!

What can we do to remain strong and faithful
when bad things happen in our lives?

DON'T FORGET TO PRAY AND HAVE A GREAT DAY!

Day 191

 Today's Reading:
Job 9:1-35

As we skip ahead a little in the story of Job, his friends have continued to accuse him of wrongdoing and demand that he repent. Bildad has rightly stated that God's integrity is unquestionable, and His judgment is perfectly righteous. However, he has incorrectly assumed that Job's suffering is the result of that righteous judgment upon some unconfessed sin in Job's life. Job's response represents what is probably his lowest point, both spiritually and emotionally. While he readily acknowledges God's righteousness, he continues to hold fast to his own innocence. Using legal imagery, Job pictures God as occupying every role in the divine courtroom. He is the prosecuting attorney, the judge, and the jury. Standing before this majestic court as the defendant, Job has no grounds on which to argue his case. His only hope is to throw himself on the mercy of the court and trust in God to affirm his uprightness. Job's desperate desire is for one to stand between him and God to act as a mediator. The legal quandary that Job envisions in this text is a perfect illustration of our own spiritual circumstances. As sinners, we all stand guilty before God, the righteous judge. We have no right to approach him and no grounds on which to plead innocence. All that we can hope for is his mercy and for a mediator to come to our aid. Thankfully, we have that mediator in Jesus Christ. He stands with and for us as the One who has paid for our sins and can declare us justified before God. Without him, we have no hope, but with him we have the assurance of victory!

Knowing that we stand before God as guilty
sinners, how can we have confidence in salvation?

DON'T FORGET TO PRAY AND HAVE A GREAT DAY!

DAY 192

 Today's Reading:
Job 13:1-28

As the accusations of Job's friends grow more and more direct, so does Job's determination to be heard by God. Turning the tables on his advisors, he accuses them of being unjust before God and of falsely representing God. In fact, he says they have put themselves in the place of God and made themselves judges. Surely, Job gives them pause when he asks, "Will it be well with you when he searches you out?" What then follows is a defense of Job's desire to be heard before God. He seeks an audience with the Almighty, convinced that that audience, in and of itself, will be his vindication since nothing and no one who is unjust can stand before the Almighty. If God would only hear him and respond, if he would only answer Job's questions and list his sins and iniquities, then Job might feel some comfort. Job is not claiming to be sinless, but rather seeking to understand what, if anything in his own life, has caused this calamity to come upon him. As the story of Job continues to progress, we see a growing confidence in God displayed in Job's words. He knows God to be a just and righteous judge. He knows that his suffering is not by the hand of God's anger or retribution. It is interesting to note that Job is more concerned with being vindicated and found just than he is with having his suffering relieved. If you look closely, you can see the growth that is occurring in Job's faith and relationship with God through the course of these trials. He is learning to trust God more and more while the physical things of life have faded into the background. Thus is the lesson of this great story—though God may not be directly responsible for the suffering that we encounter in life, he can certainly use that suffering to strengthen us and to draw us closer to him.

Thinking back over the times of suffering in your life, can you see any growth that occurred in your faith during or as a result of those events?

DON'T FORGET TO PRAY AND HAVE A GREAT DAY!

Day 193

 Today's Reading:
Job 19:1-29

Job's losses were not limited to possessions, children, and health. He had also been robbed of every meaningful relationship that he enjoyed in this life along with the respect and honor with which he was once viewed. He had become a man detested, mocked, and scorned among those whom he once considered friends and loved ones. Job had seemingly conceded that his life was over; it was only a matter of time until he would no longer be among the living. But in the midst of this recognition of hopelessness, there was one beam of hope that burned brightly. "For I know that my Redeemer lives…" Regardless of what might become of Job's life, he was supremely confident that God, his Redeemer, Vindicator, and Defender was alive and well, and that one day, he would meet him face to face. Furthermore, Job was confident that, on that day, the truth would be known, and he would be found to be just. What a beautiful picture of the hope that we have as Christians! Life in this world is often trying. There are times when we find ourselves in the midst of trials, struggling to understand and feeling dreadfully alone. But we can know that, come what may in this life, our Redeemer lives and that, when all is said and done, we will see him face to face as we are gathered to him to be found just through Christ and to rest in his glorious presence for all eternity. How wonderful it is to be able to have that hope and confidence!

How does the hope of Heaven affect your outlook on life in this world?

DON'T FORGET TO PRAY AND HAVE A GREAT DAY!

Day 194

 Today's Reading:
Job 21:1-34

Earlier in our study of the book of Job, we noted the common belief of the day that a good life would be blessed while a wicked life would meet with God's wrath. This belief was the basis of the arguments that were made against Job by his accusers. In this text, Job points out the obvious fact that there are many clear contradictions to that theory all around us. While there are certainly spiritual, and sometimes physical, consequences to sin, the fact of the matter is that there are and always have been wicked men in the world who God allows to live and even prosper. Likewise, there are many God-fearing, faithful Christians who suffer hardship, loss, trials, and difficulties in life. God has made many great and precious promises to those who choose to give their lives to him. Those promises affect this life as well as the life to come. But in many ways as it pertains to this world, God is no respecter of persons. As we have already seen, God sends sunshine and rain on both the evil and the good (see Matthew 5:45). There are certain blessings of God that are given freely to all men so that they might see his goodness and desire to seek after him. Likewise, life necessarily involves hardships that all are subject to as part of the human experience. Those trials are not a sign of God's displeasure or forsaking of us, but rather an indication of God's love and desire to see us grow closer to him. The challenge that we each face is to accept both the good and the bad with grace and faith, giving thanks to God and putting our faith in him in every situation. May he help us to do just that.

What are some things that we can thank God for in times of suffering?

DON'T FORGET TO PRAY AND HAVE A GREAT DAY!

Day 195

 Today's Reading:
Job 26:1-14

Have you ever stopped to really consider the greatness of God? In this short chapter, Job extols the greatness and majesty of God while recognizing the frailty of mankind. There are many incredible examples given in this text of God's amazing power as Job considers how great God truly is, but maybe the greatest statement of all comes in the final verse: "Behold, these are but the outskirts of his ways, and how small a whisper do we hear of him! But the thunder of his power who can understand?" Do you get what Job is saying? All that we know of God—all that we can see in his creation and all that he has revealed to us in his word—is only a tiny glimpse into the greatness of God. Our understanding of God's greatness barely touches the hem of the garment of whom and what he truly is! Our frail minds are simply not capable of comprehending the immenseness of God's wisdom, power, and majesty. What an incredible thought that is! And what is even more incredible is that he—the God who is wise, powerful, majestic, holy, and great beyond our ability to know or comprehend—he loves us! The immensely, unfathomably great God of the universe wants to have a relationship with us. He wants to care for us, provide for us, walk with us, live in us, and save us. What an amazing God he is!

Why do you think that God is so interested
in having a relationship with us?

DON'T FORGET TO PRAY AND HAVE A GREAT DAY!

Day 196

 Today's Reading:
Job 33:1-33

T he speeches of Elihu serve as a prologue to the words of God and
bring some much needed clarity and reason to the conversation.
As a younger man, Elihu has respectfully waited for the older and more
experienced men to have their say, but when he sees that nothing is being
accomplished, he ceases to hold back. The nature of Elihu's speeches
is different than the others. While Job and his accusers focused their
thoughts primarily on Job's circumstances and the goodness or badness of
his life, Elihu's speeches are primarily centered on God. In a kind but firm
way, he declares the greatness and sovereignty of God while condemning
the focus of Job on his own righteousness. Elihu's premise in this chapter
is simply that God is above all, that his wisdom is unquestionable, and that
his purposes are always perfect and in man's best interest. As humans, ours
is not to question or even understand all that God allows to take place in
our lives, but simply to submit to his will, trusting in his love and relying
on his care. Whether a person lived in the patriarchal days of Job or in our
present day world, the understanding of God that Elihu expresses is true.
Unfortunately, it is also a truth that we often forget as we question or blame
God in the face of adversity. But, oh what comfort and hope there is in
knowing that we serve a God who is the all-powerful Creator and Sustainer
of the universe, who knows every detail of our lives and hearts, and whose
perfect will and purposes always reign supreme.

How can we learn to trust and lean on God even
when we don't understand his purposes in our struggles?

DON'T FORGET TO PRAY AND HAVE A GREAT DAY!

Day 197

 Today's Reading:
Job 36:1-33

Throughout Elihu's speeches, he continues to extol the awesome power of God but look closely at this chapter, and you might notice another element of God's character that is equally as incredible and amazing as his infinite power. It is the heart of God that is firmly focused on mankind and his desire for their good. You see, even as God's power commands all of nature, his heart is always with man, to instruct, discipline, care for, bless, and protect him. The book of Job teaches us many things about the wisdom, strength, and sovereignty of God. It impresses us with the fact that nothing is beyond God's ability or control and that every element of both the physical and spiritual worlds bows before him and submits to his will. But against that amazing backdrop is the realization that the all-powerful and all-knowing Creator and Master of the universe looks down upon mankind with sincere love and concern. He does not neglect his children but blesses them with good, nor does he turn a blind eye to the evil of sinful man but works to instruct them and turn them from their ungodly ways. God does all of this because of his desire to have a relationship with man. It is mind-boggling to consider that God would care for the well-being of lowly man, but I am so thankful that he does, and I am thankful for the word that he has provided to tell us of that love.

What are some specific ways in which God has cared for you?

DON'T FORGET TO PRAY AND HAVE A GREAT DAY!

Day 198

 Today's Reading:
Job 38:1-41

In all of his pleading for God to acknowledge his complaints, Job probably never expected that God would actually respond, so you can imagine the shock and amazement (not to mention fear) that must have accompanied the thundering voice of God. Job was no novice. He was a respected man of vast experience and much sought after wisdom. Yet, as God's onslaught of questions begins, Job is immediately and completely overwhelmed by the lack of knowledge and ability that he is suddenly confronted with. Do not make the mistake of reading through this chapter so quickly that you miss the glorious majesty of God that is on full display in this beautiful description of his creative wisdom and power. All of the wonders of nature—the intricate design of the universe, the complex systems that support life in this world, the wondrous inner-workings of a magnificent planet—are beyond man's ability to create or replicate and, in many cases, even to fully understand. Yet, it is amazing how often mankind wants to revel in his own knowledge and ability. In our arrogance, we boast of our power to invent, manufacture, and even "create". But, God's point to Job, and to us, is that only God is God and only he has the power and wisdom to create. Certainly, he has created us with the great ability to think, reason, and discover, but our striving is only to understand and to make use of the things that God has already created. Anything that we discover or invent, and even those things that man has not even imagined yet, were all perfectly understood by God from the very beginning. What an awesome God he is!

What are some impressions that come to your mind
as you read the questions from God in this chapter?

DON'T FORGET TO PRAY AND HAVE A GREAT DAY!

DAY 199

 Today's Reading:
Job 40:1-24

Like the punishing blows of a prize fighter, God has come upon Job with an endless barrage of questions and challenges that have eaten away at the ego and confidence of Job until he is completely dumbfounded. But God is not finished with Job yet. The great depth of knowledge and ability that God reminds Job is reserved for Him alone gives way in this chapter to a more direct line of questioning that has one primary point—can you save yourself? In his desperation to defend his integrity before his accusers, Job had argued vehemently that if given the opportunity to plead his case his righteousness would prove him to be just. God's reminder to Job, and to all of us, is that none of us are able to stand before God as those who have been justified by our own strength or goodness. In our own lives, it is amazingly easy, even in our recognition of Christ's atoning sacrifice, for us to begin to look to our own goodness and obedience as a means of justification. We, like Job, may look at the world around us or even at our own circumstances and dare to question God's judgment and purposes. But, lest we fall into that trap, let us consider the words of the Lord as an exhortation to our own lives: "Will you even put me in the wrong? Will you condemn me that you may be in the right?" There are certainly many times when we are at a loss to understand why God allows certain things to happen as they do in this world. There may even be times when we question the events of our own lives and wonder, "why?" God allows us to ponder those things, as he did with his servant, Job, but we must never question God's wisdom, power, or purposes. Rather, we must learn to trust his perfect will in all things.

Why do you think that we are so prone to depend on our own goodness for justification? How can we defeat that temptation?

DON'T FORGET TO PRAY AND HAVE A GREAT DAY!

Day 200

 Today's Reading:
Job 42:1-17

G od has spoken in a way that is both unexpected and remarkable. He has not explained the cause and purposes of Job's suffering; he has not rebuked Job's questions and complaints (at least not directly); and he has not revealed some deep and hidden truth about the universe and human life. He gives Job exactly what he has asked for—his day in court. God places Job on the witness stand and questions him with queries that seem to have nothing to do with Job's suffering; although, in reality, his questions have everything to do with, well, everything. God's point and purpose is to help Job understand that not everything that happens in this world can be understood. Sometimes, we can't know why things happen as they do, but God always knows! His knowledge is perfect, and his purposes are resolute. Ours is not always to understand but simply to trust God's wisdom and will for our lives. Job gets the point, and his response is powerful! "I know that you can do all things, and that no purpose of yours can be thwarted...I had heard of you by the hearing of the ear but now my eye sees you; therefore, I despise myself and repent in dust and ashes." Remember, this is the same man that God testified of in the beginning of the book with the words: "there is none like him on the earth, a blameless and upright man, who fears God and turns away from evil." This blameless man of faith now stands before God with the humbling realization that prior to God's questioning, he had only known about God but had not been blessed with the opportunity to truly know God. Through the process of his suffering, and by God's response, Job had grown into a greater knowledge and faith in his Lord. What a wonderful lesson for us!

How can our suffering help us to come to a
greater understanding and faith in God?

DON'T FORGET TO PRAY AND HAVE A GREAT DAY!

Day 201

 **Today's Reading:
Psalm 1:1-6**

"B lessed is the man…" Who would not want their lives to be described by those words? We all long to live blessed lives full of goodness and joy. For as long as time has existed, mankind has searched for the secret to just that kind of life. As the Psalms begin, they are very appropriately introduced with a psalm that reveals that very information—the secret to an abundant life. The key to a blessed life is the path that we choose to travel through this world. (And remember that Jesus told us that there are only two paths to choose from. See Matthew 7:13-14.) The one who chooses to avoid the path of wickedness and sin and chooses rather to follow the path laid out in the word of God will live an abundant life full of God's blessings. That is not to say that his life will never encounter hardship or loss, but his relationship with God will provide strength, courage, and comfort in any circumstances, not to mention the blessed hope of an eternal home with God. On the other hand, the one who chooses that path of sinfulness that is so popular in the world will miss out on all of the marvelous spiritual blessings of God and the physical blessings that come along with a relationship with God in this world. Throughout the Psalms, there will be much said about God and the blessings of a relationship with him, and as we begin, the Psalmist asks us to consider the crucial question: which path are we on?

*What are some of the blessings that come
from following a path of godliness?*

DON'T FORGET TO PRAY AND HAVE A GREAT DAY!

Day 202

 Today's Reading:
Psalm 2:1-12

The scenario described in the beginning of this psalm is one that is very familiar to us, and one that has existed for all of time. "Why do the nations rage?" asks the psalmist. Our news feeds are filled every day with this raging of the nations as nations, factions, and leaders vie for dominance and control in the global theatre. Governments and groups are constantly trying to gain some financial, geographic, political, or military advantage over their adversaries in the world. It is a never-ending struggle. On a smaller, yet much more personal level, we as individuals are often involved in the same striving for control in our own lives and against our own fellow man. We struggle to succeed, to achieve greatness, to outperform our contemporaries, and thus to establish our own dominance and control over our lives. That struggle to succeed and achieve is one of the greatest sources of stress that we encounter in our lives today. But the psalmist points out that "He who sits in the heavens laughs" at this constant struggle for superiority and control. He laughs, not because he is amused or entertained by the raging of the nations, but because the very idea that we can truly control our lives and circumstances by our own strength and ability is preposterous. There is only One who is in control, and he is God! The best that we can do is to be diligent to be faithful to him and to fulfill our responsibilities in this world and then, to trust him to care for us by his gracious hand. To God be the glory!

Why do you think that it is so often difficult for us to put our lives into the hands of God and to trust him to provide and care for us?

DON'T FORGET TO PRAY AND HAVE A GREAT DAY!

Day 203

 Today's Reading:
Psalm 3:1-8

This beautiful psalm is attributed to King David as he was fleeing from his son, Absalom. Can you imagine how disheartened David must have been to have become the target of his own son? Even while he feared for his life, David's heart must have been filled with sorrow at the realization that Absalom looked on him with such hatred and malice. Given these circumstances, it is significant that David says of God that he is "the lifter of my head." You see, God was more to David than just a shield of protection and One to fight for him and ensure his victory. God was an encourager to David. He comforted him in his sorrow and despair. When David's head was hung in mourning for the lost relationship with his son, God was there to lift his head and to give him strength. What about us? We often struggle to associate psalms such as this with our own lives because when we read them, we envision David on a battlefield, engaged in physical warfare. The battles that we fight throughout life are not fought with swords and spears. Rather, they are emotional and spiritual battles that often cause us to hang our heads in shame, sorrow, or despair. In this way, we are well acquainted with David's struggles. God is always there to be our strength and shield. He is our protector, provider, and salvation. When we are disheartened and discouraged, God is there to be the lifter of our heads—to comfort us, to encourage us, to strengthen us, and to help us endure the battles of life. Thank God for his mighty power and his loving care!

Can you think of a time in your life when God was the lifter of your head? How were you strengthened by his presence and help?

DON'T FORGET TO PRAY AND HAVE A GREAT DAY!

Day 204

Today's Reading:
Psalm 4:1-8

This psalm has the common theme of beseeching of God's attentive ear and protective care, along with an underlying element of a deep trust in and love for God. Among the many statements of confidence and adoration given to God in these verses, there is one, in particular, that jumps out at me. Toward the end of the psalm, David says to the Lord, "You have put more joy in my heart than they have when their grain and wine abound." In our day and time, and I suppose in most any period of history, there is nothing that seems to bring joy to the hearts of man like an abundance of things. You know that feeling you have when you find out that you are getting the big promotion or the generous bonus? That feeling of joy and gladness because of things is common and undeniable. But David says that there is more joy in his relationship with God than can be found in the hearts of men because of worldly abundance. It occurs to me that even we as Christians miss out so often on that joy. We know and love God, we are devoted to him, we worship him regularly and try to live for him each day, but does he, and our relationship with him, fill our hearts with that kind of joy? Are we able to rejoice, even when faced with challenges and hardship, because of the blessing of God's love and grace? May we continue to grow in our love for God, and may we find true joy in him!

How can we as Christians learn to find greater joy in our relationship with God than in the things of the world?

DON'T FORGET TO PRAY AND HAVE A GREAT DAY!

Day 205

 Today's Reading:
Psalm 8:1-9

This wonderful psalm of praise is one that exalts and magnifies the name of God, proclaiming his majesty and glory. As we think about all the beauty of creation or gaze into a star-filled night sky, it is not difficult for us to understand the awe and praise of David, to whom this psalm is attributed. But as soon as David begins to consider the greatness of God and of his creation, he is overwhelmed with a deep sense of awe and humility at the realization that among all of the glorious creations of God in this world, man is at the center of His heart and mind. How minuscule we are in comparison to the vastness of the universe, and yet God is mindful of each of us. He has placed us in a position of glory and honor above all of creation and given us authority over everything in the physical realm. David is baffled by this knowledge and seemingly feels unworthy to be in such a position. Truly, it is a thought that boggles the mind. God, the all-powerful, all-knowing, perfect in every way, Creator and Master of the universe has looked upon us with favor. He created us in his own image, breathed into us the breath of life, and from the beginning, has sought a relationship with us. He has paid for our sins through the blood of his Son and prepared a glorious home for us in Heaven with him. There is no doubt that we do not deserve and can never merit such love and favor, but God is a God of grace. Therefore, ours is simply to live lives of thankfulness, appreciation, and devotion for all that God has done for us.

How can we show our appreciation and
gratitude for God's love and grace toward us?

DON'T FORGET TO PRAY AND HAVE A GREAT DAY!

DAY 206

Today's Reading:
Psalm 10:1-18

Though written thousands of years ago, this psalm describes all too accurately the sort of people and forces that have become far too familiar to us in our world today. Whether it is the worldly sort that desire to see God and Christianity disappear from our world, power-hungry governments looking to control the world, or religious extremists with the goal of eradicating Christianity, we certainly have our fair share of enemies in this world. While our current times may present some new and different threats than many of us have seen in our lifetimes, the truth of the matter is that there have always been people, governments, and forces that have looked to defy God and force their beliefs and ways of life on others. But the other thing that has always been true is that God is the sovereign ruler of the world. He sees every wicked act and knows every defiant heart. Though at times it may seem as though the odds are stacked against God's people and that there is no one who is willing to defend us, we must remember that we serve a God who holds all things in his hands. His will is perfect, and his power is infinite. Though enemies may come and seem formidable, make no mistake—the Lord will arise to bring vindication to his people and judgment to the ungodly!

Why do you think that there have always been those who were determined to deny or to defy God? What can the Christian do to remain faithful when faced with those adversaries?

DON'T FORGET TO PRAY AND HAVE A GREAT DAY!

DAY 207

**Today's Reading:
Psalm 14:1-7**

A s I read the words of this psalm, I cannot help but imagine the scenario that is described. It is a picture of God looking down upon the earth and searching for those who desire to know him and who are devoted to doing his will in their lives. I imagine the sadness with which God must view our present circumstances—a world overwhelmed with wickedness, hatred, and violence. It is a world that is filled with people that the psalmist describes as "fools," saying that there is no God. How sorrowful God must be at the vast number of souls who are journeying toward an eternity of condemnation and punishment. I wonder if, even in his omnipotence, God feels powerless to save a world that is determined to deny, forsake, and abandon him. Thankfully, all is not lost. There are still those in this world who love God and his word; those who have been washed in the blood of his Son and who have taken on the righteousness of Christ; those who have devoted themselves to living faithful lives of obedience and service. There is still the availability of atonement and forgiveness through the sacrificial gift of Christ on the cross and the saving power of his blood. There is still, at least for the moment, life and time, and with that time, the opportunity to repent and turn to God. Finally, there is still the merciful heart of God who desperately desires the salvation of mankind, and though he watches over this world with much sorrow and disappointment, he also watches with hope for the souls of those who might still turn to him for salvation.

*What can we, as Christians, do to help turn the
minds and hearts of unbelievers toward God?*

DON'T FORGET TO PRAY AND HAVE A GREAT DAY!

Day 208

 Today's Reading:
Psalm 15:1-5

Who can dwell with the Lord? It is a question that many people ask, and it is the subject of this short psalm. Often, as humble and conscientious Christians, we struggle to see ourselves as worthy of approaching God, much less continually dwelling with him. After all, he is a holy and righteous God in whom is found no sin or shortcoming. He is light, and no darkness exists in him, neither can it exist in his presence. We are therefore, as sinful creatures, dependent upon the redeeming blood of Christ to cleanse us of the darkness that invades our lives through sin. Only through Christ can we hope to come into God's presence and dwell with him eternally. But what is our part? Surely there is some responsibility that we have in finding our way into God's presence. In this short psalm, David gives several attributes of the life and heart that are acceptable to God. In the overall analysis of the psalmist's teachings, the one who is able to dwell with God is not the one who is sinless of his own strength, for we would all fail that test. Rather, it is the one whose heart is firmly centered on God and whose life is devoted to godly conduct. You see, in our striving to live with and for God, our hands might from time to time be dirtied by unintentional sin, but our hearts should always remain pure. With a pure and holy heart and the good life that that heart produces, we cannot merely approach God, but we can find our permanent dwelling place with him, both in this life and in the life to come. What a glorious thought!

What are some of the specific things that you can think of that the New Testament tells us to do in order find our way into God's presence?

DON'T FORGET TO PRAY AND HAVE A GREAT DAY!

Day 209

 Today's Reading:
Psalm 19:1-14

Psalm 19 is a beautiful psalm that follows a simple, yet profound progression of thought. David first establishes the power, majesty, and authority of God (verses 1-6). He does so by pointing to the heavens and allowing God's creation to speak. God put the celestial bodies of the heavens in their places and commands their movements. Surely, his power and authority cannot be questioned. David then makes the powerful point that God has created and commands us with the same power and authority with which he rules the skies (verses 7-11). His law instructs and warns us in order to direct our paths in his righteous ways. From there and in light of God's perfect law, David realizes the shortcomings of his own life and of all mankind (verses 12-13). When placed alongside God's holy word, the sinfulness of our lives is clearly evident, and we find ourselves with nothing to offer but our humble pleas for God's mercy and grace. Finally, David turns his attention back to God with only one desire—to be found acceptable in his sight (verse 14). How often do we fail to see the glory of God in our world? How often do we take God's word for granted and not appreciate the great blessing that it is to our lives? How often are we unwilling to confess our wrongdoings but look to justify ourselves instead? May this psalm remind us of all of those things and bring us in humble submission before the throne of God to acknowledge, praise, and adore him.

Do you think that it is important for us to acknowledge the power and majesty of God in order to truly appreciate his place in our lives? Why or why not?

DON'T FORGET TO PRAY AND HAVE A GREAT DAY!

DAY 210

 Today's Reading:
Psalm 23:1-6

It is one of the most well-known and beloved passages in all of the Bible. Time and time again, it has offered comfort and strength to those who are struggling with the trials of life. Often called "the Shepherd's Psalm," these words of David paint a beautiful picture of God's constant care, provision, and protection of his people. While the bulk of this psalm is about God and all that he does for his people, think with me about the effects of that great care as revealed in three "I" statements made by David. First he says, "I shall not want." Because of God's wonderful provision, his children want for nothing and, therefore, find contentment in their Shepherd. Second, David says, "I will fear no evil." Though enemies abound and dangers threaten, the sheep are safely under the protective care of the Shepherd. As the apostle Paul would later write: "If God is for us, who can be against us" (Romans 8:31). Knowing that we are guarded by the mighty hand of God, we find courage to face the struggles of life. Finally, David concludes this psalm with the words, "I shall dwell in the house of the Lord forever." We thought a couple of days ago about the idea of dwelling with the Lord and what was involved in accomplishing that goal. David, here, voices a great confidence in the fact that through God's grace and goodness he will have that glorious dwelling place with the Lord. And thus it is with us. If we will submit our lives to the care and guidance of God as our good Shepherd, we will find the contentment, courage, and confidence that can only be attained through him.

In what ways has God blessed your life and allowed you to have the contentment, courage, and confidence that this psalm talks about?

DON'T FORGET TO PRAY AND HAVE A GREAT DAY!

DAY 211

Today's Reading:
Psalm 24:1-10

Some of the sentiments of this psalm are similar to those of Psalm 15. However, there is a much greater emphasis in this psalm on the greatness and glory of God as the reason for the questions, "Who shall ascend the hill of the Lord? And who shall stand in his holy place?" I believe that there is a powerful and vitally important principle contained within this psalm that we would do well to remember. So often in our lives, whether we intend to or not, our Christianity is reduced to the keeping of obligations and abiding by rules. As long as we worship and live properly, then our relationship with God is safe and everything is okay. What often gets lost in that mindset, however, is God. We are so focused on our lives and doing everything correctly that we lose sight of the overwhelming awesomeness and glory of God that is supposed to be the motivation for our doing right. You see, a religion that is based entirely on the desire to be right is doomed to fail, but a faith and life that is totally consumed with the goodness and majesty of God and with a deep and abiding love for him will motivate the heartfelt worship, constant communication (study and prayer), and humble submission that a faithful relationship with God calls for. After all, didn't Jesus say that the greatest and most important of all the commands was: "You shall love the Lord your God with all your heart and with all your soul and with all your mind" (Matthew 22:37)?

How would it change your Christian life if you lived, worshipped, and served each day out of a profound and overwhelming awe, appreciation, and love for God?

DON'T FORGET TO PRAY AND HAVE A GREAT DAY!

Day 212

 Today's Reading:
Psalm 25:1-22

What impresses me most about this psalm is the deep yearning that David expresses for God. David had all the advantages of a faithful relationship with God that one could enjoy under the old covenant. He was "a man after God's own heart," he had been chosen to lead God's people as their king, and he had been greatly blessed by God in many ways. He loved God and was committed to being faithful to him. But David's love was not just a "thank you Lord for being so good to me. I love you" type of love. It was a love that caused him to yearn and hunger to be ever closer to God. He desired with all of his heart to be nearer, more faithful, and more dependent upon God. David's relationship with God brought a satisfaction and filling to his life that nothing else could bring. I am struck by the fact that I seldom see, either in my own life or in the lives of others, that deep yearning for God. Far too often, we seem to be satisfied with the depth of our relationship with him, regardless of how shallow that depth might actually be. People in our world today seem to desire the benefits of a relationship with God—forgiveness, blessings, salvation—but without the "inconvenience" that closeness with God would bring to their daily lives. How sad that must make God, who wants so badly to be able to draw us near to him and who paid such a great price to make it possible for us to draw near to him. May we have a yearning for God that brings us ever closer to him.

Why do you think that we often fail to have that deep yearning for God? What can we do to have a greater desire for God in our daily lives?

DON'T FORGET TO PRAY AND HAVE A GREAT DAY!

Day 213

 Today's Reading:
Psalm 27:1-14

T he Lord is my light and my salvation; whom shall I fear? The Lord is the stronghold of my life; of whom shall I be afraid." I must admit that when I look at the direction of our world today, I am afraid. I am afraid of what the future holds for God's people, of what persecution or hardship might await us, of what my children will be forced to endure in order to be faithful to God. But then I am reminded of words like these from David. I am reminded that, whatever may come in this world, God reigns supreme and his people are safe in his care. I am reminded that, even if the whole world were to rise up against us, we still have the victory through Christ. I am reminded that no amount of unbelief or ill-will toward God can defeat his purposes or overwhelm his will. You see, God has never promised his people a life free from hardship, pain, or suffering; he has never promised us that we will not have to stand in the face of persecution or even lose our lives for his sake. However, what he has promised us through his word is that there is no power in this world that can take us away from him or rob us of our eternal home. Our challenge is simply to trust—to faithfully endure this life and trust God's perfect will and time. This beautiful psalm ends with the simple expression: "Wait for the Lord!" God is on his throne, and our victory and salvation is sure if we will only wait faithfully for the Lord.

What can we, as Christians, do to find greater
courage and faith to face the challenges of our world?

DON'T FORGET TO PRAY AND HAVE A GREAT DAY!

Day 214

 Today's Reading:
Psalm 28:1-9

Have you ever, in a time of concern or hardship, taken your cares to God in prayer and then witnessed the answering of those prayers in a powerful and marvelous way? If so, what was your reaction? Unfortunately, it is far too often the case that we go to God for his care and protection during difficult times in our lives, but then fail to recognize or acknowledge him when those petitions are granted. It seems that we would sometimes prefer to credit our blessings to luck, fortune, fate, or coincidence rather than to the God of Heaven. What a shame it is when God's own people are unwilling to give him the glory and praise for the blessings in their lives. In today's psalm, there is a sharp and definite turn that takes place as the writer considers God's involvement in his life. In the first part of the psalm, we find the fervent pleas of the psalmist for God's help and deliverance. But then suddenly, the psalmist completely changes the sentiment of the psalm: "Blessed be the Lord! For He has heard the voice of my pleas for mercy." Not only is he quick to call on the Lord when he finds himself in need, he is quick to recognize God's goodness when his prayers are answered. May we follow that wonderful example of trust and reliance upon God and his goodness!

Can you think of a time when God answered your prayers?
What was your reaction?

DON'T FORGET TO PRAY AND HAVE A GREAT DAY!

Day 215

 Today's Reading:
Psalm 32:1-11

This psalm is often thought to be a companion to psalm 51, David's beautiful psalm of confession and repentance concerning his sins with Bathsheba and Uriah. Whether it actually relates to those events or not, its sentiments certainly express the relief and joy that come with forgiveness from sin. The forgiveness of transgression, the covering of sin, freedom from iniquity—what a wonderful feeling it is to be released from the guilt of sin through the mercy and grace of God! But in stark contrast to the joy and peace that freedom from sin brings, David also describes the pain and suffering that comes with abiding sin. "For when I kept silent, my bones wasted away through my groaning all day long." Oh, the agony of being separated from God by sin, of trying to pretend that all is well while inwardly struggling to hide the transgressions of our lives! But, the question is, do we feel that pain that comes with sin and separation from God? Unfortunately, it seems that many people live in sin with no thought for the fractured state of their relationship with God. There seems to be no regret or sorrow over sin. May this attitude not be ours. When we find ourselves in sin, may we recognize its pain so that we can experience the joy of forgiveness.

Why do you think that we often do not feel the sting of sin?

DON'T FORGET TO PRAY AND HAVE A GREAT DAY!

DAY 216

Today's Reading:
Psalm 34:1-22

What do you want? It is a very broad question with answers as varied as the people who would offer them. But one thing is universal—everyone wants something. We spend our lives pursuing the things that we long for and need. Acceptance, honor, riches, relationships, success, pleasure, fulfillment, and the list goes on and on. Our wants or perceived needs often dictate our actions, drive our decision making, and direct our paths in life. But what if the things that we want are not the things that we need? What if the things that we long for are actually detrimental to the greater purpose of our lives? This psalm focuses in on God as the greatest need in any life. Whether we realize it or are willing to admit it or not, there is nothing that we need more than the presence of God in our lives. In the final analysis, any other pursuit is nothing more than a chasing after the wind. But in the Lord is to be found purpose, blessing, joy, help, and hope—all the things that we truly need. Therefore, the psalmist says, seek the Lord. Praise him, exalt his name, submit your life to his rule, knowing that the rewards of that relationship are greater than any earthly prize or human accomplishment. So, again, what do you want? What is your greatest desire? May our hearts always desire God, and may we constantly strive to be closer to him in our lives.

What can you do today to help someone
in your life to have a greater desire for God?

DON'T FORGET TO PRAY AND HAVE A GREAT DAY!

Day 217

 Today's Reading:
Psalm 39:1-13

This psalm brings to mind a truth that we all know but that is difficult to admit: life is short and futile. At its very best, life is but a brief moment. As James would later write, it is just "a mist that appears for a little time and then vanishes" (James 4:14). We struggle with this truth. We want to think that our lives mean something and that the work we do and accomplishments we achieve make a real difference. We often do not want to admit that, while all of our physical struggles and work and accomplishments have a purpose and place within this world, so much of the labor, pursuits, and accumulating of possessions that we strive after have no lasting worth beyond this life. So, what is life about then? What is to be our focus and desire? God! A striving after God and the relationship that we form with him through his Son is the only thing that we will take with us into eternity. That simple fact places God above everything else that we can pursue. The most important work that we can do, the only work that makes a lasting impression, is the work that we do for God. As we live the Christian life, serve others, show Christ to the world through our example, teach others about him and lead them to him, we are, indeed, making an eternal difference in the lives of those around us. The lesson here is not for us to consider life to be pointless and without meaning but, rather, to understand that God is the meaning and purpose of life, and therefore, he should be the most important thing and primary focus of our lives.

What can we do to help keep our focus on
God as the primary purpose of our lives?

DON'T FORGET TO PRAY AND HAVE A GREAT DAY!

Day 218

 Today's Reading:
Psalm 42:1-11

What a beautiful picture is painted in this psalm of the deep desire and yearning for communion with God that is felt by the psalmist. In a time of heat and drought, how deeply does the panting deer pictured in this psalm desire to drink from the flowing waters of a gentle brook? How desperate is that animal for refreshment and nourishment? In the same way the psalmist says his soul yearns and thirsts for communion and closeness with God. He is desperate for the fellowship of God's people and desires to join his heart and voice with them in worship to the Almighty. In his time of trouble, he longs for the saving hand of God to be his deliverer. Some have suggested that this psalm was written at a time when the psalmist was in exile from his people and suffering under the oppressive hand of his enemies, and there are certainly some lines within the psalm that seem to indicate that scenario. But, as others have stated, for the sincere lover of God who truly realizes the blessings of communion with God, an earnest longing for closeness with God and his people should be a constant state of being. Oh what a challenge that is for us as we are daily confronted with so many things that vie for our attention and affection. But as we grow to understand the greatness of God and the greatness of his love toward us, maybe we can yearn more and more for a closer communion with him.

Have you ever found yourself in a situation where you desperately yearned for God and his people? How were you affected by those feelings and how did you react to them?

DON'T FORGET TO PRAY AND HAVE A GREAT DAY!

Day 219

 Today's Reading:
Psalm 46:1-11

This psalm is a beautiful tribute to the protective power of God, but there is one particularly poignant phrase that I would like to focus on. Verse 10 says, "Be still and know that I am God…" What a profound and meaningful thought! The idea of "be still" is that of relying upon God's care instead of trusting in your own ability and letting go of the anxiety that difficulties often cause. Essentially, God is saying, "Stop trying to take care of all of your problems yourself; trust me to care for you and stop worrying!" I don't know about you, but I need to take those words to heart! It is not an easy thing to "be still" when we find ourselves in the midst of adversity. How often do we fret and worry and struggle with the circumstances of our lives, all the while praying to God for his help, but never really trusting him to take care of us? Then, as we are consumed with desperately trying to solve our own problems, we miss the providential care that God provides and fail to give him the glory. You see, in my mind, this statement is not so much about leaving room for God to work; God is God, and he can do whatever he wants regardless of what I do. I believe that it is more about us being calm and trusting enough to recognize the things that God does for us so that we can give him the glory and exalt his name. May God help us to be still and know that he is God.

Acknowledging that it is very difficult to "be still" in times of worry and anxiety, what can we do to help us lean on God in those troubling times?

DON'T FORGET TO PRAY AND HAVE A GREAT DAY!

DAY 220

 Today's Reading:
Psalm 51:1-19

What do you do when you have failed everyone and everything that you held dear? I'm not sure that there is any way to overstate the devastation, sorrow, and loss that David was experiencing as he penned the words of this psalm. He had betrayed a friend, hurt the kingdom, and brought shame on himself, but most importantly, he had forfeited the relationship with God that he had so badly yearned for and coveted. Much of the wrong that David had been guilty of in his dealings with Bathsheba and Uriah had been done in an effort to hide or escape the consequences of his initial sin of adultery. He had blindly carried out a series of sinful deeds with seemingly no recognition of the downward spiral of his spiritual life. But now, there was no denying his sin and no escaping its consequences, and David was not interested in either. His only concern, as he wrote this psalm, was the cleansing of his soul and the restoration of his relationship with God. He could accept the consequences that his sins would bring, but he could not fathom a life without God. So, through the words of this psalm, David threw himself before the mercy seat of God and pled for his forgiveness and cleansing. I sometimes wonder how a man as close to God as David was could be guilty of such grievous sins, but then I remember that I, too, have much to seek forgiveness for. Thankfully, the beautiful lesson that we learn from David is that God is merciful and forgiving toward those who come to him with humble and repentant hearts. What a blessing it is to know that our failures don't have to be final!

What lessons can we learn from this period in David's life
and from the sentiments he expresses in this psalm?

DON'T FORGET TO PRAY AND HAVE A GREAT DAY!

Day 221

 Today's Reading:
Psalm 53:1-6

This psalm, which is almost identical to Psalm 14, is an indictment on the evil and godless world of David's day, and it has much to teach our world today as well. As we think about the world that we live in today, it is easy to see that many are proclaiming loudly, "There is no God." What is interesting in this psalm is to see what God, through the psalmist, says about those who deny the existence of God. There is, he says, a necessary and inevitable progression that occurs when one denies God's existence and Godhead. The heart that has rejected God will produce a life that deteriorates into one of corruption and abomination. This is true whether it is applied to an individual or to an entire society. In our world today, we bemoan the fact that violence, hatred, and immorality have become so prevalent. In our frustration, we look for where to place the blame, often settling on political parties, governmental leaders, activist groups, celebrities, or the media as the target of our blame and disdain. The truth of the matter is that underlying all of these people and groups a very basic problem exists: it seems that the very heart of our nation is rejecting God. What God teaches us in Psalm 53 is that a system of laws that are based on morality, respect, and human decency, such as ours is cannot be sustained in a society that does not acknowledge God, for God is the very basis of the morality, respect, and decency undergirding those laws. As Christians, we must do what we can do: continue to be what God would have us to be and through our lives show the world the way back to God.

What are some specific ways that Christians and
the church make a difference in our world today?

DON'T FORGET TO PRAY AND HAVE A GREAT DAY!

DAY 222

Today's Reading:
Psalm 54:1-7

Life often has a way of reminding us that we are not in control. It can beat us up and leave us feeling hopeless and helpless. When faced with the trials of life, we find ourselves in search of solace, many grasping for anything and everything that offers any semblance of hope or relief from their struggles. What are we to do when our world falls apart and life becomes unbearable? David, the human author of this psalm, was certainly a man that was well acquainted with hardship and suffering. In the days in which this psalm was written, David was running for his life and hiding from Saul. But despite the difficulties of his life, David knew where to find the help and shelter that he so badly needed, and in his words we find the answer to our own search for solace. "Behold, God is my helper; the Lord is the upholder of my life." Whenever tragedy and sorrow find their way into our world, we can be sure that God is there with us, to strengthen and comfort us. He is our shelter and our strength. He holds us up and allows us to overcome the struggles that we face. He comforts us and provides a peace that passes understanding. He promises to never leave nor forsake us. Yes, life is often difficult; there is no escaping that difficult truth. But what a comfort it is to know that, in those difficult moments, we are held safely in the hands of a loving and merciful God!

What encouragement would you give to someone
who was struggling with some great trial of life?

DON'T FORGET TO PRAY AND HAVE A GREAT DAY!

Day 223

 Today's Reading:
Psalm 61:1-8

Have you ever felt overwhelmed by the circumstances of life—weighed down with worry and concern for a loved one, burdened by a health, family, or financial crisis of your own, or just simply struggling with the everyday stress and strain of life? If you have ever felt like you were at the end of your rope and unable to take any more (and most of us have at some point), then you can relate to the words of the psalmist: "from the end of the earth I will call to you when my heart is faint. Lead me to the rock that is higher than I." David, to whom this psalm is ascribed, cries out to God from "the end of the earth" — a place of isolation, despair, and desperation. In this helpless state, he pleads with God to provide refuge and shelter for his life by leading him to "a rock that is higher." The imagery of this psalm is beautiful, depicting the carrying away of the troubled soul to a place of safety and refuge under the shelter of God's wings, a place that is closer to God and farther from the problems of life. Though much time has passed since the penning of this psalm, it remains true that God offers a place of refuge from the storms of life. When our hearts are overwhelmed by trouble or sorrow and we are helpless to meet our own needs, God knows, and he is always there to offer the comfort and peace that we so badly need. So in our time of need, let us, like the psalmist, cry out to God to relieve us from our faintness of heart by leading us to a rock that is higher than we.

In addition to our prayers, where can we go to find
the help and comfort of God in our times of need?

DON'T FORGET TO PRAY AND HAVE A GREAT DAY!

Day 224

 Today's Reading:
Psalm 62:1-12

Within this psalm of trust in God's presence and abiding care, the psalmist confidently states, "God is a refuge for us." In that statement and in the overall sentiment of this psalm, the presence of hardship, danger, or suffering is implied. So often, we are tempted to wrongly believe that God's presence and care means that our lives will be protected from all harm and from every struggle. But remember that a refuge is a place or thing that offers shelter and protection from a storm or danger. A person doesn't seek refuge when there is no threat. Refuge is for those who are frightened, suffering, or afflicted. God never promises us a life without trials, at least not in this world. Surely, life has a way of reminding us of that reality. However, God does promise us that during those times of suffering, heartache, affliction, or trial, he will always be there to shelter us, to care for us, to strengthen us, and to lift us up. Surely, as the psalmist declares, God is our rock, our salvation, our defense, and our refuge. He is a good and merciful God. So, when we encounter the challenges and trials of life, we can confidently trust in him even as we struggle to "wait silently for God alone." May he give us the strength and courage to do so.

How has God sheltered you in times of storm in your life?

DON'T FORGET TO PRAY AND HAVE A GREAT DAY!

Day 225

Today's Reading:
Psalm 63:1-11

Many of the psalms are psalms of intercession, pleading with God to come to the aid of the psalmist or of His people as they face hardships or enemies. This psalm, however, is strictly a psalm of praise for the help and blessings that God has already provided. As the psalmist reflects on God's many acts of love and goodness, he is overwhelmed with gratitude and a yearning to be even closer to the God that has so completely filled and satisfied his life. This psalm causes me to reflect on my own life and on a general attitude that is so prevalent in our world today as I ask the question, "What would it take to satisfy me?" So often, in so many lives, the answer to that question can be summed up in one word: more. More money, more possessions, more fame, more pleasure, and on and on the list goes. It seems that so many of us are never satisfied. In contrast, the psalmist, David, needs nothing more than the presence of God in his life to be content and satisfied. Notice that according to the introductory statement this psalm was written "when he [David] was in the wilderness of Judah." In a time when David was away from the comfort and security of home and was fleeing for his life (probably either from Saul or from Absalom), his only desire was for God. What a humbling and challenging example that is for us. The New Testament, in warning us about the dangers of loving riches (worldly things), states that "godliness with contentment is great gain" (see 1 Timothy 6:6). May we learn to find our contentment and satisfaction in God alone!

Why does our desire for worldly things often overshadow our yearning for God? What can we do to improve that area of our lives?

DON'T FORGET TO PRAY AND HAVE A GREAT DAY!

Day 226

 Today's Reading:
Psalm 66:1-20

When we speak of the transcendent power and mighty works of God, we often point to the creation as evidence of those things, and rightly so, for the beauty, intricacy, and design of this world is certainly testament to the wisdom, power, and majesty of God. Yet, as the psalmist words this beautiful psalm of praise to God for his mighty deeds, it is his working in the lives of his people that the psalmist praises. This causes me to wonder if we don't sometimes take for granted and fail to acknowledge all that God has done for us. If we want to see a demonstration of the love that God has for mankind and of the powerful presence that God has in our world today, we need look no further than our own lives to find it. Beginning with the supreme sacrifice of his Son for the cleansing of our sins, and including every big and small thing that God provides for us through his providential care, our lives are a constant testament to the wonderful love and mighty works of God. This fact ought to motivate our heartfelt worship as we give thanks and praise to him for all of his blessings. As any group of Christians gathers for worship, each individual present has many things for which to be thankful. As the recognition of God's goodness and love fills each heart to overflowing, our voices blend in beautiful worship to the Giver of all good things. In this psalm, the writer's earnest desire is to give praise and worship to God for his goodness and might. May our desire always be the same.

Do you think that our worship typically reflects a genuine
and heartfelt expression of loving praise? Why or why not?

DON'T FORGET TO PRAY AND HAVE A GREAT DAY!

Day 227

 Today's Reading:
Psalm 68:1-35

This psalm is particularly poignant given the circumstances of our world today. From Islamic terrorism to ungodly and immoral agendas within our own society, it seems as if our world's opposition to God and his people is increasing at an alarming rate and that we, as Christians, are becoming more and more isolated and hated for our faith. But in the midst of these seemingly hopeless circumstances, the beginning words of this psalm bring triumphant hope to dark and desperate circumstances. "God shall arise, his enemies shall be scattered; and those who hate him shall flee before him!" You see, it can be easy for us to feel overwhelmed by the world and develop that attitude of desperation and hopelessness, but we must remember that God is God, and he will reign victorious! As long as we stand with him, we have nothing to fear for we are never alone. This psalm pictures God as the leader of his people, going before them into the fray and leading them to victory. We must remember, as the apostle Paul tells us, that "we do not wrestle against flesh and blood, but against the rulers, against the authorities, against the cosmic power over the present darkness, against the spiritual forces of evil in the heavenly places" (Ephesians 6:12). In other words, our true enemy is Satan, and while it may seem that he has won over the hearts of many in our world today, he will ultimately face defeat. So, what are we to do? Continue to walk with God, trusting him to lead us to victory, and always praising him for his goodness, mercy, and might as we patiently wait for our heavenly reward.

What are some things that we can do to maintain
courage and hope in our present world?

DON'T FORGET TO PRAY AND HAVE A GREAT DAY!

Day 228

Today's Reading:
Psalm 72:1-20

As we saw in yesterday's reading, we live in a time and world that in many ways can be very discouraging to Christians with problems such as terrorist organizations that are violently opposed to Christianity, a culture that seems to be plummeting headfirst into a moral and religious abyss, and even a religious world that is laden with confusion, error, and moral compromise. It can often seem as if God is losing his foothold in this world and is in danger of being defeated completely. But as I consider these things, I can't help but think about how much more hopeless and defiled David's world must have seemed as he penned this psalm. Surrounded by a godless world that constantly mocked and ridiculed the God of Israel, he often felt alone, despised, and defeated. But despite the deplorable circumstances of David's world, or of ours, his message is true and powerful and one that we need to constantly be reminded of. It can be summed up in two words—God reigns! Despite the attitudes and actions of those who would reject and oppose him, God is sovereign in his power and authority as he continues to rule over the earth and provide care and blessings to his people. There is no power on earth that can dethrone God, and in the end, all will fall before him and worship at his feet. What a comfort that promise is to those who are striving to faithfully serve him in the midst of an unbelieving world!

What do you think will be the reaction of a godless world
when they are finally confronted with the reality of God?

DON'T FORGET TO PRAY AND HAVE A GREAT DAY!

Day 229

 Today's Reading:
Psalm 84:1-12

This psalm represents a beautiful declaration of the psalmist's love for God and his desire to be in the house of the Lord. It is the presence of God that the writer craved, and under the old covenant, the house of God (the tabernacle or temple) offered that blessing. It was God's dwelling place among his people. Time spent in that special place brought a special closeness and communion with the Lord. As a Christian parallel to this thought, it is now the people of God and not a physical structure that represents the dwelling place of God among us. If one wants to be in the presence of God and enjoy that communion that the psalmist expresses a desire for, then being among the people of God is the equivalent of the psalmist's being in the house of the Lord. In an environment in which it seems that we must plead with and entice people to gather with the church, oh how we need a revival of that desire to be with God and among his people! In a day when many have become disgruntled with organized religion and others have come to see the church as optional to their faith and relationship with God, how we need to crave and yearn for the closeness and communion with God and his people that only the church can provide. May we find within ourselves the yearning desire to share in the communion with God that comes by being with his people.

Why do you think that so many have developed a negative or apathetic attitude toward the church? What can be done to turn that situation around?

DON'T FORGET TO PRAY AND HAVE A GREAT DAY!

Day 230

 Today's Reading:
Psalm 86:1-17

One of the greatest sources of comfort and strength for the Christian is prayer. We take our joys and our sorrows, our heartaches and our thanksgiving before God as we praise him for his goodness and petition his help in our times of need. Through prayer, we communicate with God and strengthen our relationship with him. Unfortunately, we sometimes struggle to believe with confidence that God is listening to our pleas or that he is willing to help with, what must seem to him to be, our petty concerns. These fears and thoughts can often hinder our prayer life and, ultimately, worsen our struggles. This psalm, ascribed to David, is a prayer for God's help and guidance in a time of difficulty. As you read it, pay particular attention to the unwavering confidence that the psalmist expresses in the faithfulness of God in hearing and answering his prayers. Intermingled with his petitions are words of praise and thanksgiving for the goodness and power of God. David is supremely confident in God's ability and willingness to grant his requests and to meet his needs. Thus it should be with us. As we go to God in prayer and lay the cares of our hearts at his feet, we, too, need to be supremely confident of his ability and willingness to meet our needs. God is a God of love and mercy who knows his children's needs and is ready to meet those needs according to his perfect will and in his perfect time. May we learn to trust and rely upon his gracious care.

Are you satisfied with your current prayer life?
If not, what can you do to improve it?

DON'T FORGET TO PRAY AND HAVE A GREAT DAY!

Day 231

 Today's Reading:
Psalm 90:1-17

Man—the pinnacle of all that exists; the most intelligent, most powerful, and most creative being in existence; with limitless potential and complete independence from any controlling force. This is the way that many would view man's place within the world and universe, and admittedly, if God were to be removed from the equation, much of it would be true. However, as diligently as many have tried, God is not and cannot be removed from the equation. He is the almighty creator and sustainer of the universe. He is the maker and sovereign ruler of all that is; the eternal God, the great I AM. Comparatively, we are powerless and finite in every way. Our thoughts, our abilities, and even our very lives are but a minuscule speck in comparison to God. Our time on this earth, at its very best, is brief and uncertain, and whether we realize it or not, our very existence is constantly dependent upon God's sustaining power and care. Given this reality, the best and most profitable thing that we can do in this life is to submit ourselves to God and trust in his almighty hand. We would be wise to implore of the Lord that he might "teach us to number our days that we may get a heart of wisdom," for in that numbering of days we find reliance upon the loving hand of a mighty God.

Why do you think that so many have developed a negative or apathetic attitude toward the church? What can be done to turn that situation around?

DON'T FORGET TO PRAY AND HAVE A GREAT DAY!

Day 232

Today's Reading:
Psalm 95:1-11

Why do we worship? Far too often, worship in our world has become about us—the worshippers. We look for worship that is convenient, comfortable, enjoyable, fulfilling, inspiring, and motivating to us. Don't get me wrong—I firmly believe that sincere, heartfelt, and scriptural worship ought to be encouraging and beneficial to us in many ways. I believe that God designed it that way. Our worship provides a sort of spiritual refueling for our lives as we join our hearts and voices together with other Christians to give praise and honor to God. However, if our only focus in worship is to please and benefit ourselves, then we have missed the point altogether. You see, while we might reap some spiritual and emotional rewards from it, our worship must never be about us. It is always to be completely for and about God! Psalm 95 is all about worship, but notice the reasons that the psalmist gives that we should worship, indicated by the word "for" in the psalm. We should worship God because of who God is (verses 3-5); he is the all-powerful Creator and Sustainer of the universe, the great God above all gods, our maker, our provider, and our savior. We should also worship God because of who we are (verse 7); we are his people, chosen and redeemed by him to be his precious children. Given all of this evidence of God's greatness and worthiness of our worship, the psalmist concludes with a warning about not giving our hearts to God. He is certainly worthy of our thanksgiving, our praise, and our worship. May we ever be devoted to worshipping him with sincere and thankful hearts.

Why do you think that so much of the worship in our world is focused on the worshipper instead of on God?

DON'T FORGET TO PRAY AND HAVE A GREAT DAY!

Day 233

Today's Reading:
Psalm 96:1-13

O f all the psalms, some of the most beautiful are the wonderful psalms of praise and worship to the Lord. With a heart overflowing with awe and wonder, the psalmist gushes forth with words of adoration for his Lord. As you read the words of this beautiful psalm, let me ask you to stop and consider all that God is and all that he has done in your life. There is no doubt that, for each and every one of us, there is more than sufficient reason for us to praise and worship God for the goodness and mercy that he has shown toward us. Given that fact, it is both sad and concerning that we so often worship him with so little joy and heartfelt sincerity. Boredom often seems to characterize our praise more than enthusiasm. But, as the psalmist exclaims, "the Lord is great and greatly to be praised." All honor, majesty, and glory are due him. As his people, those who have been redeemed from sin by the blood of his own Son, we above all people should recognize his goodness and love and be determined to give him the praise and worship he deserves. May we be overwhelmed with the knowledge of God's goodness and love, and may all praise, worship, and honor be given to him!

How can we bring more joy and enthusiasm into
our worship without losing our focus on God?

DON'T FORGET TO PRAY AND HAVE A GREAT DAY!

Day 234

Today's Reading:
Psalm 99:1-9

There is one sentiment that is prominently displayed throughout this psalm. "Holy is He." The holiness of God is exalted in this psalm of praise, but what does it mean to declare that God is holy? The word "holy" can be used to refer to simply the character of God's existence or to his moral and ethical character, but in either sense the word denotes absoluteness or perfection. In every aspect of his being, God is absolute and perfect. There is no shortcoming, no weakness, no imperfection. His power, wisdom, and presence are all infinite. As high as the heavens are above the earth, so is God above any of his creations in any aspect of his character. God is equally holy in his moral and ethical character. His spiritual purity is without blemish. In his holiness, he is incapable of dishonesty, deception, greed, or any of the other unethical qualities that often plague mankind. God is holy and his holiness is reason for our rejoicing and praise. Because of his holiness, we can have confidence in his promises. Because of his holiness, we can trust in his benevolent care. Because of his holiness, we can know that his judgments are just and that his will is for our good. What a wonderful God he is, and what a blessing it is to be able to call him "Father."

In your own words, how would you explain to
someone what it means to say that God is holy?

DON'T FORGET TO PRAY AND HAVE A GREAT DAY!

Day 235

 Today's Reading:
Psalm 100:1-5

This familiar psalm of praise is a beautiful call to worship for those who love God and recognize his goodness. As the psalm states, "he is God" and as such, he is certainly worthy of our worship and devotion for many reasons. In today's thought, I would like to focus on just one of those reasons, as indicated in the text. Concerning God, the psalmist declares: "It is he who made us, and we are his." We are his. Have you ever stopped to consider all that is contained within such a short and simple statement? We are his because he made us. We are God's creative handiwork— designed in his infinite wisdom, created by his powerful hand, and sustained by his immutable will. We are his to possess, control, and command, but the amazing thing about God is that he chooses not to exercise that right. He has chosen, rather, to allow us to choose him. He has provided for us, instructed us, warned us, and pleaded with us, but he leaves the choosing to us. God's desire is for our relationship with him to be not one of domineering ownership but of loving devotion. Thus, the psalmist follows "we are his" by clarifying that "we are his people, and the sheep of his pasture." God does not view us as merely possessions to be used and controlled at his whims, but rather as children to be lovingly cared for and nurtured, and who will lovingly devote themselves to him in return. To belong to God is surely one of life's greatest blessings and joys. May we never take it for granted.

Why do you think that it is important to God that
we have the freedom to choose a relationship with Him?

DON'T FORGET TO PRAY AND HAVE A GREAT DAY!

Day 236

 Today's Reading:
Psalm 103:1-22

"Bless the Lord, O my soul, and forget not all his benefits." This is a phrase that has been wrongly applied in the minds and lives of many today. When we think of the word "benefits," we are often drawn to the question, "What's in it for me?" Unfortunately, that is exactly how some people view a relationship with God. "If I choose to follow God, what do I get out of it? A better job, more money, improved health...?" Certainly, there are many physical blessings associated with a life of faithfulness to God, but, interestingly, David, to whom this psalm is credited and who had been greatly blessed by God from a physical perspective, is not focused on physical things in this psalm. The "benefits" that have prompted David's attitude of worship in this psalm are the spiritual blessings that God has provided—forgiveness, redemption, mercy, and love just to name a few. Certainly, of all that God has done for us and blessed us with, these blessings are the greatest. Yet, it seems that, so often, when we are asked to consider or list what we are thankful for, the physical things seem to come first while the spiritual blessings are an afterthought. The truth of the matter is that if we had nothing from a physical point of view but had the forgiveness of our sins leading to a relationship with God and eternal salvation, we would still be, of all men, most blessed. May we never forget the great privilege and blessing of being a redeemed child of God through Jesus Christ!

What can we do to be more focused on and
appreciative of the spiritual blessings of God?

DON'T FORGET TO PRAY AND HAVE A GREAT DAY!

Day 237

 Today's Reading:
Psalm 106:1-48

This is one of the longest psalms that we have covered in our reading, but amidst all the words and sentiments of these verses, there is one word that stands out to me; one possibly surprising word that sums up, in my mind, the meaning of this psalm. That word is "nevertheless." I know that's probably not the word you were expecting or thinking but consider the great amount of meaning it has in the context of this psalm. This psalm is about two things: Israel's sin and God's forgiveness. Much of the psalm is devoted to detailing the sins and transgressions of God's people—idolatry, rebellion, unfaithfulness, and disobedience. Israel had certainly given God plenty of reasons to destroy them, but he did not. Though he punished them and allowed them to be defeated by enemies, he never forsook them. He continually forgave and restored them. But lying between their sinfulness and God's mercy is the word "nevertheless" (or the very similar word "yet" also used in this psalm). They deserved God's wrath. They deserved to be destroyed. They deserved to be forsaken by God as they had forsaken him; nevertheless, God showed mercy. This word is very meaningful to me because it applies to me in the same way. I am a sinner—weak, sometimes rebellious, often falling short, always imperfect. I deserve nothing more than God's wrath and punishment. Nevertheless, God loves me. He continues to bless me, forgive me, and show unfathomable mercy toward me. And he also does so for you! Aren't you thankful that the word "nevertheless" is a part of your story?

In what ways has God's mercy and forgiveness been a blessing to your life?

DON'T FORGET TO PRAY AND HAVE A GREAT DAY!

Day 238

 Today's Reading:
Psalm 115:1-18

It has long been the ambition of man to find glory and praise for himself. At least as far back as the tower of Babel (Genesis 11), humans have sought to make a name for themselves and, in so doing, to secure the respect, admiration, and honor of others. Throughout the centuries and in today's world, that type of self-centeredness has often manifested itself in some form of idolatry—the placing of some object of our own invention or desire on a pedestal, as it were, and devoting our hearts and lives to it. However, a proper understanding and appreciation of God should cause us to desire that God receive the praise and glory instead of ourselves. After all, there is no good thing that we enjoy or achieve in this life for which God is not ultimately responsible. As the New Testament reminds us, "every good gift and every perfect gift is from above…" (James 1:17). So often, we are guilty of attributing the good things and events in our lives to luck, fortune, coincidence, or to our own talent and hard work. In contrast to that, consider what a message it would send to the unbelieving world if we would, as we celebrate the joyous occasions and accomplishments of our lives, acknowledge the goodness of God and express our thankfulness for his many blessings. May we strive to have the attitude of the psalmist: "Not to us, O Lord, not to us, but to your name give glory, for the sake of your steadfast love and your faithfulness!"

What would you consider the greatest physical blessings of your life?
How is God to be credited and praised for those blessings?

DON'T FORGET TO PRAY AND HAVE A GREAT DAY!

DAY 239

 Today's Reading:
Psalm 117:1-2

This is the shortest of all the recorded psalms and may seem hardly worth our attention, but this brief psalm, consisting of only 30 words in the English language, has a great and powerful message for mankind. When we think of the glory and praiseworthiness of God, we often think of his infinite power and wisdom. We think of him as the creator of the universe and the sovereign ruler of the world. While these traits are certainly worthy of our awe and adoration, there are still greater and more incredible traits to God's character—traits that are directly related to our relationship with him. This short psalm highlights two of those praiseworthy traits. There is, first of all, the greatness of God's merciful kindness toward us. In all of his power and wisdom, God is still a God of compassion and mercy, patient with our imperfections and forgiving of our shortcomings. Secondly, there is the perfect and everlasting truth of God's word. Prompted by his merciful kindness, God revealed his truth to us and preserved it by his mighty hand with the firm promise that it would never pass away. Through that truth, we learn all that we need to know to accept a relationship with God that leads to eternal life. Thanks to this brief psalm, we have an everlasting reminder of these magnificent traits of God that give us reason to lift our hearts and voices to him in praise!

What are some of the characteristics of God
that you are most thankful for and why?

DON'T FORGET TO PRAY AND HAVE A GREAT DAY!

DAY 240

Today's Reading:
Psalm 119:97-104

Of all the psalms that have been preserved for us, Psalm 119 is, by far, the longest. Yet despite its length, it is among the most cohesive of psalms with regard to theme. The entire psalm is one of praise to God for his glorious word. With only a couple of exceptions, every single verse of this psalm makes some direct mention of the word of God—his word, his testimonies, his precepts, his law, his commandments, his statutes, or his testimonies. Over and over again, the psalmist declares his love for the word of God and his desire for God to teach him that word. He also proclaims his commitment to his own study of and meditation on the word of God so that he may faithfully abide by it in his life. What a shame it is that there is not more love for the word of God today. As easily accessible as it is in our modern world, far too many people, including many Christians, are simply not interested in knowing what it has to say. But, oh how badly we need the precepts of God! How desperately our world needs to listen to and apply the instructions that God has provided for our lives. How much better and happier we would be if we would only develop a greater love and appreciation for God's holy word. As Christians, we may become frustrated at our world's lack of concern for God and his word, but we must continue to be lights in the darkness by pursuing a greater understanding of God's word and diligently striving to live it out in our everyday lives. May God help us to do just that.

In your opinion, what are some of the greatest blessings of God's word?

DON'T FORGET TO PRAY AND HAVE A GREAT DAY!

Day 241

 **Today's Reading:**
Psalm 121:1-8

When your world is turned upside down and you do not know what to do, where do you go for help? When there seem to be no answers to your questions and no purpose in your struggles, who do you look to for wisdom and guidance? When you feel all alone and your strength is failing, who is there to hold you up? These are the types of questions that seem to prompt this great psalm. "From where does my help come?" But, almost as soon as it is asked, this question is answered with utmost confidence and assurance. "My help comes from the Lord…" The psalmist says, in the middle of the psalm, "The Lord is my keeper," and it is this picture of God that is carried through the remainder of the text. There is much involved in this idea of "keeper." As our keeper, God is our provider and protector, our comforter and encourager, our strength and savior. Truly, he is all of these things and many, many more. In fact, there is no limit to the help that God can and will provide for us as his children. We must only learn to trust his perfect will and submit ourselves to his abundant care. That is the real challenge for us, for when we are overwhelmed by the trials of life, it is easy to feel alone, helpless, and hopeless. But faith knows better! An abiding faith in God knows that he is always there with his mighty hand and caring heart to meet our needs and to "keep" us in our day of trouble. Thank God for his overwhelming love and grace!

What is the greatest challenge for you in trusting in the will of God?

DON'T FORGET TO PRAY AND HAVE A GREAT DAY!

DAY 242

 Today's Reading:
Psalm 124:1-8

"I f it had not been the Lord who was on our side..." This is the phrase that begins and sets the tone for this psalm of David. Notice that he is not exalting the Lord for keeping them from all trouble. He is not saying that no difficulty or hardship had come upon them because of God's loving care. They had, in fact, encountered the wrath of their enemies. They had been surrounded by trouble and harassed by hardships. They had experienced difficult and perilous times. The beauty and comfort of this psalm is not that God had kept them from all harm, for that is a concept that none of us can relate to. Instead, what this psalm so beautifully states is that, in the midst of that trouble as enemies were pressing in and the floods were threatening to overtake them, the Lord was with them, to be on their side to comfort, strengthen, and bless them. What David is so eloquently stating is that, if God had not been there with them during these difficulties, they surely would have been overcome and perished. It is a beautiful truth that every faithful child of God can easily understand and relate to, for in varying degrees we have all experienced the abiding presence of God during our darkest hours. We have felt his strength and have been comforted by his peace. Oh, what a blessing it is to know that the Lord is on our side!

Think of a time of trouble when the Lord was on your side.
What comfort and help did you receive from him?

DON'T FORGET TO PRAY AND HAVE A GREAT DAY!

Day 243

 Today's Reading:
Psalm 133:1-3

The thrust of this short psalm is summed up in the first verse and opening statement: "Behold, how good and pleasant it is when brothers dwell together in unity!" The remainder of the psalm paints word pictures that would surely have brought to mind beautiful images familiar to its ancient readers. As I consider these words of David, I am reminded of what were surely very difficult times in his life when he longed for the unity that this psalm exults—his relationship with King Saul, which began as one of love and devotion but ended in Saul's determined attempts to kill David; or his tumultuous and adversarial relationship with his son, Absalom. Oh, how David must have mourned these broken relationships and longed for the unity that he speaks of in this psalm. Then, I remember that these words, though penned by David, are actually the product of the mind and voice of God's Spirit. How saddened God must be when his people treat one another with disregard, anger, and hatred, and how greatly he must long for them to love one another and to dwell together in unity. May God help us to constantly strive to harness our human emotions and imperfections and to dwell together in peace and unity as his people.

Why would it be important to God that his people dwell together in unity?

DON'T FORGET TO PRAY AND HAVE A GREAT DAY!

Day 244

Today's Reading:
Psalm 139:1-24

For the heart that yearns to be close to God, can there be any more comforting thought than to know that God knows our most intimate thoughts and feelings and that there is nowhere that we can find ourselves that God is not with us? There is no heartache that God does not understand, there is no trouble in which God is not present, and there is no darkness that God cannot illuminate. He knows our fears, our doubts, and our struggles. He knows our sorrows and our joys. And, yes, he knows our weaknesses, shortcomings, and failures. But even in that realization, there is no fear, for God's love is everlasting, and his grace is abundant. What an unfathomable thought it is to consider that God, the creator of all that is, the sustainer of life and ruler of the universe, could be concerned with me—that he would take the time to listen to my prayers and comfort my fears, that he walks beside me and before me to guide, protect, and provide. There is only one possible explanation for God's relationship with mankind—love. He loves us! As improbable as it may seem and as unlovable as we may feel at times, God loves us. Love is the attribute of God that sets him apart from every false god that has ever been devised by man, and it is the quality of his character that makes our relationship with him possible. I am thankful for the unlimited power, wisdom, and presence of God. I am thankful for the perfection that defines every attribute of his character. But, most of all, I am thankful for his amazing love that causes him to constantly surround me and know everything about me and, yet, be kind and merciful to me anyway.

What is the most amazing thing to you about the love of God?

DON'T FORGET TO PRAY AND HAVE A GREAT DAY!

Day 245

 Today's Reading:
Psalm 148:1-14

P raise the Lord!" That is the obvious theme and continual command of this psalm. Twelve times in this short psalm all of creation is called upon to give praise to the Lord! All of nature, the psalmist proclaims, owes to God their praise and honor for by his hand they were created and exist. And, in fact, all of creation does exalt the name of God and give him praise and glory for in their very design, functioning, and beauty, they testify of the majesty, wisdom, and power of God. As the New Testament reminds us, "For his invisible attributes, namely, his eternal power and divine nature, have been clearly perceived, ever since the creation of the world, in the things that have been made" (Romans 1:20). One need only look around at the wonders of our world to see God and to know that he is a good and glorious God! I love the statement made by Jesus when upon his entry into Jerusalem amidst the praises of those lining the streets he is told by the Jewish leaders to rebuke them. His response was: "I tell you, if these were silent, the very stones would cry out" (Luke 19:40). Still today, there are many in our world who would silence the voices of those who give glory and honor to God, but just as has always been, there is no star in the sky, no mountain top or seashore, and no living plant or animal that does not proclaim and exalt the name of God. May we, as God's people, never be guilty of allowing our surroundings to be alone in praising the name of the Lord!

How does our natural world exalt and praise the name of God?

DON'T FORGET TO PRAY AND HAVE A GREAT DAY!

Day 246

 Today's Reading:
Psalm 150:1-6

How appropriate it is that the divine collection of psalms concludes with one powerful thought: "Praise the Lord!" You see, whatever sorrows and trials might come our way, whatever reasons man might find to mock, ridicule, or deny God, whatever evils might exist in this world, the fact remains that God is great and deserving of our praise! All of creation testifies of his mighty power and wisdom, and there can be no denying of his sovereign rule. Greater, yet, is the truth of God's overwhelming love and mercy toward mankind in his desire to see our salvation from sin and death. In a world that is filled with reasons to fear, worry, dread, and doubt, what a blessing it is to know that we have a God who is worthy to be praised! Unfortunately, far too often, even we as God's people fail to give him the praise and worship he deserves. But if our study of the Old Testament this year has taught us anything at all, surely it has reminded us of the greatness of God and of his worthiness to be praised. Therefore, let us resolve to give him the very best of our praise and adoration. Praise the Lord!

How can our daily lives be used to bring praise to the Lord?

DON'T FORGET TO PRAY AND HAVE A GREAT DAY!

Day 247

 **Today's Reading:**
Proverbs 1:1-33

Wisdom, understanding, meaning—they are still among the most valuable and treasured of human possessions. Men spend their lives seeking and striving to gain wisdom, recognizing that it cannot be purchased with money but only earned through the process of experience, learning, and growth. Unfortunately, many never gain true wisdom because they are searching in the wrong places and striving after the wrong things. As this great book of wisdom begins, we learn a vitally important lesson about the source of knowledge: "The fear of the Lord is the beginning of knowledge." In a world where so many have turned away from God and reject any notion of his existence, it remains true that wisdom—real and genuine wisdom—begins with an acknowledgement and fearful respect of God. After all, it is he who created us and gave us the ability to learn and gain wisdom in the first place. One cannot properly understand the workings of the world or gain insight into the meaning and purpose of life without recognizing God as the architect and builder of the universe and as the God of all things. Any understanding and knowledge that does not acknowledge God is only that which is falsely called knowledge. May we always have a reverent fear of the Lord and look to him for the wisdom that only he can provide.

Why do you think that so many in our world
reject God in their searching for knowledge?

DON'T FORGET TO PRAY AND HAVE A GREAT DAY!

Day 248

 **Today's Reading:
Proverbs 2:1-22**

Wisdom is often understood to be knowledge and understanding that is, and can only be, gained through experience. If this is true, have you ever wondered why there seem to be many people who, though they have lived long and full lives, have acquired very little wisdom? This chapter gives us two reasons for that phenomenon: first, God says, a person must long for and seek after wisdom in order to find it. Wisdom doesn't just happen. It requires diligent searching and effort. This text compares wisdom to a hidden treasure that is desperately yearned for and sought out fervently. The person who has that desire for wisdom will surely find it. The second principle in this chapter concerning the gaining of wisdom is that not only must it be sought for, but it must be sought for in the right place. One who is searching for hidden treasure will never find it unless he searches in the right location. Likewise, one can search for wisdom for a lifetime and never find it unless he looks to God, for true wisdom can only be found in him. He is the source and the giver of wisdom. Therefore, if one desires wisdom, he must go to God in search of it. As the New Testament instructs us: "If any of you lacks wisdom, let him ask God, who gives generously to all without reproach, and it will be given him" (James 1:5). Blessed is the person who desires wisdom and who goes to God in search of it.

Where do people in our world often search for wisdom? Why?

DON'T FORGET TO PRAY AND HAVE A GREAT DAY!

DAY 249

 Today's Reading:
Proverbs 3:1-35

As humans, we take a great deal of pride in being self-sufficient. As we gain more and more understanding of our world and lives, we also gain more and more confidence in our ability to control our circumstances and know the paths that we ought to take in this world. We make choices and decisions with great confidence that we are doing the very best thing for ourselves and for the goals that we are trying to achieve. However, the truth of the matter is that we know very little about our own lives. We have some understanding of our past, even less knowledge of our present, and almost no understanding of what our future holds. Isn't it wonderful, then, that we have a God who has a perfect knowledge and understanding of every minute detail of our past, present, and, yes, even our future. He knows us and our lives inside and out. Therefore, we are encouraged to trust him with our lives instead of leaning on our own very limited understanding. He can guide our paths much better than we ever could. The challenge for us is found in giving up control—following his guidance even when it runs counter to what our own desires or human wisdom tells us is the best way to go. It is difficult for us to let go of our own will and submit to God's instead. So, how do we achieve it? It starts with recognizing God's perfect wisdom and our own lack of understanding. Then we must give ourselves to his will and trust him to lead us in the right way.

Why is it so difficult for us to let go of our own understanding and trust God completely?

DON'T FORGET TO PRAY AND HAVE A GREAT DAY!

DAY 250

Today's Reading:
Proverbs 4:1-27

From a medical point of view, every organ and system is important to the proper functioning of our bodies but some are given more priority than others. Among the most critical of those organs is the heart. Its role of pumping and circulating blood throughout the body is so essential to life that it is given the utmost of attention and care by healthcare professionals. The spiritual life is no different. The spiritual heart is that part of us that reflects our love, devotion, and commitment. It is the heart that will determine what things, people, or activities will be of highest priority to us, and the heart will ultimately choose the paths that we travel through life. Thus, we are told in this chapter to guard our hearts, to "keep" them "with all vigilance." We are to watch over them, to protect them from undue influences and harmful attitudes, to keep them from the evils of the world, and to guard against the desires and temptations of the flesh. So often, it seems that we are content to be exposed to all sorts of sinful activities and ungodly behavior, confident that we can keep those things from finding a place in our own lives. However, if we continue to allow those influences into our hearts, it is inevitable that they will find their way into our lives, for the life flows out of the heart. The bottom line is that our relationship with God, maintained by a faithful and godly life, must be more important to us than any thing, person, or activity in this world. If it is, then we will protect the heart so that nothing is allowed to come into it that can hinder our walk with God.

What kinds of things can we do to help protect our spiritual heart?

DON'T FORGET TO PRAY AND HAVE A GREAT DAY!

Day 251

 Today's Reading:
Proverbs 5:1-23

Chapter 5 introduces us to one of two women who will play a central role in the teaching of the Proverbs. Later on, wisdom will be personified as a beautiful and virtuous woman to be valued and loved. But first, we are introduced to the adulteress who will represent to us the many enticing, yet destructive, ways of the world. While this chapter has much to teach us about the dangers and evils of adultery, its precepts reach beyond that one situation to speak to a broad range of actions. As those who have accepted the covenant of Christ, we have committed our lives and faithfulness to God. But, there are many, many things in this world that Satan will use to attempt to entice us and lure us away from those commitments. From possessions to activities to accomplishments to relationships, there is no limit to the number of things that vie for our time, attention, affection, and commitment. Any one of those things can become the temptress that causes us to commit spiritual adultery against our God. The basic lesson of this chapter is simple: remember who you belong to and what you are committed to. Don't allow yourself to be drawn away by any of the temptations that this world might hold. Be faithful to God!

What are some of the things that are the greatest temptations in your life? What are you doing to protect yourself from those things?

DON'T FORGET TO PRAY AND HAVE A GREAT DAY!

Day 252

 **Today's Reading:
Proverbs 6:1-35**

G od is a God of love. It is, therefore, somewhat shocking to see God in the same sentence with the word "hate." In reality, however, the Scriptures tell us on several occasions that God hates, with the object of his hatred always being some form of sinfulness. The truth is that God is a holy God who hates anything that is opposed to his perfect character and nature. He is also a loving and protective Father who hates those things that separate his children from him and cause their souls to be in jeopardy. This text lists seven things that are hated by God and that are abominations in his sight. What is surprising are the types of things included in this list. If you or I were making this list, we would probably include many of the vilest, most violent, and despicable acts that we could imagine. It would be a list of the "worst of the worst" of sins, according to our thinking. While those sins would certainly be things that God hates, they are not the things that God chose to have listed in this text. Many of the things that show up here are sins that we might dismiss, thinking that they were too minor to make the cut, but maybe that's the very reason he chose them. Look at that list again (verses 16-19). A haughty look, a lying tongue, feet that are quick in running to evil, and one who sows discord, to name a few. Maybe God included these sins in order to remind us that even the "small" sins (in our eyes) are still sins, and they are hated by God. They can just as easily take us away from God and destroy us as the "big" ones. May we learn to hate the things that God hates and to always cling tightly to him!

*Why do you think that these things are specifically
mentioned as sins that God hates?*

DON'T FORGET TO PRAY AND HAVE A GREAT DAY!

DAY 253

Today's Reading:
Proverbs 7:1-27

In this chapter, the writer once again turns his attention to the luring of the adulteress. At the center of this chapter, however, is the unsuspecting young man who becomes her victim. He is described as "a young man lacking sense." He is not wise. He has not heeded the warnings of those who have tried to instruct him. He has not protected his heart, nor has he prepared himself to deal with temptation. He has wandered into the waiting arms of the temptress whose desire is to destroy him. Sadly, this scenario plays out in a multitude of ways each day in our world with unprepared and unsuspecting people who wander into the traps of Satan, only to find misery and destruction as their reward. The writer is using this foolish young man as an example to his own son, to illustrate the dangers of following in that path. He encourages him to make wisdom his constant companion so that he is protected from the advances of the temptress. We must understand that the wisdom that has been so encouraged in this great book is not simply wisdom for wisdom's sake; it is the godly wisdom that comes from drawing near to God and heeding the truth of his word—those precepts that will guide us into holiness and faithfulness and protect us from the enticements of the world around us. There are great blessings in pursuing that wisdom but also great dangers in neglecting it. May we heed the warnings of the Proverbs and seek after wisdom.

How can we heed the warnings of Scripture and avoid foolish ways?

DON'T FORGET TO PRAY AND HAVE A GREAT DAY!

DAY 254

Today's Reading:
Proverbs 8:1-36

Most of this chapter is spoken in the voice of wisdom herself, proclaiming her excellence and value and urging anyone who desires to know God to seek after her. To demonstrate her worth, she points out that she was in existence as the companion of God before the creation of the world and was witness to all of his marvelous works as he brought this world into being. She resides in the mind of God but is available to all who desire and seek after her. Moreover, she cries out to men that they might pursue her and find the priceless treasure that she offers. What is that treasure? It is the priceless understanding that is gained by the one who finds wisdom. Wisdom teaches us what is right and acceptable to God. She leads us in those paths that draw near to God. She warns us of the dangers of evil and directs us away from abominable things. Because of all that she is and all that she does in the lives of those who find her, wisdom is a vital and invaluable possession. Without her, we cannot hope to avoid the pitfalls of life and be perpetually faithful to God. But for those who love wisdom, heed her instruction, and keep her ever close, theirs is a life filled with the rich blessings of God. May we long for the wisdom that comes from God and constantly strive to find her.

What is it about wisdom that allows us to stay close to God?

DON'T FORGET TO PRAY AND HAVE A GREAT DAY!

Day 255

 Today's Reading:
Proverbs 9:1-18

It seems that life often comes down to a choice between two very different paths. In the Sermon on the Mount, Jesus describes two ways in life—a wide gate and easy way that leads to destruction or a narrow gate and hard way that leads to life (see Matthew 6:13-14). Today's chapter of Proverbs offers a similar contrast—that of the way of wisdom with the way of foolishness. Walking in the way of wisdom provides instruction, insight, and prudence for one's life. It lengthens his days and brings honor and joy to his life. Wisdom is described as a virtuous woman who seeks to do good and provide blessings for those who pass by her. She implores with them to leave their simple and ignorant ways and to receive her wise counsel. In contrast, the way of the foolish is also described as a woman—this one arrogant and obnoxious—giving wayward advice and deceiving those who pass by her door. Unlike the way of wisdom, the way of foolishness has nothing to offer but suffering and death. There are two ways—the way of wisdom and the way of foolishness. Which will we choose? If we choose the way of wisdom, we must remember that, as has been pointed out time and time again throughout the book of Proverbs, true wisdom is from God and begins with a healthy and reverent fear of him. May we always choose the way of wisdom!

What is involved in choosing the way of wisdom?

DON'T FORGET TO PRAY AND HAVE A GREAT DAY!

Day 256

 Today's Reading:
Proverbs 10:1-32

This chapter begins a section that is headed as "The proverbs of Solomon." Solomon was a man of great wisdom, divinely endowed by God. He is said to have spoken some 3,000 proverbs (1 Kings 4:32), only a fraction of which have been preserved for us. These proverbs are succinct statements that reflect a general truth and that are intended to point the reader in the way of wisdom, integrity, and righteousness. In this chapter, the proverbs are typically two line statements that reveal a contrast between good and evil or between wisdom and folly. It is amazing to consider that despite the thousands of years that have passed since these proverbs were uttered they are still incredibly accurate and relevant to our world today. What a testament to the power and wisdom of God, spoken through his servant Solomon! As you read through the proverbs in this and subsequent chapters, let me encourage you to take the time to stop and consider the message of these wise sayings. Listen to their instruction, meditate on their meaning, and allow them to be applied to your life. As this very chapter reminds us, "The wise lay up knowledge" (verse 14) and "whoever heeds instruction is on the path to life" (verse 17). May we give earnest heed to the words of God, and may we be blessed by the wisdom of the proverbs.

Which of the proverbs of this chapter do you find to be most interesting? Why?

DON'T FORGET TO PRAY AND HAVE A GREAT DAY!

Day 257

 Today's Reading:
Proverbs 11:1-31

Sprinkled throughout this chapter's proverbs are many that give wise instruction with regard to the proper attitude toward worldly things. We live in a world that is obsessed with riches and possessions, and I suppose that the world has always been that way to some extent. We love things and often devote our lives to accumulating those things that the world tells us will bring joy, fulfillment, and meaning to our lives. At times, some will even resort to dishonest, unethical, and illegal practices in order to gain more of this world's things. But these proverbs teach us that the righteous are not so in their desires or their actions. In their character, they are humble, upright, and full of integrity. In their attitudes toward worldly things, they are content, generous, and spiritually minded. In their business dealings, they are honest, fair, and kind. Essentially, these wise sayings remind us that for those who are righteous and wise in a godly way, their good character and relationship with God are of greater priority than any amount of riches or worldly possessions. Truly, one of the great challenges of being children of God is to have a proper attitude toward the things of this world and not allow our hearts to be drawn away by our physical desires. May God help us to be strong and wise in always valuing the spiritual over the physical.

What can we do to make sure that our physical desires do not overtake us?

DON'T FORGET TO PRAY AND HAVE A GREAT DAY!

Day 258

 Today's Reading:
Proverbs 12:1-28

A s with the last chapter, there is a predominant focus that seems to emerge in this grouping of proverbs. In this case, it is in giving wise instruction with regard to the relationships that fill our lives. Whether it is with a spouse, a business associate, a friend, or a neighbor, the relationships that occupy our lives are vital to our physical happiness and fulfillment. For that reason, the attitudes and actions with which we carry on those relationships are very important. The wise and righteous person who heeds the instructions of God in the proverbs and throughout the Bible will treat those around him with kindness, love, and respect. He will deal fairly with all and with concern for the well-being and needs of others. In contrast, the foolish person—the one who does not seek or heed God's instruction—will have little concern for the feelings or needs of others and will treat them with disregard. As I read these proverbs, I am reminded of Jesus' teaching: "So, whatever you wish that others would do to you, do also to them, for this is the Law and the Prophets" (Matthew 7:12). We call this statement "the Golden Rule," and it is a very simple rule of thumb with regard to our earthly relationships. How much better and happier would this world be if we would all simply follow this one precept? While much of the world may never come over to this way of thinking, we, as God's children, should certainly be examples to the world of what God desires for our earthly relationships.

How would our world be changed if everyone would obey the golden rule?

DON'T FORGET TO PRAY AND HAVE A GREAT DAY!

DAY 259

 Today's Reading:
Proverbs 13:1-25

A mong the many wise teachings on various subjects in this chapter, there are several statements made about the words of the mouth. The things that we say certainly have a great impact on our relationships and on the way that we are viewed by those around us. They also have a powerful influence on our relationship with God. Looking at the world around us, we can see the negative and hurtful results of the shameful, deceitful, and derogatory language that often characterizes the lives of people. Those words damage relationships, destroy trust, and diminish the respect with which they are viewed. The New Testament warns us of the great challenge of controlling the tongue (see James 3:1-12), and it is certainly one of the most difficult battles that we face in our physical bodies. However, the vital importance of our words becomes clear when we consider that there may be no more obvious or easily perceived measure of our character than the words that we use. By our words, our hearts, minds, motives, and desires are often made clearly visible to those around us, either confirming or betraying the relationship with Christ that we claim as Christians. May we apply the wisdom of God to our words and be diligent in controlling our tongues.

Why do you think that the tongue is so difficult to control?
What are some things that we can do to help us control our words?

DON'T FORGET TO PRAY AND HAVE A GREAT DAY!

Day 260

Today's Reading:
Proverbs 14:1-35

As with the last chapter, there is a predominant focus that seems to emerge in this grouping of proverbs. In this case, it is in giving wise instruction with regard to the relationships that fill our lives. Whether it is with a spouse, a business associate, a friend, or a neighbor, the relationships that occupy our lives are vital to our physical happiness and fulfillment. For that reason, the attitudes and actions with which we carry on those relationships are very important. The wise and righteous person who heeds the instructions of God in the proverbs and throughout the Bible will treat those around him with kindness, love, and respect. He will deal fairly with all and with concern for the well-being and needs of others. In contrast, the foolish person—the one who does not seek or heed God's instruction—will have little concern for the feelings or needs of others and will treat them with disregard. As I read these proverbs, I am reminded of Jesus' teaching: "So, whatever you wish that others would do to you, do also to them, for this is the Law and the Prophets" (Matthew 7:12). We call this statement "the Golden Rule," and it is a very simple rule of thumb with regard to our earthly relationships. How much better and happier would this world be if we would all simply follow this one precept? While much of the world may never come over to this way of thinking, we, as God's children, should certainly be examples to the world of what God desires for our earthly relationships.

Why do you think that we are so often guilty of acting too quickly?

DON'T FORGET TO PRAY AND HAVE A GREAT DAY!

DAY 261

 **Today's Reading:**
Proverbs 15:1-33

As we continue to consider the proverbs of Solomon, it occurs to me that so many of the wise sayings of this great book are not only beneficial to our spiritual lives but also to our physical lives. God, through the wisdom of Solomon, teaches us how to have better relationships, how to be happier and more successful in life, and how to avoid many of the pitfalls of the world. But beyond the specific nuggets of helpful wisdom that we gain from the proverbs, we learn something important about God. While our spiritual well-being and salvation are most important to God, he is concerned for the well-being of our physical lives as well. His ways are not meant to make our lives harder or less enjoyable. Rather, they are intended to enhance our experience in this world. God, who created us and this world, knows best what we need and how we need to conduct ourselves in order to live lives of peace, happiness, and fulfillment. So often, we want to follow our own thinking and the ideas of the world in striving to find fulfillment in life, but discover that those ways only lead to hardship and frustration. Faithfulness to God, righteous living, humility, self-control—these are the kinds of things that allow us to be happy and at peace in this world, and they are some of the things that God continually instructs us in through the proverbs. May God help us to understand that his ways are always best!

How can following God's guidance improve our physical lives?

DON'T FORGET TO PRAY AND HAVE A GREAT DAY!

Day 262

 Today's Reading:
Proverbs 16:1-33

As humans, we spend a great deal of time discussing, debating, and arguing about who is right and who is wrong on any given subject in such areas as science, politics, economics, business, and, yes, religion. We judge one's opinion, argument, or philosophy on the merit of its supporting evidence, its logical thinking, or, often, its agreement with our own ideas. Then, of course, there are those among us who claim superior knowledge, experience, or authority on certain subjects and who proclaim adamantly that their position is the correct one. All of this has led to a great deal of confusion and disagreement in our world today, causing some to conclude that there may not even be any such thing as absolute right or wrong. However, a clear-cut truth that is echoed over and over again in the proverbs of this chapter is that when all is said and done, and regardless of what man's opinion might be, God is the sovereign God who, alone, has all authority to determine and delegate truth. Ours is not to dictate right and wrong for ourselves, but rather to humble ourselves before God and allow his word to reign in our hearts and lives. Whatever we may choose to believe in this life, we must understand that God will ultimately judge us according to his perfect standard. May we, therefore, seek the wisdom that comes from God and devote our lives to his faithful service.

Can you think of some subjects in our world in which there is much debate over what is right and wrong? Has God spoken on those subjects? If so, what does he say about them?

DON'T FORGET TO PRAY AND HAVE A GREAT DAY!

Day 263

 **Today's Reading:
Proverbs 17:1-28**

One of the great principles that is repeated over and over again in many different ways throughout Proverbs is the idea that every choice, decision, and action has a consequence, either positive or negative. Those who practice wisdom, prudence, kindness, and humility in this life will reap the rewards of those attributes in many different ways, both physically and spiritually. Likewise, those who are ruthless, contentious, foolish, or greedy in their attitudes will suffer the negative effects of their actions. The New Testament phrases the same principle in this way: "whatever one sows, that will he also reap" (Galatians 6:7). So often in life, people are thoughtless with their words and careless with their actions. They abuse their bodies, take their relationships for granted, and neglect their souls. Then, when they find their lives in chaos and filled with undesirable circumstances, they become resentful and frustrated, wondering why God is not blessing them. The truth of the matter is that they are simply experiencing the natural consequences of a life lived apart from God's guidance and instruction. Conversely, while a life lived by godly precepts will not be a perfect life free from any hardship or trouble, it will be one that is full of the blessings of God and of the positive effects of a life well lived. Thank God for his loving guidance!

*What are some of the positive effects that come
from a life lived according to God's guidance?*

DON'T FORGET TO PRAY AND HAVE A GREAT DAY!

Day 264

 Today's Reading:
Proverbs 18:1-24

One of the greatest blessings that we have in life is the blessing of friendship. We alone, among God's created beings in this physical world, have the ability to selflessly love others. What a lonely world this would be if we each lived in isolation, having no concern for others and no one to care for us. But God, in his wonderful love and infinite wisdom, knew that we needed companionship and, thus, designed and created us with the capacity to give and receive love. Friendship is certainly a wonderful gift, and not one to be taken for granted. This chapter's collection of proverbs ends with this one: "A man of many companions may come to ruin, but there is a friend who sticks closer than a brother." In a world where "friend" has come to mean anyone that shows up on our social media newsfeed, God reminds us that not all friendships are equal. Though we may have a great many acquaintances and people that we might call friends, there are certainly a select few that belong in a different category. No doubt, we can all think of those special people in our lives who we trust completely and who have proven, through many trials, that they are true friends and always have our best interests at heart. What a blessing those special friends are to us. While I do not believe that this proverb is telling us that we should not be friendly and kind to all people, it is certainly reminding us that there are very special people in our lives that we should thank God for and treasure as friends.

Who are the special relationships in your life?
Have you told them lately how much you love and appreciate them?

DON'T FORGET TO PRAY AND HAVE A GREAT DAY!

Day 265

 **Today's Reading:
Proverbs 19:1-29**

You know them—those people who seem to live life "by the seat of their pants," who never seem to give much thought or planning to the future, and who are often careless in the way that they go about their daily tasks. They might make a lot of mistakes and find themselves apologizing often for their miscues, but they take it all with a grain of salt and never seem to heed the lessons that their mistakes offer to teach them. They are not usually interested in advice or listening to the wise counsel of others, preferring to live by their own rules. I must admit that I am sometimes a little envious of those people and their nonchalant view of life and wish that I could be just a little more that way. While there may certainly be some advantages to such a care-free attitude, God also warns us that there is great danger involved in living life carelessly and without thought. For almost three weeks now, we have listened to the constant imploring of the Proverbs to seek wisdom and instruction from God, with the accompanying warnings of rejecting those things. In this chapter, we read, "Desire without knowledge is not good, and whoever makes haste with his feet misses his way." It is important and vital to a good and godly life that we carefully consider our ways and value wisdom in our lives. May God help us to do just that!

*What are some of the benefits of being careful
with the choices and decisions of our lives?*

DON'T FORGET TO PRAY AND HAVE A GREAT DAY!

Day 266

 Today's Reading:
Proverbs 20:1-30

Often, as we read through the Proverbs, we focus on our outward actions and appearances—the things that we should or should not do or say. However, many of these wise sayings are actually aimed at the inward part of us that motivates our actions. The word "integrity" is mentioned in this chapter's proverbs as an important quality of the wise and righteous life. Integrity can be understood as having the strength of moral character to act upon the wisdom that we learn from God. It is certainly good and commendable to read and learn from the precepts of God's word, but that wisdom makes little difference unless we are willing to allow it to shape our lives and direct our paths. God desires to lead us in the paths of his righteousness and to have us be conformed into the image of his Son, but that transformation is one that must take place from the inside out. Without the inward strength that integrity provides, our efforts to abide by God's word will surely fall short as we face the pressures and temptations of the world. So, not only must we strive to apply God's wisdom to our outward lives, we must also work hard to develop the internal qualities of the heart that will keep us ever close to God and give us the strength to make good choices in any circumstance. May God help us to be people of faith, courage, and integrity!

Integrity is a trait that is often lacking in today's world.
Why do you think that is and what can be done to fix the problem?

DON'T FORGET TO PRAY AND HAVE A GREAT DAY!

Day 267

 Today's Reading:
Proverbs 21:1-31

One of the qualities that is continually praised throughout the Proverbs is that of humility, while haughtiness and arrogance are often condemned. In our world today, there are not many qualities that are as under-appreciated and looked down upon as humility. It is viewed by so many as being weak and detrimental to success, yet it is a quality that God, throughout the Bible, instructs his people to develop and nurture. Given this dichotomy of ideas, how are we to understand humility, and why is it so important to God? Humility is not to be viewed as weakness but rather as the natural result of a proper understanding of our relationship to God. Our humility recognizes his greatness and sovereignty and allows us to submit ourselves to his care and instruction. While arrogance is defiantly self-reliant, humility is thankfully dependent on the benevolent love of God. Humility also allows us to take on the role that God has called us to in this life—servant. To serve him by serving others is a large part of our calling as his children, but in order to joyfully fulfill that role, we must be willing to humbly put the needs and well-being of others above our own. Ultimately, in order to gain and benefit from the great wisdom of God, we must have a much different and better understanding of humility than the world has and daily strive to be humble toward God and in our interactions with those around us.

Why do you think that humility is so often looked down on in our world?

DON'T FORGET TO PRAY AND HAVE A GREAT DAY!

Day 268

 Today's Reading:
Proverbs 22:1-29

The wise sayings of each of these chapters have been very diverse, speaking to many different aspects of our lives. This chapter is no different, and while it is impossible in the few words here to consider or apply every proverb, there is often a statement that stands out as particularly poignant in our day and time and, thus, demands our attention. In verse 2 of this chapter, we read: "The rich and the poor meet together; The Lord is the maker of them all." This proverb is reminding us that when all is said and done, we are all the same and have the same maker in God. There is so much division, hatred, and violence in our world today over things such as skin color, ethnicity, language, political party, social status, occupation, and the list goes on and on. We fight and war and do harm to one another based, in many cases, on nothing more than physical appearance. When will we learn that we all have a common origin and were made by the same God? Even if someone looks differently than I do or holds to an ideology that differs from mine, we are all on a common journey through this world and deserve one another's respect and kindness. That is the example that Christ gave to us during his life and the challenge that is set before each of us. May we have the wisdom to look past our differences and see each other as God sees us.

Why do you think that physical appearance
is such a dividing force in our world?

DON'T FORGET TO PRAY AND HAVE A GREAT DAY!

Day 269

Today's Reading:
Proverbs 23:1-35

A s I read through this chapter, and through all of the Proverbs, one of the most striking things to me is how opposed the wisdom of God is to the thinking of the world. Over and over again, we read these wise sayings and realize that God's guidance leads us in a very different direction than the world is often going. Consider just a few examples: The world tells us to work as hard as it takes and put in as many hours as necessary to acquire wealth, but God says, "Do not toil to acquire wealth," understanding that physical things are fleeting. The world says that to discipline a child is abusive and unloving, but God says, "Do not withhold discipline from a child," knowing the importance of proper training. The world says to admire and strive to be like those who enjoy life the most, even if their lifestyles are immoral, but God says, "Let not your heart envy sinners" but rather fear the Lord. The world says that we should embrace and partake of those substances that will lessen our inhibitions and enhance our enjoyment of life, but God says, "Do not look at wine when it is red, when it sparkles in the cup and goes down smoothly," knowing the danger of its effect on our spiritual and physical lives. A consideration of the wisdom of God in the Proverbs quickly shows us how far our world has drifted from God and his perfect will for us. As our Father, his desire is to protect us and lead us in the right way, but we must be willing to listen and follow. May we choose God over the world!

Why do you think the world's way is often so different from God's way?

DON'T FORGET TO PRAY AND HAVE A GREAT DAY!

DAY 270

Today's Reading:
Proverbs 24:1-34

The continuity of the Bible is a beautiful and powerful testament to its divine origin. Just as God is unchanging, so is his wisdom always the same, relevant and perfect for any period of time. We are well aware of Jesus' teaching in the New Testament that we refer to as the golden rule: "So whatever you wish that others would do to you, do also to them, for this is the Law and the Prophets." The Master Teacher teaches us to deny the fleshly desire to repay evil for evil but rather to treat others as we desire to be treated. While this is certainly a precept worthy of our attention and adherence, it is not the first time that God had revealed this piece of wisdom to mankind. Over a thousand years earlier through the wise man, God had instructed those who desired to follow wisdom with these words: "Do not say, "I will do to him as he has done to me; I will pay the man back for what he has done." As strong as the urge might sometimes be for us to get revenge on those who do harm to us in some way, and while the world might tell us that that way is understandable and acceptable, God reminds us that vengeance is not the way of the wise but of the fool. Again, we are reminded that God's way is the right way and that true wisdom is always found in him.

What things can we do to help us to treat others as we want to be treated?

DON'T FORGET TO PRAY AND HAVE A GREAT DAY!

DAY 271

Today's Reading:
Proverbs 25:1-28

If we were to assign a theme to this chapter's collection of wise sayings, that theme might well be "Self-Control" for much of what is discussed in this text has to do with that noble and godly concept. Self-control is a virtue that seems to be out of vogue in today's world where we are more likely to be encouraged to pursue life with reckless abandon—say whatever you think; do whatever you want; don't hold back; and don't let anyone or anything get in the way. Yet, in stark contrast to that way of thinking, God urges us to consider carefully our words and actions and to practice self-control in all things—think before you speak; consider the consequences of your actions before taking them; control your urges instead of being controlled by them. The New Testament echoes these same sentiments with statements such as "let every person be quick to hear, slow to speak, slow to anger" (James 1:19) and "test everything; hold fast what is good. Abstain from every form of evil" (1 Thessalonians 5:21-22). Imagine how much violence and tragedy could be avoided in this world, and how much heartache could be spared, if we would only learn to follow these simple precepts. As I consider these things, I am reminded that God is a good God who, like a loving Father, desires to guide us in good and righteous paths for our own sake. May we heed his instruction and follow him.

What are some things that we can do to grow in the area of self-control?

DON'T FORGET TO PRAY AND HAVE A GREAT DAY!

Day 272

 Today's Reading:
Proverbs 26:1-28

This chapter is possibly one of the most negative groupings of proverbs as it is entirely devoted to revealing three attributes that wisdom demands be avoided. The first of these attributes is foolishness—the mindset that refuses to seek or heed the word of wisdom. There is no integrity or honor with the fool, and one must avoid attitudes of foolishness as well as companionship with fools. Secondly, the wise man exhorts us to avoid laziness. In working to support our families, in fulfilling the responsibilities of each day, and certainly in rendering service to God, the wise man is one who is industrious, dependable, and one who follows the Bible's instruction: "Whatever your hand finds to do, do it with your might" (Ecclesiastes 9:10). Finally, the deceptive and hate-filled tongue must be avoided. There is certainly no place in the lives of those who fear God for words of dishonesty and deceit. These three attributes are among those that can hinder our relationship with God, bring hardship and grief to our physical lives, and rob us of the blessings of godly wisdom. In this chapter, we are reminded that wisdom is found not only in doing those things that are in keeping with God's will, but also in avoiding those things that separate us from him. May we continually pursue wisdom!

Are there negative things that you need to work on avoiding in your life?
If so, what can you do to help you improve in those areas?

DON'T FORGET TO PRAY AND HAVE A GREAT DAY!

Day 273

 **Today's Reading:
Proverbs 27:1-27**

T his chapter is so filled with powerful truths about life that it is difficult
to choose one to focus on in this thought. I hope that, if you have time,
you will read the chapter again after considering the thought, and read it
slowly and purposefully, meditating on the wisdom of God contained in
it. More than giving instructions for a good life, this chapter focuses on
statements that help us to understand our lives by comparing situations
in life with things that we know and understand in the world. In so doing,
God helps us to consider and understand facets of our lives that we may
have never thought about before in ways that are both enlightening and
instructive. As you read through the Proverbs, be reminded that there is
no aspect of this world or of human life that God, the designer and creator
of both, does not understand perfectly. His wisdom is complete, and his
guidance is flawless. Oh, what a wonderful opportunity God gives us,
through the Proverbs, to gain knowledge and understanding that will aid
us in making wise choices and decisions, enriching our physical lives and
fortifying our spiritual lives. Our challenge is simply to give attention to his
instruction and allow his wisdom to shape our thinking and our lives. May
God bless us as we seek him!

*Which statements in this chapter were particularly meaningful to you?
What did you learn from them?*

DON'T FORGET TO PRAY AND HAVE A GREAT DAY!

DAY 274

Today's Reading:
Proverbs 28:1-28

Many of the contrasting couplets of this chapter seem to be concerned with man's attitude toward riches. It seems that there has always been a great temptation for men to chase after riches, believing them to be the key to happiness and fulfillment in life. Yet, in striving after worldly things, many find only an insatiable desire that ultimately leads to misery and discontentment. In their greed, some even resort to acts of dishonesty and treachery. As the New Testament reminds us, "the love of money is a root of all kinds of evil" (1 Timothy 6:10). Unfortunately, it seems that all too often God's warnings go unheeded and many are carried away and lost because of an unholy love of riches. On the other hand, God reminds us that a proper attitude toward riches is possible and leads to a full and happy life. While physical things are certainly necessary in this life and are, in most cases, not evil in and of themselves, we must be able to maintain a proper view of them. Self-control, contentment, honesty, and generosity are all important virtues to have when it comes to our possessions. And, of course, we must never place physical things in a position of importance above God and our relationship with him. After all, the spiritual blessings to be found in God are infinitely more important and valuable than anything that this physical world has to offer.

What attributes are needed in order to maintain
a proper attitude toward worldly things?

DON'T FORGET TO PRAY AND HAVE A GREAT DAY!

Day 275

Today's Reading:
Proverbs 29:1-27

A s I read the words of these proverbs, I am struck by how relevant they are for our time. So much of the violence, wrath, and hatred that is so prevalent in our world today could be avoided if we would only heed the wisdom of God as revealed in this text. Fairness, compassion, discipline and self-control—all of these virtues are exalted in today's reading while attitudes of lawlessness, dishonesty, and lack of restraint are condemned. What we are seeing in our world today is simply the effects of a world that has stopped listening to the wisdom of God and has decided that he has no place in their lives. We have chosen to live by our own rules, or worse yet, no rules at all, and the results have been disastrous. We need look no further than the daily news to understand that we desperately need God and his guidance. But there is hope, for God is a patient and merciful God who has revealed and preserved his wisdom for us in the pages of his word and who continues to give us time and opportunity to return to him. No amount of protesting, legislation, or political posturing is going to fix the condition of our world. Only our return to God can do that. In our striving to shine as lights in a very dark world, may God give us wisdom to seek his ways, courage to stand for right, and faith to always follow him no matter what.

What can you do to make the world a better place today?

DON'T FORGET TO PRAY AND HAVE A GREAT DAY!

Day 276

Today's Reading:
Proverbs 30:1-33

In the world that we live in, it is so easy to become infatuated with the desire for and striving after money and material things. "If I only had a little more," we think, "then my life would be so much easier and happier." So we work longer and harder, sacrifice more, spend more, and accumulate more, and in the process, we neglect our families, ignore our faith, and maybe even forfeit our integrity. But the end of that long and difficult road so often finds us still wanting more and suffering the consequences of many negative choices in our pursuit of riches. As with all things, God's way is best, and he warns us time and time again about the danger of falling into the trap of chasing after physical things. For instance, Jesus warns us that we cannot serve both God and riches, for one will always win out over the other in the vying for our devotion (see Matthew 6:24). Paul reiterates that same truth with these words: "For the love of money is a root of all kinds of evil. It is through this craving that some have wandered away from the faith and pierced themselves with many pangs" (1 Timothy 6:10). So, where does that leave those who desire to be faithful to God but who live in a world that necessitates the acquiring and using of material things? No doubt, the answer can be found in the prayerful desire of the wise man: "Give me neither poverty nor riches; feed me with the food that is needful for me, lest I be full and deny you and say, 'Who is the LORD?' or lest I be poor and steal and profane the name of my God."

Why do you think that it is such a challenge to maintain a proper attitude toward physical things? What can we, as Christians, do to help us to meet this challenge?

DON'T FORGET TO PRAY AND HAVE A GREAT DAY!

Day 277

 **Today's Reading:
Proverbs 31:1-31**

The final chapter of the Proverbs is well-known for its beautiful tribute to the excellent wife. Wise, caring, industrious, and hard-working—this woman is whole-heartedly committed to the good and well-being of her husband and children. With no thought for herself, she labors diligently to make sure that they are clothed, fed, and cared for in every way. Most importantly, she is a woman who fears the Lord and puts her trust in him. She is certainly worthy of the honor and praise given to her in this tribute. Most of us have such a special lady in our lives—maybe a wife, a mother, a grandmother, or some other special person that filled that role for us. Oh, what a debt of gratitude we owe to them! With only the reward of knowing that our needs are met and that we are safe and satisfied, they work tirelessly to make a home and to provide for us. They never seek accolades and do not desire praise. Always willing to sacrifice their own desires in order to fulfill ours, they contribute far more to our success than most of us are willing to admit. And in the midst of all of their working and providing, they somehow manage to show us what it means to truly love God and to be devoted to him above all else. These wonderful women are truly a bright and shining light in our lives, and as the text says, may we "give her of the fruit of her hands, and let her works praise her in the gates."

Is there a special lady who fills that role in your life?
What can you do today to let her know that you love and appreciate her?

DON'T FORGET TO PRAY AND HAVE A GREAT DAY!

DAY 278

 Today's Reading:
Ecclesiastes 1:1-18

Vanity—the word means empty, useless, without value. It is the key word of the book of Ecclesiastes as Solomon, its writer, declares over and over again: "All is vanity!" This book has been called the most depressing of all the Biblical books, and it very well may be, at least until the very end. Nonetheless, it is full of valuable truths and teachings that have the ability to bless our lives and to strengthen our resolve to live for God. It gives us the rare opportunity to learn from a man who was endowed by God with the gift of wisdom and who has learned many difficult lessons from the mistakes and unwise choices that he has made. As Solomon looks back over a life that was unmatched in worldly achievement, riches, or glory, he is made painfully aware that all of that labor and all of those accomplishments have no lasting value beyond this life. Possessions, honor, wisdom—they are nothing more than a part of the cycle of life and will all fade away with the passing of our lives. What is to be gained by this revelation? Simply the understanding that this physical life with all of its pursuits is temporary and cannot endure, but with that understanding comes a great appreciation of the fact that God has given us more than just this physical life. As his children, we have the wonderful blessing of pursuing a spiritual life and home that has no end. So, while this life might be vanity, thank God that our life in Christ certainly is not!

Why do you think that we place so much emphasis
and energy into the temporary things of this world?

DON'T FORGET TO PRAY AND HAVE A GREAT DAY!

DAY 279

Today's Reading:
Ecclesiastes 2:1-26

"Y ou only live once." It is a popular saying that is often used to justify immoral or ill-advised behavior. The idea behind it is that you are only here for a little while, so you better enjoy it while you can, and it is based on the premise that the only real purpose in life is pleasure and enjoyment. For many, life is about nothing more than the experience of life itself—the adventure, enjoyment, pleasure, and excitement that can be gained during one's journey through this world. As Solomon wrote, "there is nothing new under the sun," and the pursuit of pleasure is certainly no exception. In fact, the first place that Solomon says that he looked for purpose in life was pleasure. He surrounded himself with all of the riches, women, servants, extravagances, and beautiful things that the world had to offer. There was nothing that Solomon deprived himself of in an effort to experience all the pleasure that was to be had in life. Yet, with that pleasure came the realization that there was no lasting worth to be found in any of it. The lesson here is certainly not that we should never enjoy life. God designed us to experience pleasure, and he gave us a world full of things that are beautiful and enjoyable. Within the scope of what is good and godly, there is certainly nothing wrong with enjoying life. However, Solomon's point, and the lesson to be learned, is that to devote one's entire life to pursuing pleasure to the neglect of more important and lasting things is, in his words, "a striving after the wind."

Why is the pursuit of pleasure such an attractive
and popular venture in our world today?

DON'T FORGET TO PRAY AND HAVE A GREAT DAY!

Day 280

Today's Reading:
Ecclesiastes 3:1-22

It was made popular as the subject of a hit song in the 1960's, but this passage is far more than just a catchy tune. It is a declaration of sorts on the cycle of life and on the design of God's creation. While, on one hand, we are spiritual beings with an eternal existence to prepare for after this short physical life, we are also flesh and blood, designed and created to be born and to die and, in the interim, to fulfill certain purposes in our given time. After reading the first two chapters of this book, one might be tempted to wonder what purpose there is, if any at all, in working, having relationships, pursuing goals, or enjoying life. After all, if Solomon is correct, it is all just worthless vanity and not worth the effort. But in this chapter, Solomon addresses that concern and answers the question, "what is the purpose of my physical life?" Obviously, we understand that the spiritual purpose of our lives is to seek God and to prepare for eternity, but it must also be admitted that not everything that we do in life has an overtly spiritual purpose. So, what is the purpose of all of those strictly physical tasks? Solomon's answer is that God has created this world with all of its design and functions, and God has created us to live within this world. Our physical purpose in this physical world is simply to live—to carry out the tasks that make life possible and that our circumstances call for within the design of God's creation. And remember: no task is strictly physical, for every word and action gives us the opportunity to do good and to bring glory to God. As the New Testament instructs us, "and whatever you do, in word or deed, do everything in the name of the Lord Jesus, giving thanks to God the Father through him" (Colossians 3:17).

In what ways can we use our physical lives to bring glory to God?

DON'T FORGET TO PRAY AND HAVE A GREAT DAY!

Day 281

 **Today's Reading:
Ecclesiastes 4:1-16**

O f all the physical blessings that God has provided for us in this life, few provide greater joy or comfort than the gift of companionship. God has created us with the capacity to love and to accept love from others. He has allowed us to feel emotion, to share our thoughts and feelings through language, and to share the experiences of our lives with others. Whether it be family members, friends, or fellow Christians, those with whom we share relationships in this life are precious people that occupy a very special place in our hearts. Can you imagine what life would be like if we were each forced to live in isolation from one another, with no ability to communicate and no way to share our lives? What a sad and lonely life that would be! But God is a God of love, and he has created us in his image, teaching us how to love by his own efforts to make our relationship with him possible. Our need for and desire to have companionship is yet another indication of God's great love for us. He has designed us to live in community and fellowship with one another because he wants to bless us and care for us and, as Solomon reminds us in this text, to have companionship is always better than being alone. Today, if you have relationships that you treasure, thank God for the gift of companionship, and let those special people know how thankful you are for them as well.

How has your life been enriched by the relationships that you enjoy?

DON'T FORGET TO PRAY AND HAVE A GREAT DAY!

DAY 282

 Today's Reading:
Ecclesiastes 5:1-20

"There is a grievous evil that I have seen under the sun." It is a sentiment that Solomon will express several times throughout the writing of this book. In this case, that evil is the love of riches and wealth. As one who had accumulated greater riches than any other king of his day (see 1 Kings 10:23), Solomon knew a thing or two about riches, and he had, no doubt, seen some of the negative effects that a love and desire for riches could have on men. Whether in Solomon's days or our own, there is little that can bring out the ugliness in humanity more than the striving after and desire for wealth. That lust for things can cause us to neglect our families, despise our friends, sacrifice our character, and reject our God. And, as Solomon so wisely observes, the most dangerous and deadly aspect of this lust for riches is that it is a lust that can never be satisfied. The more wealth we obtain, the more we desire, and, oh, how true that great irony is in our world today. So, what is the solution to this "grievous evil?" Solomon's advice is to simply enjoy the gifts that God has given you, whether they be many or few. Whatever you have been blessed with, use it to God's glory and be happy and content. What a wonderful goal for us to strive for in our attitude toward our physical things.

Why do you think that contentment is such a challenge for us?

DON'T FORGET TO PRAY AND HAVE A GREAT DAY!

Day 283

 **Today's Reading:**
Ecclesiastes 6:1-12

In this chapter, Solomon continues in the same vein as yesterday's reading. What vanity it is for a person to labor and toil his whole life in order to obtain and store up riches and never stop to enjoy the great blessings that God has provided. Though written thousands of years ago, these words perfectly describe the lives of so many in our own time who devote the entirety of their lives to earning wealth, achievements, and honor only to discover, at the end of their lives, that they have failed to find any real meaning or joy in life. The truth that Solomon is attempting to enlighten us on in this text is that all of the labor and toil that we put into this life is really only for the purpose of providing those things that are necessary for our survival. Anything that we achieve beyond that will have no lasting value but will ultimately pass away with us. Solomon is not necessarily saying that we should not be ambitious or strive for great things in this life; he is simply reminding us that there are things which are much more important than those physical achievements. While there may be joy and fulfillment to be found in worldly achievements, chasing after the physical honors and accolades of life to the neglect of the more important spiritual things is surely vanity. Though he never uses the term, Solomon is speaking to us about priorities. May we always strive to make the most important things the most important things in our lives.

What would be the first few things on your list of priorities?
Are there changes that might need to be made to that list?

DON'T FORGET TO PRAY AND HAVE A GREAT DAY!

Day 284

Today's Reading:
Ecclesiastes 7:1-29

As Solomon discusses attributes of wisdom and folly in this text, it seems to me that the main thrust of much of what he writes is concerning the danger of extremes in our attitudes and ideas. For instance, in Solomon's world and in ours, there is an extreme notion that, concerning this physical life, the righteous will never suffer, and the wicked will always be destroyed. Yet, how often do we see exactly the opposite play out in the world around us? There is wisdom to be found in understanding that suffering and blessing will occur, to some extent, in every life, regardless of its character. Also, Solomon observes that there is danger in the extreme attitude of exalting one's own righteousness while being quick to point out and condemn the flaws in others. Wisdom reminds us that we are all sinners and to unfairly judge another will only bring God's judgment upon us. To mention one other extreme that Solomon warns about in this chapter: do not praise God in prosperity and curse him in adversity. Wisdom helps us to understand that both prosperity and adversity have been created and allowed by God in order to equip our lives with the spiritual growth that we need. Therefore, as Job stated in his suffering, "The Lord gave, and the Lord has taken away; blessed by the name of the Lord" (Job 1:21). May God bless us with wisdom and help us to avoid these dangerous extremes in our lives.

*Why do you think that we are prone to extremes in our thinking
and attitudes? How can we keep those tendencies in check?*

DON'T FORGET TO PRAY AND HAVE A GREAT DAY!

DAY 285

Today's Reading:
Ecclesiastes 8:1-17

E ven with all of his God-given wisdom, Solomon was wise enough to understand that human wisdom has its limits. Though we question and search and desire to know the ways of God, they are beyond our intellectual reach. An evil man is not punished but seems to flourish while a righteous man suffers. We ask why and look for answers, but find none. We struggle to find meaning but cannot. In his striving to gain knowledge of God's work in this world, Solomon was left to concede that God's ways were above his own and beyond his ability to understand. It is the same lesson that God sought to reveal to Job through his suffering—there are times in our lives when we simply cannot understand the purposes or ways of God. Ours is not to understand but rather to simply trust in his perfect wisdom and will. However, in order to trust him, we must know him, and to know him is certainly within our ability because God has revealed himself to us. To know God is to know that he loves us completely and unconditionally and to know of his love instills within us a perfect trust in him to care for us in the way that is best. What peace there is, even in the midst of circumstances that we can't understand, because of the constant care of a loving God!

Why do we struggle with our inability
to completely understand God and our world?

DON'T FORGET TO PRAY AND HAVE A GREAT DAY!

DAY 286

Today's Reading:
Ecclesiastes 9:1-18

One of the great, if largely unappreciated truths revealed over and over again throughout the book of Ecclesiastes is that death is an appointment that all must make. Rich and poor, wise and foolish, righteous and wicked— there is no discrimination with death. Despite the fact that this truth is abundantly clear and evident all around us, so many people continue to live as if this life, with all of its experiences and things, is all that there is. It is almost as if we believe that if we can be successful or rich enough in life, that we can avoid death. Yet, the truth of this chapter continues to show itself to be unavoidable—death comes to all. As the New Testament tells us, our lives are like "a mist that appears for a little time and then vanishes away" (James 4:14). With that grim reality established, what is Solomon's advice? Simply this: understand the blessing of life and live the life that you have been given. Enjoy the opportunities that you are given, do whatever you do to the best of your ability, treasure the love of your spouse, do good and right, and seek after wisdom. And above all, never forget that man's days are numbered. In all of your living, do not forget to prepare for your death and the judgment that will follow.

Why do you think that we struggle to come
to terms with the inevitability of death?

DON'T FORGET TO PRAY AND HAVE A GREAT DAY!

Day 287

 Today's Reading:
Ecclesiastes 10:1-20

This chapter is reminiscent of the type of instruction found in the Proverbs. Because life is short and death is inevitable, as discussed in yesterday's reading, Solomon's advice is to live a life of wisdom. Do not squander the precious time you have in this world with a life of frivolity and foolishness. In our world, as in the world of any era, folly seems to be the way of choice. It seems that our lives and worth are judged much more by our attractiveness, success, wealth, personality, or popularity, than by our character or wisdom. Yet, we are reminded often that life is difficult, full of pitfalls and obstacles, and the quality of our lives is often determined by the choices and decisions that we make in those trying moments. To avoid the dangers and overcome the hardships, we must be able to make wise choices. Therefore, wisdom is a much more valuable possession than those attributes that are often heralded in our world. So, strive for wisdom, but remember from our study of Proverbs what true wisdom is. As Solomon wrote in those wise sayings and as he will reveal at the conclusion of this writing, true wisdom and the purpose of life is none other than to fear God and walk in his ways. It is only in the pursuit of wisdom and godliness that we find real meaning in life.

What is the difference between knowledge and wisdom?
How do we gain wisdom?

DON'T FORGET TO PRAY AND HAVE A GREAT DAY!

Day 288

Today's Reading:
Ecclesiastes 11:1-10

A s with the last chapter, there is a predominant focus that seems to emerge in this grouping of proverbs. In this case, it is in giving wise instruction with regard to the relationships that fill our lives. Whether it is with a spouse, a business associate, a friend, or a neighbor, the relationships that occupy our lives are vital to our physical happiness and fulfillment. For that reason, the attitudes and actions with which we carry on those relationships are very important. The wise and righteous person who heeds the instructions of God in the proverbs and throughout the Bible will treat those around him with kindness, love, and respect. He will deal fairly with all and with concern for the well-being and needs of others. In contrast, the foolish person—the one who does not seek or heed God's instruction—will have little concern for the feelings or needs of others and will treat them with disregard. As I read these proverbs, I am reminded of Jesus' teaching: "So, whatever you wish that others would do to you, do also to them, for this is the Law and the Prophets" (Matthew 7:12). We call this statement "the Golden Rule," and it is a very simple rule of thumb with regard to our earthly relationships. How much better and happier would this world be if we would all simply follow this one precept? While much of the world may never come over to this way of thinking, we, as God's children, should certainly be examples to the world of what God desires for our earthly relationships.

What blessings are to be found in having a
God that is beyond our ability to fully comprehend?

DON'T FORGET TO PRAY AND HAVE A GREAT DAY!

Day 289

 **Today's Reading:**
Ecclesiastes 12:1-14

For most of this world's history, mankind has been searching for the answer to the question: "What is the purpose of life?" In pursuit of that discovery, many have found the truthfulness of Solomon's wisdom as revealed in the familiar words of this book, "Vanity of vanities. All is vanity!" As we began our study of Ecclesiastes, it was noted that this is often considered to be the most negative and depressing book in the Bible ...until the last chapter. Well, we have come to that final chapter, and here we find what Solomon calls "the end of the matter." When all is said and done, we find that there is one thing that is not vain, one thing that provides hope and promise, and it is in that one thing that we find the true meaning and purpose of life. That one thing, of course, is God. As always, God is the answer. If there is to be any meaning and purpose found in this life, it must be found in God. To acknowledge him with reverence and godly fear is to recognize the importance and value of the spiritual above the physical. To keep his commands is to respond to him in a way that transforms the life and saves the soul. Do you want your life to have meaning? Do you want to discover the purpose of your time in this life? Look to God for he is the answer.

Why do you think that it is often so difficult for
people to see that God is the true purpose of life?

DON'T FORGET TO PRAY AND HAVE A GREAT DAY!

Day 290

 Today's Reading:
Song of Solomon 1:1-17

The Song of Solomon, or more accurately, Song of Songs, is one of over 1,000 songs that Solomon composed. It is actually, most likely, a collection of several songs that tell a beautiful story of love and marriage. This book is probably one of the most neglected books of the Bible, largely because we struggle to understand it and fail to see its relevance and importance to our lives. There are several different theories as to the meaning of the book and who the main characters are. While all of those theories have their merits, there is one overriding truth that remains constant—this book is about pure and faithful love. God, the creator of the world and mankind, is also the creator of human love and marriage. The relationship between husband and wife is a beautiful gift from God that should be protected and treasured. In this first chapter, the Shulamite woman and her beloved express their love for one another. Though there is much imagery used that is unfamiliar to us, the passion and depth of meaning in their words comes through very clearly. She, being outwardly rough and plain from a hard life of labor, does not understand how he can be attracted to her. Yet he, seeing through the rough exterior, gazes on her inward beauty and is enamored with her. They each express their desire to be together, and thus a beautiful love story begins.

How has God's plan for love and marriage been altered by our world to-day? How can we, as Christians, remain faithful to God's original design?

DON'T FORGET TO PRAY AND HAVE A GREAT DAY!

Day 291

**Today's Reading:
Song of Solomon 6:1-13**

Though this book is largely about the beauty and holiness of wedded bliss, Solomon was certainly not a model of the godly husband. With 700 wives and 300 concubines, Solomon had defied many times over God's design for monogamous marriage, and he had allowed his relationships with these women to become a source of separation from God. There is, within the imagery of this chapter, a glimpse into the many struggles and problems that can occur when we do not follow God's prescribed design for marriage. Jealousy, bitterness, betrayal, and mistrust, along with many other negative emotions are so often the result when marriage becomes about anything other than one man and one woman fully committing themselves to one another according to God's perfect plan. Marriage is surely one of God's greatest physical blessings, but in our world, it seems to have so often lost the sense of permanence, commitment, and faithfulness that it was intended to have, and with the deterioration of that sacred institution has followed the breakdown of our society. Once again, we are confronted with the truth that God's wisdom is perfect and that his way is the best way.

What can we, as Christians, do to fortify and strengthen our marriages?

DON'T FORGET TO PRAY AND HAVE A GREAT DAY!

Day 292

Today's Reading:
Isaiah 1:1-31

During the period of Isaiah's work as a prophet, the nation of Judah was in a time of mixed devotion. On one hand, the people had continued to recognize and offer sacrifices to God, but on the other hand, they were involved with many of the false gods and abominable practices that characterized the nations around them. Seemingly, they thought it an acceptable practice to simply add Jehovah to the list of gods that they paid homage to. However, God's message to them through Isaiah was that their divided loyalties had rendered their sacrifices to Him profitless and had caused their prayers to go unheard. But God, as always, is a merciful and patient God who desires men to come to repentance rather than be destroyed. His message to Judah was that their future was in their own hands. If they were to repent of their wrongdoing and turn to him, then they would enjoy the blessings of God. But if they refused to repent and continued on their current path, they would face destruction at the hands of their enemies. While the Old Testament provides a physical example of our spiritual journey, the lessons are, nonetheless, very true and important. In our spiritual lives, our loyalties cannot be divided, and we must choose whom we will serve. May we choose God, knowing that our spiritual future depends on that choice.

How and when is the choice made as to whom we will serve?

DON'T FORGET TO PRAY AND HAVE A GREAT DAY!

Day 293

 Today's Reading:
Isaiah 5:1-30

In this chapter, Isaiah tells the story of a vineyard in order to describe the lost condition of Judah. The vineyard had been prepared, cared for, tended, and protected by the owner. The land was fertile, the vines were healthy, and everything needed for a good yield was provided. However, despite all the effort and provision of the owner, the vineyard gave forth only useless wild grapes. That vineyard, says Isaiah, represents the nation of Judah. God had planted her in the Promised Land, given her everything that she needed to thrive, watched over her, protected her, and blessed her mightily. But despite all of the advantages and blessings of God, Judah had refused to bring forth the good fruit of righteousness, faithfulness, and pure worship. Therefore, God says, the vineyard will be destroyed. God would remove his protective hand so that his people would be devoured by their enemies. Consider the application. God has provided for us all that we need from a spiritual perspective. We have the blood of Christ to cover our sins and redeem us to God. We have the inspired word of God to guide our lives and lead us in his will. We have the help and blessings of God to provide strength, hope, and peace in this world. And we have the promise of an eternal home in Heaven at the end of this life. What more could we ask for? What more could God provide? The question is, "what kind of fruit are we producing with all that God has given us?"

What kind of fruit should we be producing as God's children?

DON'T FORGET TO PRAY AND HAVE A GREAT DAY!

DAY 294

 Today's Reading:
Isaiah 6:1-13

The vision that Isaiah describes in this chapter is similar to that of the living creatures that John describes as surrounding the throne of God in the Revelation. What an incredible sight it must have been to view the majesty of God. Notice two things about Isaiah's reaction to God in this passage. First, he feels completely inadequate and unworthy in the presence of God. "Woe is me! For I am lost..." So high and holy was God that Isaiah was immediately confronted with his own sinfulness in his presence. Secondly, when God asked the question, "Whom shall I send?" Isaiah, without hesitation volunteered, "Here I am! Send me." Despite his feelings of inadequacy and shame, Isaiah was eager to serve God. What great lessons there are for us in this scene! As we consider God and as we approach him in worship and prayer, we must always remember the greatness and majesty of God and recognize our own sinfulness and unworthiness in his presence. This attitude will allow us to remain humble and to constantly be grateful for God's wonderful love and mercy. But we must also be just as eager as Isaiah was to serve God in any way possible, understanding that God has cleansed us of our sins and that he will be with us to strengthen and help us in our service to him. May we always strive to approach God with an attitude of humility and service.

What kinds of things can we do to always be ready to serve the Lord?

DON'T FORGET TO PRAY AND HAVE A GREAT DAY!

Day 295

 Today's Reading:
Isaiah 11:1-16

I saiah is often known as "the Messianic prophet," although not all of his prophecies concerned the Messiah, and he was not the only prophet to speak of the coming Christ. Nonetheless, Isaiah does write a great deal about the promise of a Redeemer, and this chapter is one of those texts. Judah was on the brink of troubling times. They would face defeat and captivity, but even while foretelling those disastrous events, God had promised to punish their enemies and deliver them. However, all of this pales in comparison to the greatest problem that Judah (and the world) faced—the problem of sin. Sin had come into the world and created an impassable gulf between God and man, and though God had implemented a plan for his people to atone for their sins, there was no permanent solution in place. But with this greatest of problems came the greatest of promises—that One would come to defeat sin once and for all and provide for the redemption of mankind. In a great demonstration of God's perfect knowledge and power and as irrefutable evidence of Christ's identity, God foretold with perfect accuracy many of the details of the Messiah's coming through prophets like Isaiah hundreds of years before the event. In a dark world given over to sin, God made the greatest promise of all, and we are all recipients of his marvelous grace.

How do the prophecies of Christ serve
as evidence to the truth of his identity?

DON'T FORGET TO PRAY AND HAVE A GREAT DAY!

Day 296

 Today's Reading:
Isaiah 25:1-12

Much of the text preceding this chapter foretold the judgment of God against the nations that had set themselves against God and his people. Though Judah had been unfaithful to God in many ways and were subject to God's punishment, they were, nonetheless, his people. As a faithful God who had claimed Judah for his own, God had promised to bring judgment upon their enemies. Chapter 25 is one of praise to God for his faithfulness and goodness toward his people in response to the foretold destruction of Judah's enemies. But beyond the physical meaning of this text, there is a deeper spiritual foreshadowing of the infinitely greater salvation that God would bring to pass through his Son. In reading the text, you probably noticed some familiar phraseology that is used in the New Testament with reference to our salvation in Christ. While the physical salvation that God provided for his people under the old covenant is certainly praiseworthy, it pales in comparison to the spiritual salvation that he has made available to all men, not from a worldly enemy but from the spiritual enemies of sin and death, through the atoning sacrifice of Christ. If you have time, read this chapter again considering it from the standpoint of your victory over sin, and give your thanks and praise to God for his faithfulness and salvation.

How do the physical attributes of God's people in the Old Testament relate to our spiritual walk with God under the covenant of Christ?

DON'T FORGET TO PRAY AND HAVE A GREAT DAY!

Day 297

 Today's Reading:
Isaiah 30:1-33

J udah faced a powerful foe in the armies of Assyria. In an effort to defend and strengthen themselves against this enemy, they formed an alliance with Egypt. From a strategic point of view, it was a move that made sense, but there was only one problem: it was a plan that did not involve God. Judah and her leaders were trusting in the human strength of the Egyptian army instead of trusting in God Almighty to be their protection. They had not consulted with God nor had they included God in their planning. Therefore, God rebuked them and foretold of their coming shame and disgrace because of their rebellion. How fitting and relevant is this rebuke for our lives today? So often, we find ourselves facing some battle in our lives and putting our trust in ourselves or in some other person or physical thing to bring us success. How can we hope to be victorious if we, like Judah of old, leave God out of our plans? As Christians, our first and greatest line of defense in any situation must be God. As we petition him through prayer and trust him through faith, we find peace and strength in knowing that the all-powerful Creator and Master of the universe is fighting for us, and while we may call on the services and talents of people and entities in this world to help in our battles, we know that it is God who is truly in control and who leads us in victory.

What can we do to make sure that our trust is in God first and foremost?

DON'T FORGET TO PRAY AND HAVE A GREAT DAY!

Day 298

 Today's Reading:
Isaiah 38:1-22

As we read of this amazing event in the life of Hezekiah, we are surely reminded of the power of prayer in our lives. What a blessing it is to know that we have a God who hears and answers our prayers! While we do not have a prophet like Isaiah to inform us of God's decisions regarding our petitions, we can so often see the hand of God at work in our lives in response to our prayerful requests. Furthermore, we can know by faith that no word is ever uttered in prayer that God does not hear and respond to. However, we must not think of God as some sort of divine fairy godfather whose job is to meet our every want and need. No, his role as our heavenly Father is to care for us and meet our needs in those ways that he knows are best and most beneficial to us. While we certainly do not have the promise that God will answer every request affirmatively, we can know without doubt that God does answer our every prayer according to his will, and God's will is, first and foremost, our spiritual well-being and salvation. In other words, he always does what is best for us. If God answers "yes," it is because our request is in keeping with his will and purposes. If he answers "no," it is because that request would be somehow detrimental to us or to someone else in our lives. May we learn to trust in the wisdom and power of God and prayerfully place our lives in his loving hands.

How can we maintain a proper attitude toward God
and his will as we take our petitions to him in prayer?

DON'T FORGET TO PRAY AND HAVE A GREAT DAY!

DAY 299

Today's Reading:
Isaiah 52:1-15

This chapter is in the middle of a larger portion of Isaiah's prophecy that deals with the salvation of the Lord. While on the surface this text appears to be focused on the physical captivity and deliverance of Judah, it is, in reality, alluding to the spiritual salvation that God will bring about through the Messiah. While the worldly elements that are described can be understood literally, they also metaphorically describe the deliverance of mankind from the shame, guilt, and destruction of sin. Beginning in the last few verses of this chapter and going through the next, Isaiah will prophesy concerning the Servant of the Lord that will come to deliver mankind from sin, but the majority of this chapter discusses the joy with which the news of the salvation of the Lord should be received. Wake up! Take off the old, dirty garments of sin and be clothed in the beauty of Christ. Leave your sinful ways behind and rejoice in the deliverance that God has provided. This is the message that God is delivering through his prophet. While much of this was still a mystery to those who first heard it, the good news of Christ has been clearly revealed to us and continues to give us every reason to rejoice. Christ has come and delivered us from sin and death! To God be the glory!

When you think about the gift of salvation through Christ,
what is it that you are most thankful for?

DON'T FORGET TO PRAY AND HAVE A GREAT DAY!

Day 300

 Today's Reading:
Isaiah 53:1-12

This chapter represents what is probably the most well-known Messianic prophecy of the Old Testament. It is a moving and powerful depiction of the sacrificial act of love initiated by the Father and carried out by the Son on behalf of all mankind. The New Testament reminds us that Jesus "emptied himself, by taking the form of a servant, being born in the likeness of men" and that "being found in human form, he humbled himself by becoming obedient to the point of death, even the death on a cross" (see Philippians 2:7-8). Isaiah 53 fleshes out those statements with vivid images that foretell the unimaginable suffering and abuse that Jesus would willingly endure for the sake of sinful man. Long before Jesus was born into this world, God had put into motion a plan that would forever change the world and offer hope to a lost and dying humanity. At great cost to himself, God would offer his Son to pay the price for sin and redeem mankind to himself, but the paying of that price would not be easy. Jesus would lay down his divinity and take on flesh. He would experience life with all of its challenges and hardships. He would be hated, rejected, humiliated, abused, beaten, and killed, but the blood that he would shed would have the power to cleanse and save all who would be covered in it. This is the story of Christ, the good news of salvation. Thank God for his marvelous gift!

Why did an omnipotent God have to
sacrifice his Son in order to take away sin?

DON'T FORGET TO PRAY AND HAVE A GREAT DAY!

Day 301

 **Today's Reading:
Isaiah 58:1-14**

Worship—honor and adoration given to God. We often think of worship as simply the fulfilling of a requirement on the Lord's day, but it is so much more than that. As Isaiah conveys the word of the Lord to the people concerning their fasting and observance of the Sabbath, he reveals that God is displeased with them, not because they had neglected the observance of the acts but because they had observed them without devoting their hearts to God in the proper way. This text should certainly cause us to pause and consider our own attitudes and hearts as we approach God in worship. The New Testament reveals that not only does God desire and command our worship, but that he is looking for a certain kind of worship—that which is done "in spirit and truth" (John 4:24). God cares as much about the spirit (heart) of worship as he does about the rightness of the acts that we perform. As we come before the throne of God in worship, we must be very careful to not do so with attitudes of arrogant pride, irreverent thoughtlessness, or unloving hearts. There is no doubt that God is worthy and deserving of our heartfelt praise and worship and to be able to offer those things to him is one of our greatest privileges as his children. May we do so in a way that brings honor to his holy name.

*In your opinion, what are some of the greatest challenges
that we face in offering sincere, heartfelt worship to God?*

DON'T FORGET TO PRAY AND HAVE A GREAT DAY!

Day 302

**Today's Reading:
Isaiah 61:1-11**

Could you use some good news? I think we all could. It often seems that everywhere we turn, there is bad news—destruction, violence, hatred, wrongdoing, and suffering. In those circumstances, it can become very easy for us to develop feelings of hopelessness and despair. I imagine that in many ways the situation and mindset in ancient Judah was much the same. Oppression, threatening enemies, and physical hardships were all around, but in the midst of those struggles, Isaiah brings a word of "good news" to them. God has seen their affliction and has promised to comfort, strengthen, and heal them. While this promise was of a physical nature, it had a much greater spiritual significance to them and to all of mankind. Of all the bad news that surrounds us, the worst is that we live in a world that is plagued by sin and doomed to eternal condemnation. But, there is good news! God has seen our affliction and has sent his Son to provide hope, healing, and salvation. While it may be that our physical world will continue to experience struggles and hardships that fill our lives with bad news, we can rejoice in the fact that God has provided good news for us through the gospel of Christ. So rejoice and be glad and give thanks to God!

How is your life made better by the "good news" of salvation through Christ?

DON'T FORGET TO PRAY AND HAVE A GREAT DAY!

Day 303

 Today's Reading:
Jeremiah 1:1-19

As we strive to live out our Christian lives of service and devotion, we can easily lose sight of the role that God plays in helping us to fulfill our calling. Instead, we often focus on our own strength or abilities as the key factor in accomplishing our goals. As we read of the calling of Jeremiah as a prophet, we catch a glimpse of the heart of God and of the relationship between God and his servant. While in many ways the things revealed in this text were specific to Jeremiah, they are, in a general sense, applicable to all of God's servants in any place and time. Those who are called to God (that's all of us) are not simply servants for whom God has no personal concern or involvement. Rather, they are children, known and chosen by God to live with him and for him. Though we cannot know the mind and purposes of God beyond what he has revealed to us, we can be assured that he does have a purpose and plan for our lives and that he will surely be with us to help us achieve those purposes. God does not call us to serve him and then abandon us to do his will without help. What a blessing it is to know that God loves us and that he has prepared a way for us, and may we never forget that he is our constant helper as we strive to do his will.

In what ways can you be a servant of God today?

DON'T FORGET TO PRAY AND HAVE A GREAT DAY!

Day 304

 Today's Reading:
Jeremiah 3:1-25

What do you do when you find yourself away from God, following after the allurements of the world, and giving your heart and devotion to other things? How can you possibly hope to find forgiveness and renewal after turning your back on God? Can there be any hope for a return to God's favor? This is the situation that God's people find themselves in. They have followed after the ways and gods of the nations around them. They have committed spiritual adultery and have rebelled against God. They have taken part in countless abominations with no regard for their covenant with God. But intermingled with his condemnations of their idolatry, God offers them an open door of invitation to return to him. As angry and disappointed as God is with the vile behavior of his people, he continues to love them and remember the covenant that he has made with them. "Return, faithless Israel, declares the Lord. I will not look on you in anger, for I am merciful, declares the Lord; I will not be angry forever." As it was with Israel, so it is with us as God's children today. Though God may be disappointed and even angry with our disobedience, his mercy is great, and his love is never-ending. What a comfort it is to know that no matter how far we might wander from God, he always welcomes our return with his love and forgiveness.

As you think about your life, what is the
greatest blessing of God's mercy and forgiveness?

DON'T FORGET TO PRAY AND HAVE A GREAT DAY!

Day 305

 Today's Reading:
Jeremiah 6:1-30

This chapter is a sad passage of foreboding concerning the destruction of Jerusalem that God would allow to come as a result of Judah's abominable and idolatrous behavior. But in the midst of this proclamation of doom, there is a word of instruction and guidance that could have made all the difference for ancient Judah and could, likewise, make all the difference in our lives. "Stand by the roads, and look, and ask for the ancient paths, where the good way is; and walk in it, and find rest for your souls." Long ago, God had delivered a law to them that was designed to keep them pure and undefiled by the idolatrous world around them. Throughout their generations, God had instructed, warned, and rebuked them continually, encouraging them to be true to their covenant with him. If only they had listened and remained faithful to God, but sadly, the very next statement in the text reveals their error: "But they said, 'We will not pay attention.'" Their desire for the ways of the world around them had taken them away from God. What an important lesson there is for us in this text! Our world is so often enamored with anything that is new or different while we tend to reject anything that is "old." But just as with ancient Judah, the key to a faithful relationship with God is to follow the precepts and commands that God has provided for us. Those "ancient paths" found, for us, in the pages of the New Testament are a sure and trusted guide if we will only follow them.

Why do you think that so many are resistant
to following God's word because it is "old"?

DON'T FORGET TO PRAY AND HAVE A GREAT DAY!

Day 306

 Today's Reading:
Jeremiah 12:1-17

In this text, Jeremiah asks a question that every follower of God has probably pondered at one time or another: "Why does the way of the wicked prosper?" We wonder why evil persists, why those who deny and reject God seem to flourish, and why sinfulness is so prevalent in our world. Why doesn't God do more to protect his people and punish the wicked? These are natural questions for our human minds to ask as we see the chaos that sin causes all around us in this world. We believe in God and trust in his perfect will and wisdom, but in our limited understanding, it often seems that much of the evil in our world is unnecessary and detrimental to God's purposes. But as we continue to read this text, we find God's three-pronged answer to Jeremiah's question, and it speaks to our concerns as well. First, God metaphorically reminds us that to question God's purposes and will is to speak of things that we cannot understand. God's ways are above our ways and our part is simply to trust him. Second, God finds no joy in the prospering of evil. To see his people suffer as sin persists is painful to the heart of God. But, finally, God says that it will not always be so, for he and his people will ultimately be victorious over evil. Through it all, the hope of God's people is to endure the hardship of this world while we trust in the power, wisdom, and will of God.

What can we do to continue to foster trust
in God in the midst of life's struggles?

DON'T FORGET TO PRAY AND HAVE A GREAT DAY!

Day 307

 Today's Reading:
Jeremiah 18:1-23

Throughout the Scriptures, God often uses powerful images to communicate his message in a visual way. In this text, he uses the work of a potter to illustrate his intent with his people. As you read this passage, you can envision the imperfectly formed clay being collapsed by the hand of the potter into a formless lump of clay, only to be reformed into a beautifully shaped piece of pottery. God's intention was not to destroy his people but rather to tear them down for the purpose of rebuilding them into a more perfect form. While this image had an immediate application to the physical circumstances of Judah, it certainly has a spiritual application for each of us. God's desire for each one of us is to destroy the sinful inner man that takes us away from him and to remake us into the glorious image of his Son. Our challenge is to submit ourselves to him and allow him to shape and mold us according to his perfect will. Sometimes, that means letting go of some things that we enjoy because they are not what God wants for us. Sometimes, it means accepting circumstances or answers to our prayers that are not what we imagined. Always, it requires our humility and commitment to God's will. While the process of being shaped by God might not always be easy, it is certain to produce in us a beautiful finished product that will bring glory to his name.

Looking back over your life, how has God
worked in your life to reform you into his image?

DON'T FORGET TO PRAY AND HAVE A GREAT DAY!

Day 308

 Today's Reading:
Jeremiah 20:1-18

Jeremiah's life was not an easy one. He had been given the task of delivering a very negative message to the nation—one of God's disapproval and of their destruction at the hands of their enemies. Naturally, that message was one that was not received well by the people of Judah. Jeremiah was rejected, hated, and abused by his own people. So mistreated and distraught was Jeremiah that he made a decision to defy God and not speak about him anymore. However, in Jeremiah's own words, "His word was in my heart like a burning fire shut up in my bones. I was weary of holding it back, and I could not." While the hardships that Jeremiah faced were difficult and discouraging, the conviction of his heart to do the work that God had called him to do was even more compelling. His attempts to be silent caused him more suffering than the consequences of his message. Therefore, Jeremiah recommitted himself to the work of proclaiming the word of God. What a great example this scene from the life of Jeremiah is for us! There are certainly times when living for God in this world can be difficult, and we can be tempted to become discouraged and give up. However, may we be like Jeremiah, with the word of God and our faith in Christ burning inside us like a fire in our bones causing us to redouble our efforts to live faithfully for Christ in this world.

Have you ever felt like giving up on God in your discouragement?
What caused you to be encouraged and recommit yourself to God?

DON'T FORGET TO PRAY AND HAVE A GREAT DAY!

Day 309

 Today's Reading:
Jeremiah 36:1-32

It is often not how we react to the teachings of God's word that we agree with but how we are affected by the truths that are convicting that most reflect our true attitude and commitment to faithfulness. God, through Jeremiah, had delivered grave warnings of coming destruction in hopes that the nation would repent and turn back to God. Unfortunately, the king's reaction was much different than desired, and in as blatant an act of disregard for God's word as can be imagined, the king cut the scroll in two and threw it into the fire even while it was being read. While we may not be so outwardly contemptible toward God, we might often be just as guilty of disregarding God's commands and warnings. By ignoring his word, justifying our own desires, and changing his commands to fit our ideas, we effectively destroy the word of God as it pertains to our lives. We must remember that God's desire and intent in delivering his word to us is that we might be faithful to him, defeating sin in our lives and conforming to his will for us, so that he might bless us and show his grace toward us. May we choose to listen to him and obey his commands.

Have you ever chosen to ignore the instruction of God's word?
How did that decision affect your life and relationship with God?

DON'T FORGET TO PRAY AND HAVE A GREAT DAY!

Day 310

 Today's Reading:
Lamentations 1:1-22

The book of Lamentations opens with a haunting description of the ruined city of Jerusalem. Pictured as a grieving widow, the city mourns her many losses and looks for comfort among those who had once been her friends, but she finds none. Let us not forget the cause of Jerusalem's mourning and one of the primary messages of this book—the destructiveness of sin. Though they were God's chosen people, Judah had been determined to follow their own path, choosing to worship other gods and take part in the abominable practices of the world rather than to be faithful to the God who had chosen them, saved them, and blessed them mightily. The destruction of Jerusalem and their resulting captivity was a fate that had long been foretold by the prophets but ignored by the people. It was not that God had forsaken them but that they had forsaken God, causing his hand of protective care to be removed. This is the cost of sin. It is a scenario that still plays out in the lives of people over and over again. Sin is just as destructive as it ever was, and so very many in our world fall victim to its alluring and deceptive ways. Though God constantly warns us of the dangers and consequences of sin, we still so often fall into its snare. In the end, willful sin has nothing for us but death and destruction, and this book stands as a grim reminder of the extent of its destructiveness.

Why is sin such a destructive and alluring force in our lives?

DON'T FORGET TO PRAY AND HAVE A GREAT DAY!

Day 311

 Today's Reading:
Lamentations 3:1-33

Interwoven into this book of heartbreak and mourning is a message of hope. Judah had forsaken God and defiled themselves with idolatry and sin. As a result, God had given them into the hands of their enemies and allowed their holy city to be destroyed. Their physical, emotional, and spiritual suffering was palpable, and through the words of this Lamentation, they stand as a testament to how much can be lost when sin has its way with our lives. But lest all hope be lost, we are reminded that "the steadfast love of the Lord never ceases." When sin has ravaged our lives and shattered our relationship with God, there is still hope. When the foundations of our faith have been torn down and we find ourselves captive to the deceitful forces of evil, there is still hope. When it seems that we have lost everything and that there is no way back, there is still hope. This hope rests not in who we are but in who God is. He is loving, merciful, and faithful. Though we might forsake him, he never forsakes us. This text reminds us that his mercies "are new every morning." With the dawning of each new day, there is the divine invitation for renewal and restoration. What a beautiful promise that is, and what hope there is in knowing that, no matter how far we may have strayed from God, he always provides a way back.

What does it mean to you to know that there is always
hope because of God's faithfulness and mercy?

DON'T FORGET TO PRAY AND HAVE A GREAT DAY!

Day 312

 Today's Reading:
Lamentations 5:1-22

In the closing chapter of this poem of mourning, we find a defeated and suffering people pleading to God for restoration, and in their words, we discover a formula for restoration that is still relevant to our lives today. We see, first, their recognition—recognition of their own sinfulness and of the fact that, if they are to be restored, it will be by God's merciful hand. Through this recognition, their hearts have been broken and their sorrow multiplied. Next, we find desire—a desire not only to be relieved of the difficult circumstances of their present lives, but more importantly, a desire to be restored to a faithful relationship with God. It is this desire that has motivated them to come to God in search of reconciliation and healing. The final step in this process of restoration is their request—a humble acknowledgement of their sins against God and of his righteousness, and a fervent plea for his mercy and forgiveness. What a great reminder for us! Having considered, yesterday, the hope that we have because of the mercy and faithfulness of God, it is important that we recognize the path by which we take advantage of that marvelous hope. By recognizing our sinfulness and need for healing that can only come from God, being motivated by a desire to be relieved of the burden of sin and reconciled to the Father, and by a confession of our sins and request for God's forgiveness, we, too, can find the joy of renewal from the sorrow of sin.

Can you think of a time in your life when you experienced the joy of renewal from sin? What was your reaction to the recognition of God's mercy and forgiveness?

DON'T FORGET TO PRAY AND HAVE A GREAT DAY!

Day 313

Today's Reading:
Ezekiel 1:1-28

I n this opening chapter of Ezekiel, we are given a description of the vision that Ezekiel receives as he is called to be a prophet for the Lord. This vision, remarkably similar to the one that John records in the Revelation (see Revelation 4), has but one purpose: to reveal the unapproachable glory of God. I am not sure that our feeble minds are capable of comprehending the true greatness of God, and I fear that we typically have a much lower image of God than is appropriate. As we consider God, we often, very naturally, attach human qualities and feelings to him, including our own limitations and imperfections. The resulting perception of God is often nothing more than a bigger and more powerful human. Oh, how insufficient that view of God is. While it may be impossible for us to comprehend all of the attributes of God to their full extent, God has certainly provided these images for us in order to impress upon us the truth that he is utterly transcendent in his power, glory, wisdom, and majesty. Every element of Ezekiel's vision is symbolic of some attribute of God's nature and sovereignty, reminding us that he is glorious and untouchable and perfect in all of his ways. As we approach him, we must do so as Ezekiel did—with the utmost of reverence and godly fear.

What are some things that we can do to help us have a
better understanding of God's glory and transcendence?

DON'T FORGET TO PRAY AND HAVE A GREAT DAY!

Day 314

Today's Reading:
Ezekiel 8:1-18

Have you ever wondered what God's view of this world must look like? We often speak of a "bird's eye view" as being a situation where we are able to see the bigger picture as if seeing it from above and at some distance. Ezekiel, in this chapter's visions, is given a "God's eye view" of the city of Jerusalem, to see all of the abominations that are taking place there. Men were worshipping false gods, defiling the temple of the Lord, and denying God's place among them. What an eye-opening and sorrowful sight this must have been for Ezekiel. All of this causes me to wonder what God sees as he looks into our world, our churches, and our lives. Certainly, there is much for him to be displeased with in our world, and even as I consider our individual lives, I am reminded of the words of the New Testament: "And no creature is hidden from his sight, but all are naked and exposed to the eyes of him to whom we must give account" (Hebrews 4:13). Knowing that God sees and knows every detail and secret of my life should be a great motivation for me to strive for purity and godliness in every aspect of my life to the best of my ability. I am also thankful for the knowledge that God still loves me despite my imperfections and weaknesses. What a wonderful assurance!

How does understanding God's view of your life affect your motivation and desire to be faithful to him?

DON'T FORGET TO PRAY AND HAVE A GREAT DAY!

Day 315

 Today's Reading:
Ezekiel 18:1-32

"For each will have to bear his own load." These are the inspired words of the apostle Paul (Galatians 6:2), and they summarize perfectly what the Lord is saying in this text. It is a very natural human instinct to blame others for our failures or hardships. We often use statements like "that's not fair" or "I don't deserve this" to imply that someone else's actions are responsible for my circumstances, and I should not be made to face their consequences. This was the attitude of Judah. They blamed their captivity on the rebellion of the kings and people who had come before them and claimed innocence on their own part. In so doing, they implied that God was being unjust in his punishment of them. The Lord's response establishes three very important truths that are as applicable to our lives as to theirs. First, we are all responsible for and will be judged by our own actions. The son is not punished for the father's sin. Judah was being punished for their own unfaithfulness, not someone else's. Second, God does not desire for men to be lost. He does not find joy or satisfaction in bringing punishment or condemnation upon people. His desire is for men to turn to him in repentance instead of face his wrath. Third, the opportunity to escape God's punishment and live is available. "Turn and live" is the exhortation that he gives to Judah. Instead of denying your wrongdoing and wallowing in self-pity, admit your sin and turn from it so that you might live. What a powerful reminder for us!

Why do you think that we are so prone to try to blame others for our mistakes? How does this attitude affect our spiritual lives?

DON'T FORGET TO PRAY AND HAVE A GREAT DAY!

DAY 316

 Today's Reading:
Ezekiel 22:1-31

In this chapter, the Lord, through his prophet Ezekiel, depicts many of the injustices and unrighteous acts that have come to characterize his people. As the chapter closes, a statement is made that provides a very sad commentary on the state of the nation. The Lord says, "I sought for a man among them who should build up the wall and stand in the breach before me for the land, that I should not destroy it, but I found none." God uses the metaphor of a wall to represent the separating and protecting of his people from the abominable attitudes and actions of the world. That wall has been breached and sin has come in. In response, the Lord has desperately searched for those who would repair the wall of righteousness around his people and stand up for the ways of God, but he found no one. Though we live in a very different world than ancient Judah, this same image certainly has an application in our own lives. In our world, in the church, and in our families, God has provided, through his Son and through his word, a wall of righteousness to separate us from the world and protect us from sin. In many cases, that wall has been broken down by the influence of evil and sin has found its way in. Even now, God is looking for those who will stand in that gap to defend the family, the church, and the world from Satan's attacks and to work to rebuild the wall. The question for us is, in our day and time, will he find anyone who is willing? What about you?

What can you do to stand in the gap and protect the church, family, and your life from the destructiveness of sin?

DON'T FORGET TO PRAY AND HAVE A GREAT DAY!

DAY 317

 Today's Reading:
Ezekiel 33:1-33

While the job of the prophet was often to remind the people of the responsibilities of their covenant with God and to warn them of the consequences of neglecting those responsibilities, this passage reminds us that there was also a great burden on the messenger of God himself, and a great price to be paid if he neglected his duties. The Lord compares the prophet to a watchman whose job it is to watch over the city and forewarn them of any approaching danger. If he fulfills his responsibility, then he will be rewarded, but if he fails to give the needed warning, then he will not be held blameless. Consider the application of this concept to our own lives. We, who have come to know Jesus and have devoted our lives to living for him, are those watchmen in this world. God, through his word, has given warnings of a coming judgment and condemnation on those who have not known him or obeyed his will. Our duty and calling is to proclaim that warning to the world and to share the good news of Christ as the source of rescue and shelter from sin and death. But, what if we neglect that duty? What if we take shelter in the cross but do not warn others to do the same? What a tragic and sorrowful situation that would be! May God help us to always be diligent as his watchmen in the world.

What can you do, in your daily life, to help
others come to know about Christ?

DON'T FORGET TO PRAY AND HAVE A GREAT DAY!

Day 318

Today's Reading:
Ezekiel 37:1-28

Israel had lost all hope. She had been defeated, taken from her land, and placed into captivity. There seemed to be no source of reprieve from the suffering that she was experiencing. But in a powerful image, God reveals to Ezekiel his plan for his people. A valley full of dry bones, long since robbed of life, stretched out before Ezekiel. God's question was a simple one: "Can these bones live?" Under normal circumstances, the answer would be an obvious "no," but there was nothing normal about these circumstances. God was in control and nothing was beyond his ability. Imagine the astonishment and wonder as Ezekiel witnessed those dry bones coming together into skeletons, being covered by muscle and skin, and then standing before him as a mighty, living army. In the same manner, God would restore life and vitality to his people. He was not finished with them yet. What a message of hope! Have you ever felt hopeless; like there was no reprieve from your sins and nothing that could be done to revive your spiritual life? If you have, then this message of hope is for you. The God who can bring a valley of dry bones to life can revive you through the power of his Son, Jesus Christ. He is in control and there is nothing that is beyond his ability. So take heart and rejoice because, just like that valley of dry bones, you can live again!

Why is the message of revival an important one for people today?

DON'T FORGET TO PRAY AND HAVE A GREAT DAY!

DAY 319

 Today's Reading:
Daniel 1:1-21

As we begin to consider the life of Daniel, there are many remarkable qualities that this young man demonstrated under very difficult circumstances, but this chapter contains one short phrase that seems to sum up the strength and character of Daniel's life. In verse 8, we read: "But Daniel resolved …" The New King James Version says that he "purposed in his heart." Long before Daniel was seated at the king's table and ordered to eat the king's meat, this young man had made a decision that he would be committed to God and follow his commands. His mind was already made up. With that conviction firmly in place, Daniel found strength to withstand the temptations placed before him and to remain pure in a very difficult situation. What about us? In a world where subjectivism and situation ethics have become the norm, we may often wait until we are faced with a difficult decision before making a choice. In that situation, it becomes very difficult to not listen to the voice of the world or of our fleshly desires. From Daniel's example, we learn the value of being resolved in our hearts to be faithful to God no matter what, and we see the blessings that can come from our commitment to doing God's will instead of following after the ways of the world. Let us be resolved!

What is the spiritual advantage of being resolved or committed to something before the situation arises?

DON'T FORGET TO PRAY AND HAVE A GREAT DAY!

Day 320

 Today's Reading:
Daniel 2:1-49

As we read this text, it may seem that there is little in it that is of any relevance to our lives. Clearly, God had given Nebuchadnezzar this dream and then allowed Daniel to interpret it as a prophecy of the nations and empires that would come. It also reveals the power and glory of God's heavenly kingdom which would be victorious over every nation and power. But certainly one of the most comforting and hopeful points of this chapter is to be found in the words of Daniel after the Lord revealed the mystery of the dream to him: "He changes times and seasons; He removes kings and sets up kings." We often fret over the state of our world and what the future might hold. We worry about our government and our enemies and the many forces of evil in the world. Amidst all of that anxiousness, we can forget who is in control. As the psalmist so aptly stated, "For kingship belongs to the Lord, and He rules over the nations" (Psalm 22:28). Whatever may come in this world, nothing happens outside of the watchful eye or ever-present hand of the Lord. Things may not always go as we would like for them to from a physical point of view, but we must remember that God is the all-knowing and all-powerful ruler of the world, and when all is said and done, we have the blessing of being part of his kingdom that will reign forever. To God be the glory!

What hope or comfort does it give you to know
that God is ultimately in control of our world?

DON'T FORGET TO PRAY AND HAVE A GREAT DAY!

Day 321

 Today's Reading:
Daniel 3:1-30

While Daniel is the focus of much of this book, the three men at the center of this chapter are certainly to be honored for their faith and commitment to God. From the beginning, they have been with Daniel, fighting the temptations of a foreign land and resolving to obey God no matter what. In this text, their commitment faces the ultimate test. Everything about this scene speaks to the remarkable strength of character found in Shadrach, Meshach, and Abednego. As they face the threat of a horrible death if they do not bow down before the graven image, their faith in God's deliverance is inspiring, but there is one simple phrase that stands out to me as being the most powerful testament to their commitment to God. That phrase is made up of three little words: "But if not…" These men of God were supremely confident in God's ability to save them from the agonizing fate of the fiery furnace, but they also understood that the will of God was immutable and that will did not guarantee their physical salvation. That little phrase, "but if not," represents a faith that trusts in God regardless of the physical consequences of obedience. It is a faith that obeys, not just because there is no danger, but in spite of the danger that exists. May God help us to have a "but if not" kind of faith so that, no matter what life might bring, our commitment to God is firm.

Why is it so challenging for us to have a "but if not" kind of faith?

DON'T FORGET TO PRAY AND HAVE A GREAT DAY!

DAY 322

Today's Reading:
Daniel 4:1-37

Another dream. Another interpretation. Another demonstration of God's mighty power and authority. God had used Nebuchadnezzar as a tool of discipline against His people, and all of the glory of the Babylonian kingdom was at the bidding of God's hand. However, Nebuchadnezzar had become arrogant and haughty in his spirit, taking all of the credit and glory for himself. This chapter's events are about the humbling of this ruler and remind us of the need for humility in our own lives. Imagine the scene and reaction as this once great king is reduced to living like a mindless animal in the fields. But Nebuchadnezzar learned his lesson. He repents of his arrogance, acknowledges God as the ruler of all that is, and gives praise and honor to his holy name. We may not be kings or occupy positions of great honor or authority; we may not rule armies or have entire empires at our command; we may not have an abundance of this world's riches or enjoy the accolades of men. However, when it comes to our own lives, be it physical or spiritual, we all run the risk of developing a mindset of independence and self-reliance. We can far too easily forget the role that God plays in our lives and the desperate need that we have for him. May we ever fight against that temptation and be diligent to maintain an attitude of humble submission before the King of kings and Lord of lords.

Why is humility such an important characteristic
of a faithful relationship with God?

DON'T FORGET TO PRAY AND HAVE A GREAT DAY!

Day 323

 Today's Reading:
Daniel 5:1-31

S ome time has passed, Nebuchadnezzar has died, and his son, Belshazzar has assumed his throne. Unfortunately, the humility and knowledge of God that Nebuchadnezzar had gained in his latter years had not been passed down to his son. During a moment of particular disregard toward God through the profane usage of sacred items confiscated from the temple, Belshazzar literally saw the handwriting on the wall, though he was not able to interpret its meaning. Again, Daniel was called to interpret the vision as he had been for the previous king. The message was a grim one: God had brought judgment upon Belshazzar and his kingdom because of his wicked ways. His kingdom would be defeated and replaced by another. As I consider this scene, I am struck by the question: how would I feel if I were in Belshazzar's position? His fate has just been announced. God has judged him and found him lacking. I am then reminded of the words of Jesus given as a warning to any who might not obey the will of God: "I never knew you; depart from me, you workers of lawlessness." What a horrifying position to consider—standing before God in judgment, hoping to inherit an eternal home, only to find out that I have been judged and found lacking. As a child of God, I am eternally grateful for the wonderful grace of God that gives me the hope of salvation, and I am also very thankful for his word which enables me to, through my faith and submission to him, be prepared to stand before God in judgment. Thanks be to God!

What can we do to prepare ourselves to stand before God in judgment?

DON'T FORGET TO PRAY AND HAVE A GREAT DAY!

Day 324

 Today's Reading:
Daniel 6:1-28

The story of Daniel in the lions' den is a favorite for children's Bible classes, but it is far more than just a good children's story; it is a beautiful story of Daniel's prayerful life and victorious faith. While we are often enthralled by the miraculous intervention of God to shut the mouths of the lions, we must not forget the life, faith, and reputation of Daniel that precipitated those events. Daniel was a man of exemplary character and faithful service to the extent that his enemies could find no grounds for accusation against him. Daniel was also well-known to be a man of prayer, relying heavily upon his relationship with God for daily strength and guidance. Daniel did not pray as an act of protest against an unfair law concocted by his enemies nor did he pray as an act of defiance against a godless nation. He prayed because he was a man of prayer—that is who he was and what he did. He was not trying to be disobedient to the law of the land, but he was not willing to allow a man-made law to keep him from his faithfulness to God. So Daniel prayed. In the face of his enemies and at the risk of severely cruel consequences, he prayed, and through his faithfulness, the name of God was glorified, and we are given a wonderful example of the power and faithfulness of a loving God toward his people.

How can the story of Daniel be applied
to our lives and in our world today?

DON'T FORGET TO PRAY AND HAVE A GREAT DAY!

Day 325

Today's Reading:
Daniel 7:1-28

T he second half of the book of Daniel contains the prophetic visions of Daniel. This chapter's visions foretell of the nations that would rise up to rule the world, each one stronger and more powerful than the one that came before it, but the kingdom that would be the most powerful and permanent of all was the one that would be established by the One called in this text the Ancient of Days. That kingdom—the Lord's church—would not be a physical kingdom but a spiritual one and would be ruled over by Christ himself, having ever-lasting dominion over all the nations and kings of the earth. We are reminded in this text that the Lord's kingdom, of which we are blessed to be a part, has always had and will always have enemies in this world. There will always be those who desire to see her downfall and who will work toward that end. There will be persecution and hardship and trials for the saints as long as this world remains. But God is a faithful God, and the Lord's kingdom will be victorious in the end, for, one day, the Lord will return to bring judgment upon the world and to deliver, once and for all, his faithful people from the hand of their enemies. What a blessing it is to have that assurance and what a wonderful, wonderful day that will be.

Why are there enemies of the Lord and his church in this world?
How can we find strength to stand firm as we face those enemies?

DON'T FORGET TO PRAY AND HAVE A GREAT DAY!

Day 326

 **Today's Reading:
Daniel 9:1-27**

A s Daniel prays to God on behalf of his people in this text, he acknowledges their sinfulness and makes an important observation that is still pertinent in our day and time. Israel's punitive captivity had not been without warning. God had, long ago, told them of the consequences of forsaking him. He had given them warning after warning of what would happen if they chose to reject his law and leadership, and he had exhorted them time and time again to turn from their evil ways and return to him. No one could accuse God of acting rashly or unfairly with his people. But can the same not be said of us? Has not God clearly communicated his will to mankind through his word which is easily obtainable and understandable? Has he not, through that word, instructed us on how to respond to his love and grace and on what he expects of us as his children? Has he not clearly explained the consequences of rejecting him and his gift of redemption through his Son? You see, there are some who might claim that a God who would cause a person to spend eternity in hell is not a loving or merciful God, but the fact of the matter is that God has, in his love and mercy, provided a way out of sin and hell through the sacrifice of his Son and has patiently and urgently warned us of the danger of hell, pleading with us to escape that fate by becoming obedient to the gospel of Christ. God has done all that he can to save us. The choice is now ours.

*Why do many people refuse to listen to
the warnings and guidance of God's word?*

DON'T FORGET TO PRAY AND HAVE A GREAT DAY!

Day 327

 Today's Reading:
Daniel 12:1-13

The writings of the last three chapters of the book of Daniel are, in many ways, perplexing. Written in apocalyptic form, they are filled with imagery and representations that are often cryptic and difficult to decipher, reminding us of the book of Revelation from the New Testament. There is much debate about the period of time and events alluded to by the Lord in these prophecies, but of more interest to us in this writing is the lesson, exhortation, and encouragement that we are able to find in these ancient words. What can we glean from Daniel's visions that can be helpful to us in our daily lives? While we may not understand the meanings of all of the elements of these visions, there is one message that comes through very clearly: God is absolute in his power, authority, and rule. He governs over the affairs of men and his will is sovereign. Whatever might happen in this world, whether it be in centuries gone by or in our own modern world, one thing is certain: when all is said and done, God will stand victorious! There is no power that has ever been or that will ever be that can defeat the will and purposes of God Almighty. And if we will stand with him, faithfully abiding in his will and persevering until the end, we will also be victorious. What a wonderful message of hope and victory God has provided for us through his word!

Why is the message of God's authority
and rule an important one for us today?

DON'T FORGET TO PRAY AND HAVE A GREAT DAY!

DAY 328

 Today's Reading:
Hosea 1:1-11

The life and work of Hosea is very interesting and unique among the prophets. While it was not uncommon for God to use real life events or situations to provide a sort of visual aid for his people, Hosea's entire life would become that metaphor for Israel's relationship with God. The story of Hosea's work opens with the very unusual command from God that he take a harlot as his wife. This marriage would no doubt have been seen as a shameful act and a disgrace in the eyes of the Israelites. After all, harlots were considered to be among the worst of sinners. God, however, uses this situation to illustrate to Israel their sin of spiritual adultery. Though "married" to God through a spiritual covenant, they had played the harlot with other nations and other gods, offering their devotion, their prayers, their worship, and their sacrifices to false deities while continuing to claim their place as God's people. It was truly a despicable set of circumstances, and God's message to them through the words and life of Hosea are rightfully harsh and condemning: "I will no more have mercy on the house of Israel, to forgive them at all." As we read these prophecies, we must remember that their purpose for us is not simply the recording of history, but a means of exhorting us, as the bride of Christ, to be faithful to our covenant with him. May we learn from those who've gone before us.

In what ways can we be unfaithful to our covenant with God today?

DON'T FORGET TO PRAY AND HAVE A GREAT DAY!

Day 329

 Today's Reading:
Hosea 4:1-19

As we look back at Israel's straying from God, we are often perplexed by their unfaithfulness. How does a nation that has been so inextricably linked to God and has been the recipient of so many blessings from him find itself forsaking him and following after useless and empty idols? We shake our heads at their unfaithfulness, confident that we will never be guilty of the same. What this chapter reveals, among other things, is the weakness that led to Israel's falling away, and it is one that continues to pose a serious threat to God's people today. The very first words of the Lord recorded in this text are: "There is no faithfulness or steadfast love, and no knowledge of God in the land." This statement is followed up in verse 6 with these chilling words: "My people are destroyed for lack of knowledge; because you have rejected knowledge, I reject you from being a priest for me. And since you have forgotten the law of your God, I also will forget your children." Lack of knowledge—something so simple and yet so devastating to them as a nation. As we look at our present world, there are many threats and dangers to the faith and faithfulness of God's people, but possibly none as imminent as a lack of knowledge. All that stands between us and the same type of apostasy that Israel experienced in the long ago is our knowledge of and faithfulness to the word of God. May it never be said of us that we were destroyed for lack of knowledge.

With the easy availability of God's word today, why do you think that lack of knowledge is still a problem?

DON'T FORGET TO PRAY AND HAVE A GREAT DAY!

Day 330

 Today's Reading:
Hosea 6:1-11

T he prophecies of Hosea are very harsh and condemning toward God's unfaithful and impenitent people. At times, it seems that God has lost all patience and inclination of mercy toward them. God's goodness and love has been betrayed and forsaken time and time again as his people have chased after other gods, shamelessly and continuously committing spiritual adultery to their own destruction. But, if there is anything that we know about God from his word, it is that he is a relentlessly loving and merciful God who is always ready and willing to forgive the penitent sinner who returns to him. It is with that understanding of God that Hosea pleads with his people to return to the Lord for forgiveness and healing and to pursue the restoration of those things that had been lost through their evil ways. What a message of hope is found in these beautiful words of the prophet! For the one who is lost in sin and estranged from God, there is hope. God will heal, revive, and raise you up. He will forgive and restore you in his love and faithfulness. You must only be willing to come to him, repenting of your transgressions and faithfully submitting yourself to obedience to him. The blessings of that decision are many and great! Thanks be to God for his unending love and mercy.

Why do you think that God is so relentless
in his love and willingness to show mercy?

DON'T FORGET TO PRAY AND HAVE A GREAT DAY!

Day 331

 Today's Reading:
Hosea 11:1-12

This is a beautiful passage portraying the tender love, desire, and compassion that God has for his people. He chose them and raised them. He led them and provided for them. He protected and blessed them. The language of this text does not just show an all-powerful God who is meeting the needs of his chosen people; it is painting a picture of the heart of God, consumed with his people and yearning for their requited love. You can easily sense the pain that God feels because of their rebellion, but even in his sorrow and frustration over their continual sin, he cannot bring himself to cut them off completely. Though he may allow them to suffer defeat and captivity, he will bring them out and reestablish them as his people. His love is never-failing. The God of this passage is the same God that we know and love today. As his chosen people under the covenant of Christ, his love and desire for us is just as strong as it ever was for his people of old. His compassion, longsuffering, and mercy are everlasting. Oh, how he must mourn our rebellion and rejection of his will for our lives. How great is his desire for us to return when we have strayed away! How full and complete is his merciful forgiveness when we return! Of all the amazing attributes of God, surely his love for us is among the greatest and most unfathomable. Thanks be to God!

How would you describe the love of God
to someone who did not know him?

DON'T FORGET TO PRAY AND HAVE A GREAT DAY!

Day 332

 Today's Reading:
Hosea 14:1-9

The book of Hosea has, in large part, been a troubling depiction of Israel's spiritual adultery against the Lord. Through the illustrative use of the prophet's life, God has painted a vivid picture of his people's unfaithfulness and of the punitive consequences of their choices. However, as the book closes, we read a beautiful and heartfelt plea for Israel's return to the Lord. Having previously seen the great and unending love that God has for his people, it should come as no surprise that he continues to pursue their repentance and restoration. The truth of the matter is that God has no greater desire than a relationship with mankind, leading to their salvation. It is his desperate yearning and the purpose of all of his redemptive work throughout time. Our world today is not much different than the world of Hosea's day. The vast majority of the world is away from God, separated from him by sins of either ignorance or rebellion. But, God is also no different than he has ever been. His fervent desire is still to do away with that separation and to draw mankind into himself. The sacrificial death of his Son paved the way and his merciful longsuffering continues to plead with mankind to come to him through Christ. Oh that our world might heed the pleadings of God and take advantage of his marvelous love.

Why do you think that our world is so resistant to the love of God?

DON'T FORGET TO PRAY AND HAVE A GREAT DAY!

Day 333

 Today's Reading:
Joel 1:1-20

The Great San Francisco earthquake of 1906; the dust bowl; the eruption of Mount St. Helens; Hurricane Katrina—our history is filled with natural disasters and tragedies that continue to be passed down from one generation to the next because of the devastating effect that they had on our own land and people. In much the same way, the plague of locusts that Joel chapter 1 records is a monumental disaster that would not be soon forgotten. Through this text, we are reminded of at least two vitally important truths that are still valid today. First of all, the disasters that often occur in our world remind us that this physical world with all of its comforts and wealth is, at its best, temporary and unreliable. It is amazing how quickly the things that we so greatly rely on can be destroyed by acts of nature. To put our trust in this world is senseless. That brings us to the second lesson learned: we are so often reminded by tragedy that God is truly in control of all things and that he is our only true source of hope. Where do we go for help when our lives are turned upside down? It is amazing to see so many who have denied or rejected God turn to him in times of desperation and calamity, but that is exactly what this text calls for and what God desires. As we face the hardships of life, may we always remember that it is God and not this world that offers the hope and security that we desire.

Considering natural disasters that have occurred in your lifetime, how have people reacted to those events with regard to God?

DON'T FORGET TO PRAY AND HAVE A GREAT DAY!

Day 334

 Today's Reading:
Joel 2:1-32

As Joel emphasizes the spiritual implications of the physical circumstances that ancient Israel found themselves in, he employs the term "day of the Lord" over and over again. However, he uses this same term in two very different ways. The first "day of the Lord" is the day of God's judgment. It is the day that God would remove his hand of blessing and protection from his people so that they might feel the pain of sin. It is the day that he would cause them to face the consequences of their rebellion. But, lest they lose all hope, God's people were assured that there would be another "day of the Lord." It is the day of God's deliverance. It is the day that God would shower his grace upon them and bless them with his loving favor. It is the day that they would once again know the glory of being God's chosen people. And so it is with us. While we might, at times, suffer the consequences of our sinful choices and face the hardships of life in this world, we have the promise of the day of the Lord in our own lives. It is the day that we come to God for cleansing and renewal through Christ, and ultimately, it is the day that we are delivered from this world of sin and enter an eternal abode with our heavenly Father. What a glorious day that will be!

What feelings do you have when considering
the coming day of the Lord? Why?

DON'T FORGET TO PRAY AND HAVE A GREAT DAY!

Day 335

 Today's Reading:
Joel 3:1-21

This text depicts the judgment of God against the enemies of his people. As these nations gather together as if for war, God's overwhelming power and sovereignty is clearly seen in the triumph and deliverance of his people. As I read this text, I am reminded of the struggle that Christians are daily engaged in against sin and the forces of Satan. As the enemies of Israel gathered their forces to wage war against God and his people, so does the devil call into action all of his resources and agents in his constant effort to take us away from God. As we face these forces of evil, we can take great comfort in knowing that the war has already been won. Notice that today's reading does not describe the actual fighting of any battle. Though the enemy forces had gathered for that purpose, God's victorious power reigns supreme, and his judgment upon them is carried out. As those who are striving to overcome Satan and remain faithful to God, it is a great source of comfort and strength to know that God has assured us of the victory through Christ. Yes, we will face struggles in this life with temptation and trials. Yes, Satan will continue to work to defeat us. But if we can persevere and remain faithful to God, then we have the promise of victory! What a wonderful blessing!

What does it mean to say that we, through
Christ, have already won the victory?

DON'T FORGET TO PRAY AND HAVE A GREAT DAY!

DAY 336

 Today's Reading:
Amos 1:1-15

The prophecy of Amos opens up with another example of the promised judgment of God against the nations that have set themselves against him and against his people. We typically think of these passages in terms of the assurance of God's power, sovereignty, and care for his people, but let's think about today's passage from a different angle. Israel is living a double life. They are worshipping God, enjoying his blessings, and relying upon his care, while, at the same time, they have followed after the sinful and idolatrous ways of their godless neighbors. As God, through Amos, warns of his coming judgment against their enemies, his words could certainly serve as a warning to his people of the consequences of following in their ways. If they persisted in paying homage to false gods and indulging in sinful activities, then they would be subject to the wrath of God just as their enemies were. Consider the application: we are constantly tempted to follow after the ways of our world. Even as we claim devotion to God as his children, we may often find ourselves carried away with the sinful desires, attitudes, and actions that we see in those around us. If so, then God's warning speaks to us as well. If we desire to escape the wrathful judgment of God, then we must avoid the enticements of the world and remain faithful to God. May he help us to do just that!

How can we live in this world without
becoming entangled in the ways of the world?

DON'T FORGET TO PRAY AND HAVE A GREAT DAY!

DAY 337

Today's Reading:
Amos 4:1-13

This chapter contains a chilling statement of warning from the Lord against a rebellious and unfaithful people: "prepare to meet your God." Israel has insisted on living in sinful ways and chasing after false gods. They have failed to heed the many warnings that have been given to them through the prophets. Therefore, God's judgment is coming upon Israel. As he has done to their enemies, so he will do to them. Therefore, they are warned to prepare themselves to meet God. While we certainly understand God to be a loving and merciful God, the prospect of coming face to face with the righteous judgment and wrath of God is a sobering and fearful thought. In the New Testament, the Hebrew writer reminds us that for the willful sinner, "it is a fearful thing to fall into the hands of the living God" (Hebrews 10:31). So, how can we have confidence and peace as we consider our standing with a just and righteous God? Preparation! Knowing that judgment is coming and that we must all stand before God, it is imperative that we prepare ourselves for that day by being washed from our sins by the blood of Christ and by then remaining faithful to God in our daily lives. Our preparation to meet God involves a daily faith in God's saving grace and walk in the light of Christ. As those who look toward the day of Christ's return, may we diligently prepare to meet our God.

What are some specific things that we should
do to prepare for our meeting with God?

DON'T FORGET TO PRAY AND HAVE A GREAT DAY!

Day 338

 Today's Reading:
Obadiah 1:1-21

The people of Edom were descendants of Esau and were, therefore, related to the people of Judah. They were also one of Judah's closest and most antagonistic neighbors. In this vision of God given to Obadiah, the Lord foretells of the destruction of Edom by the hand of their enemies. For our purposes, it might be helpful for us to learn from one of the aspects of Edom's character that had contributed to God's displeasure. Situated on the top of a rocky outcropping and surrounded on three sides by sheer cliffs, Edom considered their land to be impenetrable and became puffed up with pride. This pride would be their downfall as God promises to humble them in a devastating way, causing them to be small and despised among the nations. For as long as time has existed, pride has been a great temptation and source of sin for mankind. To become dependent and arrogant in one's own intellect, abilities, and accomplishments is a common fallacy in this world. It is very common to see athletes, business executives, government leaders, and others take full credit for their successes and boast in their extraordinary skills. However, God reminds Edom, and us, that there is no person or nation that is beyond his reach. Nations rise and fall at his command and no venture can enjoy lasting success without his blessing. One of the greatest lessons that we can learn as those who desire to be faithful and pleasing to God is to be humble before him, recognizing his greatness and our own weakness.

Why is pride such a dangerous attitude
as it pertains to our relationship with God?

DON'T FORGET TO PRAY AND HAVE A GREAT DAY!

Day 339

 Today's Reading:
Jonah 1:1-17

Have you ever tried to run away from God? Oh, maybe you didn't do so in a physical sense like Jonah did, but mentally, emotionally, or spiritually, have you ever tried to avoid God's commands, justify your own desires, or find a way around what you know to be your responsibility? Most of us probably have at times. We look into God's word, see the deficiencies of our own lives, recognize the needed corrective actions, but balk at carrying those actions out because of the selfish urging of our own hearts. Surely, one of the great lessons that we learn from the story of Jonah is that we cannot run away or hide from God. Jonah did not agree with the command of the Lord and had no desire to carry it out. He got on a ship in order to go "away from the presence of the Lord." However, he quickly learned that his attempts were futile and disastrous. As with Jonah, so it is with us. There is no place that we can go and no excuse that we can give that can remove us from our accountability to God's word. Ultimately, his will prevails. At the very core of this story, Jonah's first and worst mistake was in thinking that he knew better than God. He found fault with God's reasoning and was convinced that God's command was not appropriate. How often do we use that same reasoning in our lives, convinced that we know better than God what is best? What a foolish and sinful attitude that is! May we ever trust God's will and seek to draw near to him instead of flee from him.

Why do you think we often second guess
God and think that our ideas are better?

DON'T FORGET TO PRAY AND HAVE A GREAT DAY!

DAY 340

 Today's Reading:
Jonah 2:1-10

We often think of the great fish in this text as a part of God's punishment toward Jonah for his disobedience, but as you closely consider the words of Jonah's prayer to God in this chapter, we realize that is not the case. God's punishment was the storm which resulted in Jonah being cast into the sea. Those events would have surely led to Jonah's death were it not for the saving grace of God, shown to Jonah through the protective shelter of a great fish. Notice that Jonah did not wait until he was on dry ground to pray, but even from within the belly of the fish, he offers a prayer of thanksgiving and praise to God for his salvation. Though the form of that help was probably not the one that Jonah would have chosen, the compassion and mercy of God had brought about salvation. Consider our own lives for a moment. It is very unlikely that any of us will ever experience being swallowed by a great fish only to be spit out onto dry ground three days later. However, we have all experienced the saving grace of a compassionate and merciful God. Whether it is in the ultimate form of the sacrifice of his Son to save us from our sins, or in a plethora of smaller ways in our everyday lives, God's love and help are constantly evident in our lives. While, as in the life of Jonah, that help may take unexpected and maybe even uncomfortable forms, we must learn to be sincerely thankful to God for his benevolent care.

Has God ever helped or blessed you in some unexpected way?
What was your reaction to that blessing?

DON'T FORGET TO PRAY AND HAVE A GREAT DAY!

DAY 341

 Today's Reading:
Jonah 3:1-10

This chapter is one of repentance. First, we see the repentance of Jonah. When given the command a second time to go to Nineveh, Jonah obeyed, turning from the rebellious attitude of chapter one and fulfilling God's command. Then, we see an even greater show of repentance in the people of Nineveh. Having heard the word of God preached and having heeded the warnings of their coming destruction, this evil and godless city, a city of Gentiles, repented and turned from their evil ways. From her king to the least of her citizens, Nineveh fasted and mourned their sinfulness, imploring God to spare them from his wrath. We talk and study often about repentance, but I wonder if we do not underestimate its great power to transform our lives. Repentance saved Jonah from God's corrective discipline and saved Nineveh from total destruction. In much the same way, this changing of our minds and turning of our lives is crucial to our relationship with God and has a profound effect on both our daily walk and our eternal fate. Notice, in the examples of this chapter, that repentance involves a combination of the heeding of God's word with an appropriate response to that word. Repentance is not always easy, and at times requires real effort, but the results and rewards of repentance are always worth the work. May God help us to see the need to repent at times in our lives and to have the strength to do so.

Why is repentance often difficult for us to do? Where can we find the strength and motivation to repent even when it is difficult?

DON'T FORGET TO PRAY AND HAVE A GREAT DAY!

Day 342

 Today's Reading:
Jonah 4:1-11

What a powerful illustration of his grace and mercy God gives to Jonah in this chapter. At the heart of this entire story is the fact that Jonah did not want to see this godless foreign city be saved from God's wrath. He was resentful about being sent to preach to them, disappointed at their repentance, and angry with God for relenting on his threats to destroy them. Much like the older brother of Luke 15, he found no joy in the mercy of the Father toward one who had acted so wickedly. Using a plant, God teaches Jonah a valuable lesson about value and worthiness. While Jonah grieved the loss of a plant that he had not worked for and that had sprung up overnight, he faulted God for caring for the thousands of people of Nineveh whom he had created, known, and desired. Though they were not of God's chosen nation, they were people created in his image with eternal souls that needed saving. In the midst of the Old Testament, where it seems that all of God's focus and care is reserved for one nation of people, this book sends the powerful message that God loves and desires salvation for all. What about us? Sadly, it can often be that we find some in our world as being unworthy of God's love and undeserving of salvation. May the message of Jonah remind us that God loves all men and desires all to be saved. As modern day Jonahs, it is our responsibility to tell them of coming judgment and urge them to repent before it is too late.

In what ways can we often display a similar attitude as Jonah?

DON'T FORGET TO PRAY AND HAVE A GREAT DAY!

Day 343

 Today's Reading:
Micah 3:1-12

L ike many of the prophets, Micah is condemning the sinfulness and rebellion of God's people. In this chapter, he is specifically focusing on the sinful injustices and falsehoods of the civil and religious leaders among the people. The phrase that stands out to me, appearing over and over again in this text, is "my people." Despite the people's shameful conduct and forsaking of God, they were still his people, and he was angered by the abuse and unfairness with which they were being treated by their own leaders. God's patience and forbearance with humanity is amazing. We sin, fall short, neglect our relationship with him, and often willfully disregard his guiding word; yet, he continues to love us as his people. He does not turn his back on us at the first sight of failure or unfaithfulness on our part. He continues to faithfully wait for our return, longing to forgive us and to renew his relationship with us. There is a common and popular saying among Christians today: "God is good." This little statement is much more than cliché. It is very true, and not only when we are in his good graces. God is good even when we are not. Even when we fail him, he continues to be faithful to us, showing concern and care for us as his people. What a wonderful God he is!

In what ways does God demonstrate his goodness toward us?

DON'T FORGET TO PRAY AND HAVE A GREAT DAY!

DAY 344

 Today's Reading:
Micah 5:1-15

Micah is one of the Old Testament prophets that foretells of a coming Messiah that would deliver God's people once and for all from sin. In this chapter, it is prophesied that the promised king would be born in the city of Bethlehem. Again, as I consider the prophetic promise of the coming of God's Son into the world, I am reminded of the great and unwavering faithfulness of God. In a book of prophecy that is concerned primarily with the sinful rebellion of his people, God reiterates his intention to send his own Son into the world to suffer and die for their sins. From a human perspective it is almost unthinkable to consider making such a sacrifice in light of the willful unfaithfulness of the very ones that the sacrifice is being made for. But thankfully, God is not subject to our human frailties and inconsistencies. His great and unchanging love for mankind prompted this unequalled gift that purchased pardon for a world hopelessly lost in sin. We, as humans, may often fail to live up to the commitment that we make to God; there may even be times when we abide in darkness, with no concern for Christ or his sacrifice, but God's faithfulness is sure and steadfast. His love for us and desire that we be saved is constant, and the invitation to come to him for cleansing and salvation is always extended. Thank God for his overwhelming love and matchless grace.

How would you explain God's willingness
to sacrifice his Son for a world of sinners?

DON'T FORGET TO PRAY AND HAVE A GREAT DAY!

Day 345

 Today's Reading:
Micah 7:1-20

Who is a God like you … ?" What a profound question and thought that is. God had allowed his people to fall into the hands of their enemies because of their rebellion and unfaithfulness. He had allowed them to feel the pain of separation from his benevolent and protective hand. But, his wrath would not last forever. God's love and mercy would prevail as he would restore Israel and remove their transgressions far from them. With a tone of amazement and awe, Micah wonders at the mercy and goodness of a gracious God. In a world so filled with violence and hatred, oh how we need to experience the mercy and grace that only God can provide! There may be other gods that are touted by many in our world (false though they may be), but there is no god like God, who is compassionate, longsuffering, and genuinely interested in the salvation of mankind. He is not a god of death and destruction but rather of life and hope. In a time when our world is so desperately looking for some source of peace and hope, we need look no further than the God of Heaven, for who is a God like him?

In your opinion, what are the greatest
and most awesome attributes of God?

DON'T FORGET TO PRAY AND HAVE A GREAT DAY!

Day 346

 Today's Reading:
Nahum 1:1-15

The short book of Nahum is a book of judgment against the people of Nineveh, but it begins, very fittingly, with a tribute to the power and sovereignty of God. The fact of the matter is, if the word of warning and condemnation directed to Nineveh was to be heeded, they needed to understand that God was a God who was capable of bringing the destruction that was being promised. They needed to know that God was, in fact, the God of heaven and earth who could accomplish anything and whose will could not be denied. As I consider the meaning and purpose of those opening words of this book of prophecy, I am struck with the realization that our world today is badly in need of a reminder of the power and sovereignty of the Almighty God. We have spent so much time in either downplaying the righteousness and judgment of God, or in denying him altogether, that we have lost sight of the fact that this world is his and that, ultimately, his will reigns supreme. Maybe what our world desperately needs is a healthy and appropriate fear of God—a fear of God that could motivate repentance and a return to his ways. What a difference that would make in our world!

Is fearing God a valid concept? If so, how should it be understood?

DON'T FORGET TO PRAY AND HAVE A GREAT DAY!

DAY 347

Today's Reading:
Nahum 2:1-13

Behold, I am against you." I can think of no more frightening words when spoken by the Lord. What a harrowing thought to consider that you have found disfavor in the eyes of God and that his wrathful hand is coming down upon you. In yesterday's thought, we considered the importance of an appropriate fear of God. We must understand the distinction between two very different types of fear as it pertains to our relationship with God. The "fear" that we considered yesterday is a respectful reverence toward God that recognizes his sovereignty and submits to his will. The other type of "fear" toward God is a fearful dread of God's judgment and wrath. What the prophecies of Nahum reveal is that all will experience one of these types of fear. Those who have a respectful reverence for God will live obediently before him and will, thus, have no reason to fearfully dread him. However, those who reject God and fail to fear him in a positive way will certainly experience that fearful dread when faced with the judgment of God. All of us will experience the fear of God. The question is, will we fear him or be in fear of him?

What is the difference between fearing God and being in fear of him?

DON'T FORGET TO PRAY AND HAVE A GREAT DAY!

Day 348

 Today's Reading:
Nahum 3:1-19

This chapter is devoted to the transgressions of Nineveh and the judgment of God that is to come upon them as a result. This large and affluent city was filled with violence and wickedness and, thus, found themselves subject to the wrathful hand of God. As Nineveh is warned of their coming destruction, they are told to fortify their walls and prepare for battle, but with the obvious point that all of their strength and preparation will not save them. The simple, yet important, meaning of this point is that no amount of human strength or effort can successfully resist or defeat the will of God. If God decides to bring his judgment upon a person, group, nation, or government, there is no force that can stand in the way. This is the nature and extent of God's overwhelming power. For Christians living in a time in which opposition to Christ is becoming more and more common, it is a great source of comfort and encouragement to be reminded that our lives are safe in the hands of a loving and all-powerful God. Whatever hardships we might face in this life, we can rest assured that God's judgment is coming, whether in this life or in the next, to deliver his people and bring judgment upon his enemies.

As God's people, how should we view the judgment of God?

DON'T FORGET TO PRAY AND HAVE A GREAT DAY!

Day 349

 Today's Reading:
Habakkuk 1:1-17

Have you ever felt like God wasn't listening to you? Like your prayers were being ignored as you were struggling with some difficult circumstance in your life? If you have, then you can relate to Habakkuk and the frustration that he voices toward God. But what I would like to focus on, and learn from, is God's response to Habakkuk's questioning. "For I am doing a work in your days that you would not believe if told." Though it may seem to Habakkuk that God is not acting, silently sitting by while evil abounds, the truth of the matter is that God is working in ways that cannot be seen or recognized by the prophet, and in ways that are going to bring about the conquering of evil and the good of God's people. Thus it is with us. In those times when we cannot see God working for our good, we must not assume that he is sitting idly by. God's wisdom and power is far beyond our own, and his constant desire is for our good and spiritual success. While we may not see or know the things that he is doing to bless our lives, we can always be assured that he is with us and that he is working to meet our needs. What a blessing and comfort it is to know that we serve a God who is so willing and able to bless us in any circumstance.

In what ways are you comforted in knowing
that God is working on behalf of his people?

DON'T FORGET TO PRAY AND HAVE A GREAT DAY!

Day 350

 Today's Reading:
Habakkuk 2:1-20

Among the woes that are delivered in this text is one directed toward those who fashion and trust in idols. How hopeless is the one who trusts in an invention of his own hands, a lifeless image of stone, wood, gold, or silver? That idol has no power to hear prayers, to affect the circumstances of one's life, of blessing, caring for, strengthening, or comforting the one who has put his trust in it. What does any of this have to do with us? Well, while the type of idols that this passage refer to may not be very prevalent in our world today, there are certainly a great many idols that many in our day constantly possess, worship, trust in, and live for. Money, physical things, careers, achievements, honor, and fame are just a few of these false gods that vie for our attention and loyalty. But while our idols may take different forms than the ones that are dealt with in this text, the words of wisdom are just as true. Woe to the one that trusts in those things of his own making for those things have no life and no ability to do anything. They are nothing but idol gods that serve only to take our hearts and devotion away from the only true and living God.

What do you think are some of the most common and popular idols in our world today? Why are those things such a temptation for people?

DON'T FORGET TO PRAY AND HAVE A GREAT DAY!

Day 351

 Today's Reading:
Habakkuk 3:1-19

T he short book of Habakkuk is a beautiful book about the hope that exists in trusting in the power and the wisdom of God. He works in his own time and way according to his perfect knowledge and will. As we have read this book, we have considered the mighty work that God does in ways that we cannot see or recognize to bring about our good. We have seen the danger of trusting in false and powerless gods instead of trusting in the great I AM. Now, as the book closes, we consider the great value to be found in waiting on the Lord. We are often very impatient when we have pressing needs and desire God's help. We are often quick to make demands of God or to become frustrated with him when he doesn't act immediately. But, as Habakkuk writes these words of praise to God, he expresses a beautiful trust in God to work in a time and way that is best. Therefore, he will patiently wait on the Lord. In times of trouble and hardship, there may be no greater demonstration of faith than to be willing to patiently wait on the Lord—to trust in his perfect will and wisdom with endurance until the glory of God's work and purposes is seen. May we have the faith to trust in the Lord and to wait on him in our day of trouble.

Why do we often struggle to wait on the Lord?

DON'T FORGET TO PRAY AND HAVE A GREAT DAY!

DAY 352

 Today's Reading:
Zephaniah 1:1-18

It is a common theme among the prophets: the day of the Lord's wrath is coming. Sometimes, that day of judgment is promised toward God's people because of their unfaithfulness and rebellion. At other times, the wrath of God is to be against the enemies of God's people for their mistreatment of Israel. In the case of this chapter, the day of the Lord's wrath is to be against Judah, but the language reminds us of a much larger, more universal day of judgment involving all the nations of the world. Today, even as much of our world lives in denial of God or in defiance of his authority, the coming day of the Lord is an inescapable truth. When that day comes, there will be no denying the presence or power of God. Every eye shall see him and every tongue shall acknowledge him as all stand in his presence. Sadly, for the majority of this world, that day will be a day of wrathful judgment and the beginning of an eternity of darkness and punishment. However, as sure as the day of the Lord is, just as sure is the opportunity for salvation in that day through the sacrifice of Jesus Christ. The day of the Lord does not have to be a dreaded day of God's wrath. It can, instead, be a glorious day of reward for those who have been washed in the blood of Christ and have prepared themselves for the Lord's return. May we be prepared for that great day!

What can we do to help those around us
be aware of the coming day of the Lord?

DON'T FORGET TO PRAY AND HAVE A GREAT DAY!

DAY 353

 Today's Reading:
Zephaniah 2:1-15

In yesterday's reading, we considered the importance of being prepared for the coming day of the Lord. The questions might be asked, "How can I be prepared? What must I do?" In this chapter, the answer to those questions are given: "Seek the Lord, all you humble of the land, who do his just commands; seek righteousness, seek humility." Our preparation, or lack thereof, will be determined by what we seek in this life. If our focus is on the Lord and on those attributes and actions that bring us into conformity with his will, then the day of the Lord's appearing holds no fear for us. However, if our focus is on worldly things and on fulfilling our own desires apart from God's will, then the day of the Lord will certainly be a day to be dreaded. The good news in this situation is that God has not left us without counsel. He has revealed himself to us and has told us what to do to be prepared. In doing so, he has made it possible for us to not only seek him and his will, but to find those things which we seek. God has made himself accessible to us through his Son and has shown us the way to himself. May we seek him with all of our hearts!

What is involved in seeking the Lord?

DON'T FORGET TO PRAY AND HAVE A GREAT DAY!

Day 354

 Today's Reading:
Zephaniah 3:1-20

As is often the case, this short book of prophecy concludes on a positive note as we read of the forgiveness and restoration of God's people. Despite all of the harsh and wrathful language that is directed toward the rebellious nation of Judah, we are reminded that God is a God of mercy and love who desires to spare mankind from his wrath and show his goodness instead. We certainly like the idea of a merciful and loving God. We want to believe that God is a God who is anxious to forgive and quick to save. That desire has led, in many cases, to an understanding of God as One who, when all is said and done, will not allow anyone to suffer his wrath but will, in his mercy and grace, save everyone, regardless of the lives they have lived. Notice, though, what this text says about those who will receive God's mercy and forgiveness. "But I will leave in your midst a people humble and lowly. They shall seek refuge in the name of the LORD, those who are left in Israel; they shall do no injustice and speak no lies, nor shall there be found in their mouth a deceitful tongue." Obviously, there is a certain quality that characterizes those who find favor in God's eyes—a humble submission to the will and commands of God. While it is certainly true that God desires to show mercy toward all of mankind, his righteousness demands that his favor be reserved for those who have loved and obeyed him. May we humbly seek his mercy and salvation!

Why do you think we struggle to understand
both the love and the righteousness of God?

DON'T FORGET TO PRAY AND HAVE A GREAT DAY!

DAY 355

 Today's Reading:
Haggai 1:1-15

It is a momentous and long awaited time in Judah's history. A portion of them have been allowed to return to their homeland where they have begun to rebuild the holy city, the most important structure of which is the temple. Unfortunately, we quickly see a problem in the mindset and actions of those who have returned to Jerusalem. Instead of making the temple their first and greatest priority, they have focused on their own homes and personal desires. In doing so, they have neglected the great work of restoring the glory of God to the city. There is an important lesson to be learned from this misstep. In their desire to re-establish themselves, they have failed to put God and his will first. It is a matter of skewed priorities. How often does this same mistake become a problem in our own lives? When our physical needs and wants seem so important and crucial, it is often a difficult thing for us to put aside those desires in order to seek the will of God. Yet, Jesus tells us that if we will "seek first the kingdom of God and his righteousness," over even the most basic necessities of our physical lives, that God will meet those needs (Matthew 6:33). For us, just as for the ancient people of God, it is a matter of priorities. May we ever put God first in our hearts and lives.

Why is it important that we place the
will of God before our own desires and needs?

DON'T FORGET TO PRAY AND HAVE A GREAT DAY!

DAY 356

 Today's Reading:
Haggai 2:1-23

"Work, for I am with you." This is the reassuring word given by God to those tasked with rebuilding the temple. After rebuking them for their misplaced priorities, the Lord encourages them to renew their minds and redouble their efforts in order to return the temple to its former glory. In that short statement from the Lord, there are two very important points that we still need to keep in mind as we strive to work for and serve the Lord in our lives today. There is, first, the assurance that God is with us. As we work to fulfill our mission and share Christ with the world around us, we can still be sure that God is with us to strengthen us, guide us, and bless our efforts. As the apostle Paul would later write, though we may plant or water the seed, it is God who gives the increase (1 Corinthians 3:6). What a wonderful blessing it is to know that God is always with us. But the other important point is that, despite God's promise of his abiding presence and constant help, he tells us to "work." He doesn't give us that command because he needs us or can't accomplish his will without us, but rather because our devotion and effort for the cause of Christ is his will. Through our work, the name of God is glorified and our faith is strengthened. Therefore, God says, if you will work, I will be with you to give you success. What a wonderful promise!

In what ways do you or can you work in the service of the Lord?

DON'T FORGET TO PRAY AND HAVE A GREAT DAY!

Day 357

 Today's Reading:
Zechariah 1:1-21

R eturn to me… and I will return to you." For anyone who has ever made the decision to walk away from God and to follow a path in life that leads to sin, and ultimately destruction, it is important to understand that God, the perfectly righteous and holy God, cannot dwell in the presence of sin and therefore must separate himself from the one who has rejected a relationship with him. It is a sad and hopeless situation to be away from God and to know that God is away from you. But the words of the Lord in this passage offer hope to the hopeless. The separation of God from the sinner does not have to be the final, defining state of his life. To the one who has walked away from God, he gives this hopeful promise: if you will return to Me, then I will return to you. God does not desire to be separated from mankind, but he will not force a relationship upon anyone. What he will do, however, is offer the promise of reconciliation and renewal to anyone who desires to walk away from sin and return to him. What a great promise and what a wonderful God he is!

How does someone who has been separated from God by sin return to him?

DON'T FORGET TO PRAY AND HAVE A GREAT DAY!

Day 358

 **Today's Reading:
Zechariah 2:1-13**

As the series of visions that opens up this book continues, this chapter contains a glorious and victorious message for the people of Judah who are returning to Jerusalem from captivity. This vision is filled with wonderful promises of God's blessings, the greatest of which is his abiding presence with his people. For a nation that has been separated from their home and from God for so many years, can you imagine what a welcome and encouraging message this must have been for God's people? Such is the nature of God's redemptive grace. For the soul that is lost in captivity to sin and far away from the presence of God, there is nothing to offer hope as long as that state of separation exists. But when the decision is made to leave the land of sin and return to God, what a wonderful thought it is to know that not only will God forgive, but that he will restore completely, showering his repentant child with his bountiful love, mercy, and grace. What greater promise can there be than that of having the abiding presence of God restored after a period of absence? What a wonderful God!

In your view, what are the greatest blessings of God's abiding presence?

DON'T FORGET TO PRAY AND HAVE A GREAT DAY!

Day 359

 Today's Reading:
Zechariah 7:1-14

In his words to the people through Zechariah, the Lord poses a very challenging rhetorical question: "When you fasted and mourned... was it for me that you fasted?" During all of their time in captivity, as they bemoaned their undesirable circumstances, was it a restored relationship with God that they longed for or just their physical freedom and homeland? Though their circumstances were designed to remind them of their dependence upon God and encourage them to return to him, their hearts were "diamond-hard," and their focus was on their own needs and desires instead of on the One who could provide for their needs. It occurs to me that it is often so easy to become self-focused in our lives. Our felt needs and wants are so strong and demanding that they can easily dominate our thoughts and motives. If we are not careful, our worship, our service, and even the entirety of our spiritual lives can become about us instead of about God. Being focused on ourselves, we can look for worship that feels good or that is entertaining to us; we can serve in order to get recognition or praise; and we can live our entire lives in order to create and maintain an image of spirituality instead of nurturing a true and sincere relationship with God. Maybe the Lord's question to his people is still one that should be asked to us: when you practice your religion, is it for you or for God? May we always strive to be focused on God.

How can our religion become self-focused?
How can we avoid this danger?

DON'T FORGET TO PRAY AND HAVE A GREAT DAY!

Day 360

 Today's Reading:
Zechariah 8:1-23

A re you familiar with the excitement of anticipating a coming event or celebration? Of course you are. We have all experienced those times that we plan for, look forward to, and dream about—a vacation, the birth of a child, graduation, your wedding, or a holiday or family gathering. As we approach the Christmas holiday, you can see the excitement building in the eyes of children (and many adults) as they anticipate the special family gatherings, fun traditions, special meals, and, of course, the gift giving that typically accompanies this time of year. The excitement leading up to those events is almost as special as the events themselves. In this chapter, the people of Judah are told of a very special event that is coming. They will be delivered from their captivity, returned to their homeland, and restored to their rightful place with God. How excited they must have been as they thought about and looked forward to that glorious day! As I consider these things, I am reminded that there is a glorious day that you and I have been promised—a much greater day even than that foretold to the captive people of God. It will be the day that we are delivered from the bonds of sinful flesh and given an immortal spiritual body as we are ushered into an eternal home with God. That home in Heaven will be a place where the pain, suffering, and sorrow of this world cannot touch us and where we will dwell in the glorious presence of God and of his Son for all eternity. What a glorious day that will be, and how excited we should be as we anticipate and look forward to it!

Do you think that we look forward to Heaven
as much as we should? Why or why not?

DON'T FORGET TO PRAY AND HAVE A GREAT DAY!

Day 361

 Today's Reading:
Zechariah 10:1-12

False gods come in many different shapes, sizes, and colors in our world. There are, of course, the idols and images that people around the world pay homage and offer prayers to, but false gods can often take different, less obvious forms as well. Sometimes, they can take the form of physical things that have great earthly value and, thus, offer the promise of riches, comfort, and ease of life. At other times, they can take the form of activities that offer enjoyment, pleasure, or fulfillment. Then, there are times when false gods take the form of people of extraordinary ability, accomplishment, or flamboyance. While we may not openly call these things "gods," the adoration and devotion that we show toward them can rise to the level of worship and religion. However, whether in the ancient world or in our own, the overwhelming truth is that there is no god except the God of Heaven. False gods, no matter how popular or sought after they might be, have no power, no real wisdom, and no lasting value. The words of today's text continue to be true today: "The household gods utter nonsense, and the diviners see lies; they tell false dreams and give empty consolation." Only God can bring the spring rains to the land and provide its fruit in its season. Only God can know our cares and comfort our sorrows. Only God can redeem our souls and save us from sin. There is no god but God!

How can a physical thing, activity, or person become a god in our lives?

DON'T FORGET TO PRAY AND HAVE A GREAT DAY!

DAY 362

Today's Reading:
Zechariah 14:1-21

"On that day…" It is a phrase that is repeated over and over again throughout this chapter that foretells a glorious day in which God will be victorious and his people will regain their homeland and their glory. It is a day when no enemy shall be able to stand against the power and sovereignty of the Lord as he leads his people in victory over all of their enemies. This description of a physical day of victory reminds us, of course, of an even greater day when our Savior will appear to claim victory and to take his people home to God. Much like the day described in today's text, that day will be one when no enemy will be able to stand against Christ and everyone will acknowledge the truth of his power and godhead. He will reign victorious, and we, his redeemed people, will reign with him, having escaped the struggles and temptations of this life and having been delivered from the curse of sin and death. On that day, we will receive the prize for which we have faithfully striven, the salvation of our souls, as we rest from our labors and proclaim the praises of him who has given us the victory. On that day, our faith will become sight and our patient and unwavering devotion to God will be vindicated. What a day, glorious day, that will be!

What do you most look forward to about the return of the Lord?

DON'T FORGET TO PRAY AND HAVE A GREAT DAY!

Day 363

 Today's Reading:
Malachi 1:1-14

As this final book of prophecy begins, the sacrifices of the priests are condemned as being polluted and profane. They had offered the sick, injured, and lame to God—worthless animals that would not even be considered as a gift to an earthly governor. As we know, the story of this people is preserved for us that we might learn from their experiences. Sadly, their example is all too often of attitudes and behaviors that need to be avoided rather than emulated. So, what can we learn from them on this occasion? While it may be true that we do not offer animal sacrifices to God as they did, it is also true that God still desires sacrifices from us. In our lives, our sacrifices consist of things such as our worship, our time, our service, our money and physical things, and other things that are a part of our daily lives. The lesson for us is not to be found in the items being sacrificed but in the quality of those items. It is possible for our sacrifices to be polluted just as theirs were. If we offer the leftovers, scraps, unwanted, and unused portions of our lives to God while reserving the valuable and important parts for ourselves, we have been guilty of the same transgressions as our predecessors. God wants and certainly deserves the best that we have to offer. May we always be willing to give him our best.

How can we assure that the sacrifices that we offer to God are our very best?

DON'T FORGET TO PRAY AND HAVE A GREAT DAY!

Day 364

 Today's Reading:
Malachi 2:1-17

There is a dangerous attitude that is prevalently displayed throughout this short book of prophecy on the part of the worshippers of God. They have offered improper sacrifices to God and have profaned the altar and temple. Yet, their attitude is that they have acted righteously and their constant response to God's condemnations is, "How have we" done these things. In their hardness of heart, they have become convinced that they have done nothing wrong, though they have clearly violated God's laws. Instead of humbling themselves before God, they have become defensive and defiant. Not only are their actions sinful, but their hearts are also wrong. God has always cared deeply about the hearts of his people. He wants our obedience, but he wants that obedient life to be motivated by a pure heart that loves and is devoted to him. Likewise, he desires for our sacrifices to come from a place of love and reverence rather than a sense of obligation. How many in our world would defend their vain acts of worship or service to God by saying, "How have I wronged him? I have worshipped; I have done good; and I have served." What we see in the Scriptures, however, is that the attitudes and motivations that lie behind our actions are just as important as the actions themselves. May our hearts and our actions always be pure and pleasing to God!

Why is God so concerned with the commitment and sincerity of our hearts?

DON'T FORGET TO PRAY AND HAVE A GREAT DAY!

Day 365

 Today's Reading:
Malachi 3:1-18

"Will a man rob God?" It is one of the most well-known statements from this book, and while the idea seems to be that it is preposterous to think that someone would dare to attempt to rob the all-powerful and all-knowing God of the universe, the truth of the matter is that, from the beginning of time, mankind has been doing just that. It seems to me that our giving to God is often viewed in the same way that we view paying taxes to the government: we know that we have to give something, for that is our duty, but what inventive ways or excuses can we come up with to limit how much we have to give? The question is still a valid one, as is the answer given: "Will a man rob God? Yet you are robbing me." However, did you notice the interesting challenge that God issues to his people immediately after pointing out their thievery? "Put me to the test" the Lord says. Give yourselves fully to Me and see if I will not bless you far beyond what you have given to Me. That is the promise and challenge of God. As true as those words were for his people of old, they are certainly true for us as well. So often, we hold back from God because of concerns for our own needs and well-being, but God's challenge continues to ring true. Put him to the test and see that he will bless your life far beyond what you have given to him. That is the nature of God. He is good and benevolent. He desires to do good for us and promises to care for us as a loving Father. What a great God he is!

In what ways has God blessed you in your life?
Has your giving to him ever exceeded what he has given you?

DON'T FORGET TO PRAY AND HAVE A GREAT DAY!

Made in the USA
Charleston, SC
30 September 2016